DATE DUE

American Political Poetry in the 21st Century

AMERICAN LITERATURE READINGS IN THE 21ST CENTURY

Series Editor: Linda Wagner-Martin

American Literature Readings in the 21st Century publishes works by contemporary critics that help shape critical opinion regarding literature of the nineteenth and twentieth century in the United States.

Published by Palgrave Macmillan:

Freak Shows in Modern American Imagination: Constructing the Damaged Body from Willa Cather to Truman Capote
By Thomas Fahy

Arab American Literary Fictions, Cultures, and Politics
By Steven Salaita

Women & Race in Contemporary U.S. Writing: From Faulkner to Morrison
By Kelly Lynch Reames

American Political Poetry in the 21st Century
By Michael Dowdy

AMERICAN POLITICAL POETRY IN THE 21ST CENTURY

Michael Dowdy

AMERICAN POLITICAL POETRY IN THE 21ST CENTURY
© Michael Dowdy, 2007.

"Mariano Explains Yanqui Colonialism to Judge Collings" by Martín Espada, from Trumpets from the Islands of Their Eviction (1987) reprinted by permission of the Bilingual Press/Editorial Bilingüe, Arizona State University, Tempe, AZ.

Parts of this book have appeared in different form in the following publications:
Callaloo: A Journal of African Diaspora Arts and Letters
Popular Music and Society

Also by the author:
The Coriolis Effect: Poems (Chapbook), Bright Hill Press (forthcoming 2007)

First published in 2007 by
PALGRAVE MACMILLAN™
175 Fifth Avenue, New York, N.Y. 10010 and
Houndmills, Basingstoke, Hampshire, England RG21 6XS
Companies and representatives throughout the world.

PALGRAVE MACMILLAN is the global academic imprint of the Palgrave Macmillan division of St. Martin's Press, LLC and of Palgrave Macmillan Ltd. Macmillan® is a registered trademark in the United States, United Kingdom and other countries. Palgrave is a registered trademark in the European Union and other countries.

ISBN-13: 978–1–4039–7644–4
ISBN-10: 1–4039–7644–9

Library of Congress Cataloging-in-Publication Data

Dowdy, Michael.
    American political poetry in the 21st Century / by Michael Dowdy.
        p. cm.—(American literature readings in the 21st century)
    Includes bibliographical references.
    ISBN 1–4039–7644–9 (alk. paper)
        1. Political poetry, American—History and criticism. 2. Hip-hop—Influence. 3. American poetry—21st century—History and criticism. 4. American poetry—20th century—History and criticism. 5. Politics and literature—United States—History—21st century. 6. Politics and literature—United States—History—20th century. I. Title.

PS310.P6D69 2007
811'.609358—dc22   2006050995

A catalogue record for this book is available from the British Library.

Design by Newgen Imaging Systems (P) Ltd., Chennai, India.

First edition: March 2007

10 9 8 7 6 5 4 3 2 1

Printed in the United States of America.

To the poets of the fields, villages, mountains, city streets, stadiums, bars, clubs, prisons, rallies, and marches

CONTENTS

PREFACE

When I began reading, writing, and studying American poetry seriously many years ago, I happened upon Adrienne Rich's poem "North American Time" and the particularly bold, provocative lines, "Poetry never stood a chance / of standing outside history" (33). Reading these lines and the other poems in *Your Native Land, Your Life* (1986) set in motion the process from which this book emerged. I started considering how poetry can be political, and I began to see the ways in which poems can engage public debates about political, historical, social, and economic concerns. As my academic interests often tend, this initial inquiry led me back to my early teenage years and the development then of latent political and intellectual interests. In other words, I saw immediately the connection between the varieties of poetry I was studying in graduate classes and the poetry of my youth—hip-hop music. Listening to the hip-hop poets of the late 1980s and early 1990s set the foundation for my later understanding of how poetry *can* be and why it *should* be political. The dual genesis of this book thus reflects my conception of American poetry as a dynamic collection of startling different, yet overlapping, methods for transforming the world in verse.

I feared initially that it would be difficult to articulate points of convergence for the two controlling imperatives of this book—printed poetry and hip-hop music as potentially sociopolitically engaged texts—but I soon realized that these forms are bound together intimately. My dedication to contemporary American poetry, hip-hop music, and international political issues reaches a critical juncture under the broad designator "political poetry." Despite the opinions of some scholars, colleagues, and friends that contemporary poetry is obsolete except in a few isolated conclaves and that hip-hop music is ephemeral and vacuous, I believe that poetry—both in printed form and in hip-hop performance—is not only a powerful cultural form in the United States, but that it is perhaps the best means for exploring contemporary American culture and the ways artists make their work political. In this book I analyze the poetics of late-twentieth and early-twenty-first-century poets, including those who perform on stage and on record, as well as on the printed page. Their strategies for confronting complex political, social, and global contexts in an era of globalization, war, human rights abuses, increasing economic inequality, and a prevailing uncertainty about the future help illuminate how artists negotiate between creative purposes and real-world constraints.

I began listening to and thinking and talking about hip-hop music and culture long before I became a serious poet or critic. I went to my first hip-hop concert when I was thirteen years old, but did not read my first full-length volume of poetry until I was an undergraduate. If, therefore, I sound occasionally like an ardent fan or passionate defender of hip-hop, my stance is a product of this history. I trust that my growth from fan to critic-fan does not prevent my analyzing hip-hop music and culture in an illuminating and disciplined, scholarly way. Printed poetry, on the other hand, does not have "fans" in the same way that hip-hop does. Hip-hop is both a youth-dominated and performance-based culture, whereas the most exalted and celebrated poetic traditions in the United States have been passed along in printed form and are generally more intellectual and less accessible—so the story goes—than popular youth culture forms.

This dynamic has led many observers to view hip-hop as an evanescent art form with little long-term value. In hip-hop culture, after all, fans often think of music made prior to 1994 as "old school," whereas scholars often periodize "contemporary" poetry as any work produced from the 1960s to the present. Printed poetry, at least what critics and scholars have determined is the "best," tends to mature and gain in cultural value over time. I have come to believe that these opposite trajectories are a key to understanding contemporary political poetry and the different political potentials of printed poetry and hip-hop. Hip-hop artists are capable of accomplishing what active contemporary poets often strive to create—a public space of collective agency, potential change, and community. They have a larger stage on which to interact with their audience, to create alternative images of justice, and to build potential political movements. Printed poetry, though, appreciates more slowly. Its impacts are often not as immediate as they are in hip-hop; thus, it is often difficult for many to see printed poetry as a political form. I have thus come to think that any extensive study of contemporary poetry, especially political poetry, is incomplete if it does not consider the politics, poetics, and rhetorical strategies of hip-hop. Such a study has never been published; consequently, critics have missed the opportunity to explore what hip-hop can teach us about printed poetry and what printed poetry can tell us about the world's most popular, dynamic, and often confounding art form.

Years of attending hip-hop shows at night while reading, writing, and studying printed poetry during the day have compelled me to consider the shifting roles of both poets in society and of hip-hop as a powerful form of political poetry. I have also been grappling with the apparent desire of many critics, readers, and poets to make lyric poetry—since the Romantic period associated with introspection and isolation, and since the Modernists with an unapproachable difficulty—political. Poetry, these observers hope, should be capable of making a difference in the world. Further, although romantic and modern poetry, for example, are rightly and seriously studied, I discovered that I was drawn more to contemporary poetry's inextricability from current political and social contexts, partially, I believe, because of what Robert von Hallberg pointed out in 1987, a dictum that applies nearly twenty years later: the need of humanities scholars to make the study of poetry "obviously important" (*Politics and Poetic Value* 2). Printed poetry can be "obviously important" in the classroom, for instance, when it reverberates beyond the narrow confines of the classroom in confronting issues of social justice, war, and foreign policy—outside, between, and within the walls of the individual heart and mind. In my view, it is unnecessary to style hip-hop as "obviously important"; Patrick Neate's recent, *Where You're At: Notes from the Frontlines of a Hip-Hop Planet*, for instance, shows that hip-hop music and culture are a fascinating combination of local and global forces, what he calls "glocal," and they have sociopolitical implications in places as dissimilar as Tokyo, Cape Town, New York, and Rio de Janeiro.

Throughout my years of graduate study, I wrestled, often inconclusively, with the same question from friends, family, and colleagues. After being asked about my research interests and responding with "American poetry, especially political poetry," I often received blank stares, as if to say, *I know what poetry is and I know what politics are, but what is political poetry and who writes it? Who ever thought that poetry was political?* This book, then, is my extended answer. As Michael Bérubé discusses in *Public Access: Literary Theory and American Cultural Politics*, there is a great need for a more accessible language and a better articulation of political positions in humanities scholarship so that it has greater potential to reach a broader audience (171). As such, I hope this book contributes to academic discussions of contemporary printed poetry, cultural studies, literature and politics, applied theoretical studies of agency, and discourses about hip-hop music and culture, African American culture, and Latina/o culture. Further, I hope what follows will be capable of reaching a broader audience—those who enjoy reading poetry and those who grew up with hip-hop music, those who follow global politics, and those who are interested in art's engagement with sociopolitical conditions. As such, in this book I attempt to negotiate the constraints of scholarly literary criticism with a more accessible style.

Although I employ various extant theoretical terms and devise quite a few theoretical terms of my own, I trust that these terms will challenge and engage rather than confuse readers. Also, my theoretical and stylistic approach to the material is similar to hip-hop artists' approaches—eclectic and pragmatic. I do not hesitate to borrow from a variety of academic disciplines and scholarly approaches. Like hip-hop sampling, I sample a variety of approaches to poetry scholarship and cultural studies. When Helen Vendler writes that poets who use more than one language or register employ a "macaronic aesthetic" ("Poet of Two Worlds" 31), she derides them for their unsustainable voices. However, I believe that these voices are dynamic and creative even if they appropriate and revise previous voices and traditions. I hope that this book's "macaronic" critical approach is the best one to elucidate the complex landscape of contemporary poetry in the United States in both printed poems and hip-hop songs and performances.

Acknowledgments

In writing this book I received encouragement and advice, directly and indirectly, from the following colleagues, professors, and poets: Barbara Baines, John Balaban, David Davis, María DeGuzmán, Marcia Douglas, Nick Halpern, Trudier Harris, Robert Hass, John McGowan, Elaine Orr, John Thompson, and Linda Wagner-Martin. The Welton, Holliday, and Kirkpatrick families were kind and generous during the years of writing, and my own family has been supportive and patient with me. My parents, Janie and Dennis, and my brother, Ryan, have been more interested in my work than anyone else, and they were always careful to point out that it wasn't simply a familial obligation. I want to thank as well the entire Dowdy and Small families, especially my grandparents, for their support and inspiration. Finally, I want to thank Shelley for challenging me and championing my work.

Introduction: Political Poetry
in the United States

The age of the ignorant rapper is done
knowledge reigns supreme over nearly everyone
the stereotype must be lost
that love and peace and knowledge is soft
do away with that and understand one fact
for love, peace must attack
and attack real strong, stronger than war
to conquer it and its law
—Boogie Down Productions, "Why Is That?"
(KRS-One: A Retrospective 1989)

For poetry makes nothing happen: it survives
In the valley of its making where executives
Would never want to tamper, flows on south
From ranches of isolation and the busy griefs,
Raw towns that we believe and die in; it survives,
A way of happening, a mouth.
—W.H. Auden, "In Memory of W.B. Yeats"
(1939) (247–249)

Poet and critic Edward Hirsch once wrote that poetry embodies a
"magical potency" (*How to* 1–5). In this book I explore the ways that
contemporary American poets and hip-hop artists[1] transmit, impart,
and create political potency in their work without losing the magic
and dynamism that is usually the province of poetry but less often of
politics. I begin, then, with two epigraphs, one by a rapper and one by
a poet who made the United States home for most of his adult life.
Both suggest some critical departure points for this study uncovering
the rhetorical strategies for making poetry political. It is often
thought, as Auden implies in his elegy for Yeats, that poetry "makes

nothing happen" because it is isolated from the domains of political power and from the executives who make decisions about the future of nations. Nevertheless, Auden claims, poetry "survives" as a "way of happening," an action in its own right that persists and retains a power and mystery with which the powerful "would never want to tamper." For KRS-One (Kris Parker), the rapper for the influential Bronx-based Boogie Down Productions and one of the culture's most respected innovators and political voices, hip-hop artists must use positive, powerful language to "attack" the forces of "war." This poetic language, KRS-One believes, is capable of helping to "conquer" the "law" of war that upholds inequality in a world rife with racism, violence, poverty, and oppression. This optimism and abiding belief in language as a force of resistance to injustice differs from Auden's suggestion that a poem is ultimately an ineffective social act.

I begin with these two epigraphs because they illustrate centuries-long questions about the usefulness of political poetry and the survival of poetry in the face of substantial doubts about its viability. Moreover, they illustrate the ways that poets alternate between swaggering braggadocio and despondency about their poetry's making something "happen" politically or socially. The divide between naïve optimism and pessimism, though, should not be understood as one between hip-hop songs and printed poems. Numerous hip-hop artists bemoan their inability to affect change in their communities, whereas other poets, such as those of the Black Arts Movement, challenge and deftly proclaim the power of language. Poems such as Quincy Troupe's "Boomerang: A Blatantly Political Poem," which claims that "absolutely nothing / will have been undone" (665–666) by the poems of resistance during the civil rights movement, and José Montoya's "The Movement Has Gone for its Ph.D. over at the University, or the Gang Wars are Back" (95–96) suggest that progressive change is compromised by the institutionalization in which poets are complicit. But rarely, if ever, is any printed poem as unabashedly swaggering as a rap song. Even if tongue-in-cheek, one of hip-hop's primary tropes asserts the power of language as a weapon for change and as a metonym of the artist's linguistic dexterity. For instance, Edan's "Promised Land" (*Beauty and the Beat* 2005) proclaims both the power of hip-hop and the impact of his verse: "my power settled the clash between races / and put good people on the magazine faces."

Most importantly, though, these epigraphs point to an overarching warrant for writing about the political strategies of printed poetry and hip-hop music instead of some other expressive form such as folk music, film, fiction, or blogging. Auden implies that poetry is and always will be primarily countercultural. Similarly, hip-hop music began as a countercultural art, but has since lapsed (or progressed, depending on your perspective) into a cornerstone of popular culture. The most politically and socially adept hip-hop is still countercultural—both within the culture itself and within the larger American culture—and is often recorded on independent record labels and performed at smaller, independent clubs and concert spaces. These artists are able to comment on both the dominant American culture and the hypermaterialistic commercial hip-hop that often implicitly supports it. In chapter 4 I explore some of these artists' work and the implications of hip-hop's movement into the mainstream. Precisely because the printed poetry and the hip-hop I discuss are countercultural, they are able to comment on the larger culture in unique and penetrating ways. At the same time, poets themselves still have a large amount of cultural currency and prestige even if their work often does not. Independent hip-hop and printed poetry, therefore, survive and remain countercultural while maintaining prestige and credibility.

These two epigraphs, finally, are apt departure points for a rhetorical mapping of the strategies and figures of voice contemporary poets use to write political poems. Today's poets and critics capture three primary centuries-long concerns about political poetry, two of which I discuss thoroughly in this introduction: (1) the efficacy of poetry as public discourse; (2) the functions of poets and poetry in society; and (3) the potential for political poetry to remain important across cultural and historical borders.

There is no satisfactory method for determining the efficacy of poetry. Denise Levertov, one of the United States' most controversial and outspoken political poets during the Vietnam War, claimed, somewhat tenuously, that poetry can "indirectly" affect the course of events by "awakening pity, terror, compassion and the conscience of a leader" and by "strengthening the morale of persons working for a common cause" (174). How should "indirectly" be expanded or understood? Does poetry retain elements of mystery and subtlety that prevent such certainty? I argue here that cause-and-effect criteria are too limiting a means for understanding poetry's powers. Establishing a poem as a primary motivator of an agent's (or group of agents') actions would be a remarkable achievement, one that would likely require extrapolation and reductivism. Though I do not elide the question of audience in the discussions that follow, especially in the hip-hop chapter, determining an art form's verifiable efficacy is largely speculative. More importantly, such a focus would distract from the main purpose of my book—to study poetic strategies, specifically the figures of voice employed in political poems. Regardless, the difficult question remains and will likely remain in perpetuity: are poems capable of creating change? While discussing poems *per se*, I concentrate on the strategies poets use to engage political and socioeconomic issues, conditions, and problems. If we can map and understand poets' rhetorical strategies for making political poems, we can perhaps begin to understand the potential for poetry as a form of political speech, as a form of speech that can influence people to act in certain ways in the public and political spheres.

Poets, Political Poetry, and the American Public

What, then, are the functions and the roles of poetry in the broadly defined contemporary U.S. culture? In "Responsibilities of the Poet," Robert Pinsky explores the dialectic between the poet and her culture; he claims that poets must continually revise the definitions of the "poetic" that the culture reifies, sustains, and encourages. The poet's job, he claims, is to make social judgments prior to the actual writing of a poem, and more crucially, to re-envision the poetic and thereby transform values by, in Pinsky's words, "looking away" from the ways that the culture represents the poetic ("Responsibilities" 12, 19). Poetry, then—and I consider both printed poetry and hip-hop music "poetry"—is thoroughly countercultural and resistant to the structures of both the dominant discourse and the sociocultural norms it supports. Poet, translator, and critic Kenneth Rexroth made a comparable claim in 1936 when he said that the poet, "by the very nature of his art, has been an enemy of society, that is, of the privileged and the powerful" ("The Function" 1).

In a similar vein, in *Praises & Dispraises: Poetry and Politics, the 20th Century*, Terrence Des Pres grapples with the "impact of political havoc" on poetry in the twentieth century. He claims that poetry, often the territory of hope and praise, now "finds more exercise in cursing" and "dispraises." Though he points out that the "patron saints of poetry in dark times"—Anna Akhmatova, Boris Pasternak, Pablo Neruda, César Vallejo, and Nazim Hikmet among others— come to North Americans through translations from places ravaged by political upheaval, he also suggests that the poet's role has fundamentally changed, largely due to what he calls the "miracles of modern communications," including the work of television's "instant replay of events" and horrific images captured by photojournalists. He asserts that "a wretchedness of global extent has come into view; the spectacle of man-created suffering is *known*, observed with such constancy that a new shape of knowing invades the mind" (xiv–xv; original emphasis). From the vantage point of 2006 and the almost immediate access to images of horror that an Internet connection can provide, Des Pres's assessment of the onslaught of media images in 1988 seems tame by comparison.

Five years earlier, in 1983, Czeslaw Milosz wrote in *The Witness of Poetry* that poets' roles have changed, largely because of an exponential expansion of their "knowledge of reality"; once limited to perhaps a single village, now subject to the catastrophes of the globe, poets, he suggests, bear an increased burden, especially when the U.S. role in conflicts around the world is palpable and often negative. Is it not surprising, Milosz asks, that poets are "morally indignant"? He continues with a final commentary on the trajectory of twentieth-century poetry toward dark visions: poets, he says, have a difficult time imagining a future devoid of economic crises and wars (116). Similarly, in the late 1980s, Chuck D, lead rapper of one of hip-hop's most acclaimed groups, Public Enemy, explained many rappers' dark visions as "the Black CNN" (Saddik 110–112), because they described with gritty realism actual urban living conditions that mainstream news consistently ignored, or when they did report on them, essentialized. Des Pres, moreover, describes the imperative for a "diction" that can challenge and outlast these dire events and support through "the stamina of language" the trials of the twentieth, and now, by extrapolation, the twenty-first century (xv). What, then, is this "diction" that Des Pres invokes? An analysis of the strategies for inscribing the political in poems moves toward understanding any such diction, or, I would argue, *dictions.*

In *The Uses of Poetry*, Denys Thompson provides a sweeping description of the poet's role in society, one that boldly suggests the poet's superiority and a preexisting societal consensus: "In the past the poet has often been the spokesman of his society, saying what it wanted said but could not voice for itself" (202). Similarly, and often dangerously, many hip-hop artists are often styled as the spokespeople for their communities, sometimes to negative effect, whereas poets are often considered "outsiders." Although slightly misguided, Thompson's broad definition is helpful as an initial departure point. Social theorist Anthony Giddens rejects the functionalist conception that social systems have "needs" or "reasons" of their own, as Thompson suggests, when he implies that society "wants" to "say" something (109–115). Perhaps Thompson simply chooses some unfortunate words—"society" instead of "people"—and if he avoided the implication that there are only spokesmen and not *spokeswomen*, then the definition may be more helpful.

Poets are often seen as charged with speaking on behalf of their people, which is quite a lofty task, albeit one that Latin American poets such as Neruda and Ernesto Cardenal took on willingly in the twentieth century.[2] As Suzanne Gardinier points out, Neruda's *Canto general* (1950) was an attempt to summon forth power on "his people's behalf." Furthermore, the *Canto general*, she says, was made both to be beautiful and "a force of nature, a testimony, a pamphlet, a letter, a sword" (18). However, especially given the debates concerning a poet's right to speak on behalf of others—cogently outlined by Hélène Cixous in her essay "Conversations," Hirsch in *How to Read a Poem*, and by the various theorists of the Latin American *testimonio* (which I discuss thoroughly in chapter 1)—the wisdom and propriety of writing on behalf of others is now viewed suspiciously, especially by those living in postcolonial nations. To paraphrase Eudora Welty's 1965 essay: "*Must* the poet crusade?" Hirsch calls into question the poet's function as voice of the people because of "compelling reasons" for poets "to resist any public or ideological pressure to speak for anyone besides oneself" (180). Referring primarily to the dangers of writing political poetry on behalf of others in World War II–era Poland, he shows the dangers, both to life and liberty, of writing to promote the needs and rights of others. Is there an inherent danger, then, in political poetry, or is this factor heavily dependent on context? Can political poems speak simply on behalf of the poet rather than on behalf of a community? I believe that even poems that speak on behalf of one person are nonetheless read by others who may see them as speaking on behalf of themselves or others. In other words, once a poem is written and published or performed, it leaves the boundedness of the author's world.

Political Poetry's Historical-Cultural Contexts

The question of temporality has long been problematic for political poetry. Is political poetry timeless, or is it time- and context-bound, mutable, decaying in meaning over temporal, geographical, and historical borders? If the roles and functions of the poet in American society are contested and ever-shifting, so too is the import of political poems when they are removed from historical or cultural context. In "Poetics of the Americas," Charles Bernstein indicates that it is important not to remove poems from the local contexts that give them meaning (3), which is always a danger when a critic embarks on a wide-ranging exploration of political poetry. Removing poems from their political context can shift or recontextualize their political import; however, it should not prevent the critic from charting the political *strategies* of poems. Moreover, as Günter Grass has suggested, much good writing depends on a hearing at some point forward in time (cited in Des Pres *Praises & Dispraises* 225), which is especially important for printed poems that may slowly appreciate in value. Even though much political poetry becomes dated—I think especially of many protest poems from the 1960s—the transferability of poetry to a point forward in time can reinvigorate political poems and stretch their meanings across contexts.[3] Hip-hop, on the other hand, may be most vibrant in the cultural and historical moment of its transmission, especially if it is in a live performance, which I explore at length in chapter 4. Hans-Georg Gadamer's hermeneutics highlight the instability of all texts because meaning changes from one historical context to the next. He points out that all interpretations of a text consist of a dialogue between past and present; consequently, all understanding is productive and adds to the meaning of a specific poem.[4]

Following the September 11, 2001, terrorist attacks on the World Trade Centers in New York City, Auden's "September 1, 1939," originally written from Manhattan to mark the date of Germany's invasion of Poland, had a renaissance due to its eerie reverberations with the aftermath of terror sixty-two years later. In a recent essay, Stephen Burt explores the public's increased interest in poetry after the attacks, and the way that the poem was presented following 9/11 as "an ideal-typical example of the kind of poetic object academic readers now seek," one that "described shared, urgent, clearly public concerns for a large body of people" (535). Thus, whereas some poems, such as Don L. Lee's "From a Black Perspective" (1969) about George Wallace, which utilizes African American traditions of signifying and playing the dozens, become depoliticized over thirty years later when Wallace is largely forgotten, others, such as "September 1, 1939," become more than just great poems or pertinent cultural/historical documents—they re-become poignant political poems.[5]

In an essay on Nicaraguan poet Ernesto Cardenal and political poetry, Reginald Gibbons discusses the penetrating specificity of Cardenal's poetry, but subsequently allows for what I understand as a transhistorical and transtemporal movement of the poem. Depending on the context, a poem may be politically important when it is published, but it may also *become* important politically. For instance, historian Howard Zinn points out that the International Ladies Garment

Workers Union used Shelley's "Mask of Anarchy" as a rallying cry during strikes in New York at the beginning of the twentieth century (326).[6] In his analysis of a Cardenal poem in which the speaker names Nicaragua's dictator, Gibbons claims that a substitution of a different tyrannical political or historical figure known by an audience as a violent dictator will not change the poem's meaning, "only its focus" (282–283), just as the focus of Shelley's poem changed in the decades after its writing. The recent revival of Shakespeare's *The Tempest* and Charlotte Bronte's *Jane Eyre* as postcolonial texts can be understood through a similar lens.

Although there have been many arguments that the role and cultural esteem of poets in the United States since the 1960s has changed greatly (mostly for the worse, critics and observers claim), in the aftermath of 9/11 and the events that have followed such as the incursions into Afghanistan and Iraq, the role of poets has rekindled some of the public spirit of 1960s poets. The evidence is circumstantial but prodigious: Galway Kinnell's "When the Towers Fell," which first appeared in *The New Yorker* a year after the attacks; Amiri Baraka's confrontational "Somebody Blew Up America," which incited a flurry of anti-Semitic accusations; performance poet Saul Williams's project against the war in Afghanistan called *Not in My Name*; Sam Hamill's project *Poets against the War*; the cancelled poetry-month celebration to be hosted by Laura Bush at the White House; and the speaking appearances of poets at rallies across the country, such as Robert Hass in Berkeley in September 2001. These examples indicate a greater public role for poets when dramatic events impinge on everyday living. Why do we turn to poets such as Hass, a former U.S. Poet Laureate (1993–1995) better known—if somewhat inaccurately—for poems of introspection than political poems, when we are faced with uncertainty? Poets, we still seem to believe, can access truth by stripping back superficial appearances for deeper meanings and by giving revelatory insight into public issues in ways that politicians and journalists cannot.

Gibbons indirectly points out one of the potential consequences of poets being charged with commenting on political and social issues. He discusses Cardenal's self-imposed requirement that his staunchly political poetry refer to a tangible world outside the poem. Such an approach skirts the possibility of pulling poetic creation into the domain of referentiality and away from the imagination. Leonard M. Scigaj points out a similar problematic in his monograph on American "ecopoetry" (poems by A.R. Ammons, Wendell Berry, W.S. Merwin, and Gary Snyder) when he conjectures that environmental poetry has received less attention from theorists due to a widely held assumption that it depends on mimesis and the idea that language always conveys the unmediated presence of the speaker, essentialized referents, and a passive representation of the natural world (xiv). Nevertheless, for political poems, concrete referentiality and the tangible world outside the poem dilate attention on the "occasion" of poems, whether the occasion is terrorist attacks in the United States or the abuses of a Nicaraguan dictator. Do events create the need for poems or do poets recreate events, or a combination of the two? The answer must be an affirmative to both poles. For example, Carolyn Forché's poems of El Salvador seem to substantiate the first whereas those of Charles Simic's WWII Yugoslavia seem to affirm the later. In hip-hop, The Perceptionists's "Memorial Day" (*Black Dialogue* 2005), which berates President Bush for going to war in Iraq, demands an explanation for the "missing" weapons of mass destruction. In this case, the event itself spurred the creative response.

POLITICAL POETRY AND INDIRECTION

There has been much debate about the public functions of poetry, a debate that converges with another important theoretical concern in the discussion of political poetry—the interstices between direction and indirection, or the supposed binary opposition between direct public speech and lyric poetry.[7] The latter usually works through figurative language, indirection, and obliquity, often displaying clarity and referentiality only intermittently. In a strike against poetry written specifically to move others to a certain action or set of actions, Hirsch claims that "voice in written poetry is always metaphorical, never literal" (*How to* 103), whereas Barbara Herrnstein-Smith brings up another problem for some political poetry when she writes that lyric poetry must affect its audience even as it must pretend that it has no audience to affect (141). Jenny Goodman, on the other hand, disrupts any private/public divide when she foregrounds her essay on Joy Harjo with a reference to the false dividing line between poetic and public discourses. Poetry, she claims, links to Aristotle's understanding of "language as a process in which a speaker uses language in an attempt to move people toward action in public settings," even if for Aristotle art is cathartic and a way to prevent regular citizens from engaging in public action (37).

Goodman also refers to Kenneth Burke's definition of rhetoric and its inclusion of literary forms. According to Burke, poetry as rhetoric is "the use of words by human agents to form attitudes or to induce actions in other agents." This definition is appropriate in a study of political poetry "even though the kinds of assent evoked have no overt, practical outcome" (41, 50). Mutlu Konuk Blasing further erodes a strict divide between private poetry and public speech when she argues that poetic rhetoric is at once figuration and persuasion, which allows the critic to negotiate poetry's uneasy relationship between indirection and direct political message. She appears to agree with Gibbons, who says that political rhetoric values persuasion, whereas poetry values perception and insight. Blasing writes, "poetry's public function is to grant a perspective on how all meanings are rhetorical and therefore political" (21–22). Both suggest that poetry's role is to strip away surface veneer in order to create new perspectives, meanings that are present but must be unveiled through poetry—"the sight of what is visible" and "the understanding of what is hidden" (Gibbons 294). Political poetry, then, appears to have as its charge the role of revelation. Yet if lyric poetry is always indirect, must it also obscure what it reveals? I implicitly explore this question in chapter 2 when I discuss poems that are often indirect and equivocal.

WAYS OF TALKING ABOUT
POLITICAL POETRY

In addition to understanding the roles of poetry in society and the public responsibilities of poets, a book about political poetry should interrogate the array of signifiers, terminology, and confusion for what counts as "political" poetry. Some readers may wonder, as did the interlocutors I mentioned in the preface, how exactly to identify a political poem. What should be considered *political* poetry? What shapes do political poems take? What kinds of political work do they attempt? What kinds of voices? What kinds of speakers? I begin with a simple but expansive definition, a "broader view" of politics, put forth by Michael Parenti:

> Politics is more than just something politicians do. It is the process of struggle over conflicting interests carried into the public arena. It also involves muting and suppressing conflicting interests. Politics involves not only the competition among groups within the system but the struggle to change the system itself, not only the desire to achieve predefined ends but the struggle to redefine ends and pose alternatives to the existing politico-economic structure. (3)

Drawing from Parenti's view of politics, my definition of political poems is inclusive and far-ranging. For me, the line between what is "political" and what is "social" blurs. Political poems, moreover, may not narrowly comment on a certain issue, but may comment on "the system itself." For instance, a poem does not have to be about a specific political issue such as affirmative action; instead, it may comment on the broader conditions that make a specific political policy such as affirmative action a necessary corrective. Further, political poems may not have a "predefined end" but may instead "redefine ends" and "pose alternatives" to the existing economic, political, and social structures that currently govern our lives. They are also struggles carried into the public arena, actions themselves put into print, onto record, or into performance.

Political poems, though, do not have to be explicitly oppositional. Gibbons's examination of the tension in Cardenal's work between poems that speak "against" and those that speak "for" helps illuminate the ways that poems can be political without being narrowly oppositional. Those that speak *against* speak against injustice, suffering, materialism, oppression, and so on, whereas those that speak *for* speak for compassion, justice, and so on (279). But it seems likely that most poems, even those that are primarily personal and introspective, speak for, against, and sometimes in the same poem, for and against something or somethings. Robert Frost's "The Road Not Taken," for instance, generally not considered a political poem, in the popular (but specious) reading speaks for an independent spirit of daring even as it speaks against conformity and timidity. So, if the speaker's stance is important, it may be secondarily so; a political poem is one that speaks to political issues (if only indirectly), one that consciously engages political and socioeconomic conditions, its energy directed, at least partially, beyond the poem itself.

Contemporary American poetry understood as political by poets, critics, and theorists tends toward consciously issue-engaged, lyric-narrative poetry of personal experience; that is, the poem's political content must be transparent to be designated "political"—some clear issue such as the outrages of war, racism, or oppression must be readily apparent. Further, many poets and critics narrowly define political poetry as poetry that "takes its stand on the side of liberty" (Levertov 166) or that "speaks for the party of humanity" (Forché "Against" 46), thereby bracketing the functional political work of poetry that does not challenge dominant political structures or social conventions, but implicitly or explicitly supports them. Robert Bly insists that political poems "do not order us to take specific acts," a notion that seems to contradict many of his most forceful Vietnam-era antiwar poems; rather, he asserts that they move only to deepen awareness, a notion that departs fully from any notion of a poem as a facilitator of action ("Leaping" 134). Poems, then, can be part of (or symbolic of) a culture's consciousness shift. Similarly, Robert Duncan draws from William Blake's ideas about poetry and politics as he contends that great political poetry is "visionary" in its presentation of events as "part of larger and more universal paradigms." He positions poetry as an imaginative endeavor that must not "become a mouthpiece for a righteous cause" or offer cures for political issues (cited in Perloff "Poetry in Time" 209). Duncan would likely discount Cardenal's "tactical" poems, as the term has been used by Thomas McGrath, as poems, since they stand in certain opposition to both of his imperatives. Duncan's position reveals more about his preference for what McGrath calls "strategic" poems, which are poems that work to expand consciousness, rather than tactical poems, which often speak for a cause and diagnose political problems (McGrath 28–29).

A further conundrum in the discourse surrounding contemporary political poetry is the multitude of signifiers for the political poem. Mary K. DeShazer's study of women's "resistance" poetry, Forché's anthology of "witness" poetry, Hirsch's discussion of "transpersonal" poetry, McGrath's "tactical" (context-specific poems) and "strategic" political poems, and John Gery's study of contemporary poetry's embeddedness in the nuclear age as a "discourse of survival," amongst others, provide thorny departure points for any study of political poetry. When these signifiers are viewed in conjunction with the prevailing disregard for polemical poetry, political poetry occupies an overdetermined but murkily defined place in the criticism. Rather than open up a platform of debate, these signifiers for politically and socially engaged poetry often reduce it to one of two spaces—active opposition or consciousness raising, a problematic that dovetails with the illusory either/or proposition of McGrath's dualistic "strategic" and "tactical" political poetry. Bly's insistence that the political poem "comes out of the deepest privacy" ("Leaping" 132), which collapses what is often seen as a divide between the personal poem and the political poem, is much different from Adrienne Rich's proclamation that "the personal is political."[8] Again, these assumptions limit the range of political poetry to either an autonomous realm of assertion or one of contestation. In the chapters that follow, I discuss poems that could be understood as assertive, contestatory, and various combinations thereof. I hope that my discussions will help move us away from this dichotomy toward an understanding of political poetry as a collection of multiple rhetorical strategies, with unique, but overlapping figures of voice.

Though defining the political is important for my book, defining the broader subject of poetry is equally so. "American" poetry is itself a loaded term. I am against, in Bernstein's words, an American literature understood as a positive, expressive "totalization" (2). What we usually consider American literature ignores a large percentage of the literature created in *América*, below the Rio Grande in Central and South America and in the Caribbean, as well as in Canada. The limited use of this term also privileges English as the language, literary and otherwise, of the Americas, whereas Spanish is spoken by the majority of *América*'s citizens. As early as 1889, Walt Whitman saw a difference between "American literature" and "United States literature." As Ed Folsom wrote on the one hundred and fiftieth anniversary of *Leaves of Grass* (1855), Whitman "heard something in the term 'America' " that most U.S. citizens "do not hear today, in part because the term has been so fully appropriated by the US as a synonym for itself, 'at somebody else's expense' as Whitman would remind us" (110). Many citizens of Latin America often think of themselves as "Americans" in the broadest sense of the term, whereas in the United States we often think of the term only in reference to ourselves. In this book, then, I use the term "American" for convenience's sake, but I do so understanding that it is compromised, limiting, and inferior to the Spanish *estadounidense*, for which English-speaking North Americans have no equivalent.

Bernstein's notion that disparate poetic practices comprise a shifting poetic space is also important here, especially because I discuss both printed poetry and performed hip-hop lyrics. He writes that "disparate practices" occupy "a poetic space that is grounded not in an identical social position but in the English language itself as the material with which we make our regroupings and refoundings" (8). I draw from this notion in establishing some theoretical guidelines for this book, about which I speak in detail later in this introduction. First, by focusing on *how* poems work as texts rather than on what their objects of study are (for example, themes and subjects) or what the identities of their writers are (for example, African American or female), I implicitly argue that *language* is the thing that makes the debate. In other words, we "make" our groupings and foundings in language, and we understand identity positions in and through language. Why not study the language, voices, and rhetoric of poems as a first-order concern rather than approach American political poetry through the lens of identity, subject matter, or theme? Is it not limiting to approach the work of Yusef Komunyakaa simply as an African American poet or a Vietnam War poet or Mark Doty solely as a gay poet? Though both of these identity positions may reveal something about their interests, concerns, and language, they also limit the critic's frame and bias their readings. They also prevent potentially revealing juxtapositions between diverse writers who share, if not identity positions and thematic concerns, then similar poetics.

Second, though I also agree with Bernstein that disparate practices and rhetorical strategies are grounded in the materials of language, I do not agree that these practices begin and end with English. It is also important to consider the influences and materiality of Spanish for not only the Latina/o poets who utilize both English and Spanish, some of whom I discuss in chapter 3, but also for many wholly English-language poems that may be influenced by Spanish-speaking cultures. For instance, many twentieth-century U.S. poets have been greatly influenced by Neruda, Vallejo, Julio Cortázar, Jorge Luis Borges, and other Latin American writers (many of whom themselves were greatly influenced by Whitman), and yet others have been influenced by the techniques and sensibilities of magic realism. I argue that the scope of political poetry in the United States must be broadened to include poetic strategies that foreground language choice and language interchange. Social positions and geographic locations, then, can be viewed within the materiality of *languages* and their criss-crossings. "America" and "American poetry," like the boundaries between English and Spanish, and like the shape-shifting signifier and its signified "political poetry," are contested spaces. Many readers may also contest that hip-hop is "poetry," a claim that I hope is refuted in chapter 4.

Political Poetry and Interiority

A primary obstacle for political poetry is the widely held notion that poetry is foremost a private expression. This belief can be attributed to a variety of factors: a hangover from the Romantic era (although Jerome McGann's *The Romantic Ideology* suggests otherwise);[9] the false assumption that poets are antisocial outcasts, partially inherited from the reception for the Beats in the 1950s; the aesthetic promi-nence of the lyric in contemporary poetry, which is often viewed as a form appropriate primarily for introspection; the legacy inherited from high modernism that poetry should be both difficult and a mon-ument to the individual; and the defensible notion that "poetry is often seen as a 'natural' medium for the recounting and examining of personal experience" (Roberts and Allison 1). Jenny Goodman writes that "mainstream thinking" views poetry as "culturally apart" and "impotent" to engage the public sphere (39). Hirsch writes that poetry is primarily a communication between strangers and a private exchange between writer and reader (*How to* 16), and Walter Kalaidjian points out that contemporary poetry has reproduced rather than contested formalism's "swerve from social change" as he claims that the poetics of private lyricism are the "symbolic form par excellence of the more recent American impulse to contain and repress the social text of contemporary history" (*Languages* 4). Vernon Shetley, for his part, suggests that the modernist legacy of "difficult" poetry has been inherited by post-WWII poets and audiences (14). Potential audiences may avoid poetry because they see it as difficult and inaccessible, a perception that has opened a gap between poets and audiences, a gap that hip-hop artists have seized upon. It is not outrageous to claim that teenagers and college students may have read poetry in the 1960s, but now listen to hip-hop. Even so, Shetley argues that poetry should become *more* difficult. Further, the "romantic persistence" of American poetry, as described by Pinsky in *The Situation of Poetry*, can prevent poetry's engagement with social and political spheres if it is viewed as insular and primarily concerned with internal mind states rather than public issues.

Similarly, poet and current NEA chair Dana Gioia describes "the energy of American poetry" as focused inward toward a self-contained community of relatively homogenous readers, which leads to (and is a product of) a lack of a broader public role for poets (2), something we see changing with a broader public activist role for many hip-hop artists. Further, Goodman points out, then elides, the fact that Joy Harjo and other engaged poets address their poetry to two audiences—the broad literary community and those readers who share the poet's political perspectives. Problematically, she discusses how Harjo's poems work to transform readers' attitudes, without acknowledging the circularity of her argument (41–42). This situation seems pertinent for many political poems—who reads them but those who already agree with the political positions and sensibilities therein? How is this form of address a political *strategy*, unless a political poem is intended simply to mobilize people and to crystallize or articulate their views?

Hip-hop music, on the other hand, has a greater potential to mold latent opinions, generate interests, and spur burgeoning educations. Partly because teenagers listen to hip-hop music at impressionable ages, hip-hop lyrics can lead them in a variety of directions. Hip-hop, unlike much political poetry, often does not merely "preach to the choir," a problem that engaged artists often bemoan about their work and its audiences. Hip-hop can literally bring its listeners to new knowledge and ideas and to ignored historical figures. Of course, some hip-hop can potentially have a negative impact on impressionable youth too. In junior high and in high school everything I learned about African American history, the Civil Rights Movement, and radical movements of the 1960s came from listening to hip-hop. Because I was not learning about them in history classes, these glimpses of a broader American history were, I see now, crucial in forming my views about the world and my interests as a poet, scholar, and teacher. Listening to artists such as Boogie Down Productions, Just-Ice, X Clan, Public Enemy, Brand Nubian, Paris, Pete Rock and C.L. Smooth, and Poor Righteous Teachers—some when I was as young as twelve years old—had an immeasurable impact on my sense of justice and my desire to learn about cultural and political figures rarely mentioned in school. MC Slug of the rap group Atmosphere sums up these influences, both positive and negative: "as a child hip-hop made me read books / and hip-hop made me want to be a crook / and hip-hop gave me the way and something to say" ("Party for the Fight to Write" *Lucy Ford* 1998). In contrast, I did not begin reading poetry seriously until college when hip-hop had already staked its claim on my consciousness, a situation I believe is true for many twenty-somethings and college students over the last decade.

Political Poetry and Poetic Form

Interiority may be a potential impediment to poets speaking to sociopolitical conditions; however, poetic form is often wrongly considered a yoke that must be rejected in order to write politically engaged verse. While the common perception styles an easy correlation between form and political motivation—metrical voice is conservative, free verse is politically progressive—this understanding is inaccurate. Both Shetley and Blasing point out that poetic form and political values do not always align neatly. Blasing writes that "techniques serve political rather than revelatory functions . . . without any inherent authority" (10). A specific poetic strategy can be contestatory *or* politically hegemonic. "Making it new" is many decades past, and free verse is the norm and, some would argue, politically neutralized. In the 1960s poets such as Kinnell, Bly, Rich, Merwin, James Wright, Philip Levine, and Donald Hall began writing free verse partly in response to the political climate and partly in rejection of New Criticism, formalism, and their training in them, but they often did so for personal as much as political reasons. Any essential alliance of techniques with specific political values is faulty because many poets uninterested in politics made the same shift. Free verse, then, was radical for Whitman, the French Symbolists, and even for the Beats, but beginning with the 1960s free verse became conventional. It is now the dominant, hegemonic form for printed poetry. Therefore, it is important to note that the politics of free forms is unstable and does not align precisely with oppositional values.

Hip-hop lyrics, which embody a range of implicit and explicit political values, are mostly in strict form with rhyming couplets, straight rhyme, assonance, and as one book puts it, "the verse's syntax and meter often tortured for rhythmic gain" (Costello and Wallace 24). Hip-hop, then, is more formal than most contemporary poetry, and it is often much more explicitly political. However, Robert Hass writes that since free verse is now "neutral" there is "an enormous impulse" for poets "to establish tone rather than to make form." He claims that a free verse poem does not have an imposed "specific character" so poets often "make a character in it" by working hard to establish a distinctive tone (*Twentieth* 71). His claim rings true for many poems I discuss in this book, regardless of their specific strategy. Tone, I argue, is important for political poems because it gives them distinctive figures of voice. Like a politician or rapper, a poem needs a distinctive voice in order for it to be memorable for its audience. Hass concludes that "on the level of form the difference between the strategies of free and metrical verse is not very great" (*Twentieth* 122). Metrical poems, he notes, immediately announce their patterns but free verse patterns emerge as they develop. Many free verse poems in fact have a pattern—of beats per line, of line lengths—discernible in a full reading.

Studies of political poetry should delve further than an alignment of certain forms with certain sociopolitical commitments. Gibbons notes that Ezra Pound and Ernesto Cardenal were diametrically opposed politically, the latter leftist utilizing the poetic innovations of the fascist, but they shared both technique and the "assumptions that the structure of a society and of institutions, if changed, could improve the spiritual and material conditions of man, and that poetry may participate in the attempt to change what exists" (280). So, while it is unwise to align form with politics, it seems important to understand how both Pound and Cardenal understood poetry's potential energies and its meliorist functions. Even if there is no strict alignment of ideological values with forms, Blasing calls to account the possibility of political resonance in the choice of forms. She believes that metrical verse has more political potential because it flaunts artifice and thus commands greater distance from cultural discourses—the more nonutilitarian and special poetry sounds, the more it fulfills its political function (19). I agree with Blasing to an extent, but she does not go far enough in considering the potential of various informal languages, working-class languages, and the languages used on numerous city streets where rhythm and rhyme are highly regarded for their differences from standard discourses; she also appears to overstress the power of elevated literary language. For instance, hip-hop both confirms and subverts her claim; rule bound, it has extremely rigid forms and does not sound at all like "normal" speech, but it is usually not "high" diction. Hip-hop language is nonstandard English, and it exploits a variety of appropriated linguistic and cultural discourses. However, Blasing's point is significant: Robert Lowell's strongest political poems were generally written in form—albeit innovative and experimental form—such as sonnets, even as free verse was beginning to carry the day, whereas poems such as Rita Dove's "Parsley" rework traditional forms.[10] Though I discuss mostly free verse poems in this study, many of the poems I consider experiment with form and hold on to it in interesting, innovative ways.

VARIETIES OF AND STRATEGIES FOR POLITICAL POETRY

What, then, are the advantages of a comprehensive study of contemporary American political poetry, including its most popular form— hip-hop music—through an argument about the major rhetorical strategies poets use to engage the political? Precisely because poetry and politics are at odds in so many ways, a broad understanding of poets' strategies, especially their figures of voice, may reveal clues about how politics can be made poetic, how something so unappealing to so many (politics, broadly understood) can be made striking, memorable, and actionable.

In *Nuclear Annihilation and Contemporary American Poetry: Ways of Nothingness*, John Gery approaches the relationship of poetry to the nuclear age so as to allow for strategy's prominence. Gery classifies the techniques and stylistic devices poets have used to envision the nuclear age, and he explains this method as the best alternative among others, including approaches that outline a history of American poetry after 1945 and that identify poems written explicitly in reaction to events and subject matter. Gery's four chapters explore poems that, respectively, speak "*against, through, around,* and *from within* potential nuclear annihilation*" (13; original emphasis). Each chapter title doubles as a new signifier for a poetic technique and strategy: "Nuclear Protest Poetry," "The Apocalyptic Lyric," "Psychohistorical Poetry in the Nuclear Age," and "The Poetry of Destinerrance" are departure points for Gery's exploration of poems. This organization allows the author "to underscore *how* poets have imagined the nuclear world more than what they explicitly say about it" (12; my emphasis). I use Gery's method as a departure point and focus here on *how* poets make their poems political. Such an approach inevitably leads away from a primary emphasis on content or on an event-based perspective and to an emphasis on the imaginative strategies and voices poets use to be political. Bernstein writes that "poetry can be a process of thinking rather than a report of things already settled, an investigation of figuration rather than a picture of something already figured out" (5), a claim that converges with both my approach and with Gery's exploration of *how* poets imagine nuclear threats instead of *what* they say about them.

My primary aim in this book is to elucidate the primary techniques of contemporary American political poetry by doing extensive readings of specific representative poems. For each strategy, I choose five to six poems that I believe best represent the characteristics of the particular rhetorical strategy. I consider strategies for engagement the primary departure point for my study of American political poems, with their sites of engagement and issues of engagement secondary variables for understanding the work they attempt. Gibbons's proposition that political poetry is "inextricable" from specific poems at "particular historical moments" leads to his suggestion that it is apt only to discuss *examples* of political poems (207) rather than to explicate political poetry with broad critical strokes. The examples I choose to write about range from the Vietnam-era to the present; I occasionally select poems that appear in anthologies such as *The Norton Anthology of Modern and Contemporary Poetry*, whereas others I choose are lesser-known poems that exhibit a range of qualities important to my study. In choosing both Norton "worthy" poems by "canonical" poets, those that have been published only in magazines and journals, and those that have been anthologized in books such as *Postmodern American Poetry: A Norton Anthology, Poetry Like Bread: Poets of the Political Imagination from Curbstone Press*, and other lesser-known anthologies, I hope to engage a broad cross-section of American poetic practices, engagements, and strategies. Most of the hip-hop artists I discuss are independent artists, iconic figures in the culture, or politically resonant ones. My choices generally align with my aesthetic preferences and knowledge base, and my approach in this book allows for a tangible sacrifice in depth—of a specific poet or hip-hop artist, specific "school" of poetry, or a defined period of literary history—for breadth.

My framework for reading contemporary political poetry is twofold. My first consideration is the distinctive rhetorical strategies and figures of voice that characterize political poems. Categorizing strategies of political poetry makes *rhetorical* strategy primary. The categories depart from previous formulations of political poetry in that they foreground the uses of language in poems—figures of voice, kinds of narrative trajectory, types of "evidence," tones of authority, and the types of images and rhetorical figures. I set out to see how poems act politically. These categories, moreover, are not self-contained; there is significant overlap and slippage between strategies. In the conclusion I discuss a poem that actualizes multiple strategies. My categories are not nearly as rigid as Northrop Frye's four narrative categories into which any work of literature can fit. One poem may embody multiple strategies; however, I choose the one that governs the poem, that shapes its action, power, impact, and this reader's response to it. Further, there are significant changes in strategy from poem to poem or from volume to volume in a poet's career. For instance, Forché abandoned her lyric-narrative, free verse poetry of *The Country between Us* for the staging of multiple voices in *The Angel of History*,[11] and rappers often change their voice, style, and persona from song to song. Most importantly, the categories are not poet-generated; instead, I formulated them in order to clarify and illuminate the political work of contemporary American poetry. But to be clear, the poetry is generative of the strategies—I did not read poetry and listen to hip-hop for years with this framework in mind; rather, the framework comes from years of trying to understand the political work of printed poetry and hip-hop.

While the categories are an emergent quality of the poetry itself, this book certainly reveals my preferences. Gibbons claims that the "evaluation of political poetry" must always lead to the phrase "political evaluation of poetry" (297). My evaluative methods and choices are political in that I do not evaluate politically conservative poems, and I occasionally value representative breadth above aesthetic brilliance. Explicitly conservative poems (in terms of viewpoint, rather than in terms of style) are, in any case, difficult to find. Poets generally seem a progressive lot these days, even if not stylistically. Further, though I do not evaluate what I consider "bad" poems, I do not feel indebted to traditional Western, Anglo-European aesthetic paradigms. Giving space and consideration to poems that refute Western aesthetics for "alternative" aesthetics, such as Native American, Latina/o, spoken word and voice-driven aesthetics, and the African American aesthetics of hip-hop and the Black Arts Movement, which draw from African American and west African traditions of signifying and playing the dozens, foregrounds rhetorical strategy instead of any "inherent" poetic value. This approach also allows me to bracket the somewhat specious universal question of whether a poem must be "good" (whose good, it begs) to be a strong political poem. The traditional Western aesthetic is inadequate for evaluating political poetry; unlike Levertov, von Hallberg, and Alicia Ostriker, who imply (some more strongly than others) that political poetry must be judged by the same standards by which we judge all poetry, I contend that if we follow their directive, some of the most powerful political poetry being written in this country would be ignored.[12] Hip-hop artists, I argue, probably have much more political potential at their disposal than poets who work in printed form. Unlike poets, many of the rappers I discuss have larger, more enthusiastic, loyal audiences, participatory live shows, and more cultural capital as the bards of contemporary culture.

AGENCY: A FRAMEWORK FOR READING POLITICAL POETRY

My framework for reading poems and understanding their strategies is derived from theories of agency that work to negotiate the individual agent's ability to act according to her purposes in relation to the determining material, political, and social forces that constrain action. Theories of agency can tease out the nuanced sensibilities of individual and collective agency—of paramount importance in political action—in contemporary American poetry. I understand poems as actions, as engagements with agents in various social fields. In an interview with *American Poetry Review*, Yusef Komunyakaa claims that "poetry is an action" that "reconnects us to the act of dreaming ourselves into existence" (Hass et al. "How Poetry" 21–27). Komunyakaa refers, deliberately or otherwise, to Burke's notion of literature as "symbolic action" where action in the "real" world is practically difficult (for example, in stopping a war or a widespread invidious way of thinking) but conceivable in language.[13] Poetry as action can be both creative and referential action; in Komunyakaa's words, poems can call potential future actions into existence. Therefore, they make conceivable in language what is difficult to achieve in the "real" world; they show us not what *is*, but what could be or might have been, through images of justice, peace, community, and progressive change. They also expose what in the larger world is often concealed in the discourses of "progress" and "freedom," the first concept of which I discuss in relation to several poems in this book.

Agency provides two frameworks for understanding political poetry. First, the subjects of poems—speakers, characters, the witnessed—can be seen as agents acting in response to various other agents, material constraints, and the social fields in which they are embedded. In reading a Cardenal poem, Gibbons interprets the poem's speaker and spoken-of as political agents in their "participation in Nicaraguan society" (283). In a shift in what Anthony Giddens would call "two-way power relations" where power is, in part, transformative capacity, the dictator is voiceless while the speaker, an agent with little power in society, has the voice of the poem to act symbolically (Giddens 88, 93). Whereas symbolic action is categorically different than action in the world, to bracket symbolic action as a consolation prize or wishful thinking denies the power of symbolic action in politics. (For a recent example of symbolic action in politics one need look no further than George W. Bush's "mission accomplished" speech aboard an aircraft carrier after the "fall" of Iraq.) In any case, Giddens's sense of agency elucidates the complex conditions for action for speakers in a space where agents, as William James and James Dewey might have argued, are entangled in relation to material conditions, social and political networks, preestablished meanings, and other agents. Like agents, political poems are entangled with these conditions, networks, meanings, and realities as well. Second, agency provides a way to generate categories of political poetry through a formulation of the various types of agency represented in poets' strategies, specifically in their voices. For example, the source of agency in a first-person, lyric-narrative poem of witness or personal experience is the experience itself.

Before I outline the strategies for making political poetry, I want to outline how I use theories of agency in my readings. Giddens suggests that human practices—the habitual acts we engage in on a daily basis—rather than roles "should be regarded as the points of articulation between actors and structures" (117), a principle that leads away from understanding agents in poems as occupying essential or representative roles (as an African American, as a poor person, as a dictator, and so on); instead, subjects, speakers, and characters in poems are better understood by their practices, language, and their actions and consequences. Focusing on actions and practices allows for greater nuance and creativity than does mechanistic role or identity fulfillment. Moreover, an agential reading of political poetry redirects the extant criticism about the isolated, speaking "I" of lyric poetry into social and political space: the Pragmatists, Hannah Arendt, Pierre Bourdieu, and Brian Massumi all see individual identity as activated in and through action, where action transforms the relations of the field. Action does not express a preexisting identity; rather, action creates and forms identity. Arendt also pointed out that individual identity is possible only in a matrix of social and political relations because identity emerges out of interrelations rather than out of isolation, a notion that is key to the theories I lay out about live hip-hop in chapter 4. The notion of action as creative and productive rather than referential opens up political poetry to a more expansive paradigm than the opposition between imagination and reality, wherein a poem represents either the product of imagination or the witness to actual events.

A framework of agency further assists in elucidating poems as objects in the mix of social and political space, as contestation points between actors, structures, and material realities. It helps to illustrate the ways in which poems display the constraints limiting agents' actions and the way that social and political forces shape action and individual and collective agency and identity. Massumi's work on movement is meaningful for my understanding of politics and agency in poetry. He sees positionality—the individual's roles and positions in society—as an emergent quality of movement, where the field of emergence for the agent is "open-endedly social." With every move, with every change, there is something new to the world, an added reality so that the world is self-augmenting. Every experience carries a "fringe of active indetermination" (232). Just like those (real, imagined, or recreated) experiences related in a political poem, the sense of active indetermination centers a poem in public space, where the experience inside the poem is also in some sense outside it in public, social, political spaces, and with other readers, listeners. Political poems, I argue, often track a speaker's awareness of what Dewey, Massumi, James, Arendt, and Giddens all tackle: our awareness is always of an "already ongoing participation" in developing relations as "we become conscious of a situation in its midst, already actively engaged in it" (Massumi 231). For live hip-hop this immersion is requisite for the creation of a vibrant political space and audience–performer interaction.

Types of Agency in Political Poetry

In chapter 1 I discuss two types of poems that utilize personal experience as a poetic strategy. I group them under the chapter heading *embodied agency* because both *experiential agency* and *authoritative agency* rely on the speaker-poets' lived experiences demonstrable through the human body and memory; as Massumi might argue, human agency is bodily. Poems that foreground individual and collective experience insist that the first-person perceptions, testimonies, and memories of historical actors provide the most powerful political agency for poetry. Like my understanding of how poems can be "political," my understanding of what experience *is* is broad. Simply put, these poems generally use the lived experiences of real historical actors. As Walter Benjamin believed, personal experience is the content and "source" of storytelling. It can be "passed on from mouth to mouth." For Benjamin, the horrors of the twentieth century did much to endanger our "ability to exchange experiences" with each other through stories (83). Poems of experiential agency are thus acts of exchanging (and transforming) experience with readers.

My understanding of experience, moreover, is influenced greatly by the Latin American *testimonio* and its scholars. I say more about the testimonio in chapter 1, but here I want to make two points about experience. George Yúdice argues that testimonial writing "promotes expression of personal experience" that is through and through a "*collective* experience of struggle against oppression" (54; original emphasis). Many poems I analyze suggest that the speaker-poet's experiences are part of a larger community's experience of the world. Experience, then, is not only personal; it can be shared, exchanged, and lived together. However, as Santiago Colás writes, in testimonio the speaking "agent is not identical to the other members of the community, precisely because he or she has chosen to speak" (166), in this case because he or she is a poet. As such, the speaker-poet is always somewhat apart from that represented community. Second, John Beverley shows that the testimonio is able to produce a peculiar sensation in readers that fiction cannot. He writes, "it produces if not the real then certainly a sensation of *experiencing the real*" (34; original emphasis). Poems that are centered by and in experience, unlike testimonios, do not seek to produce "the real"—whatever exactly that may mean—but they can impact the reader with something akin to "*experiencing the real.*"

As I wrote earlier, "poetry is often seen as a 'natural' medium for the recounting and examining of personal experience" (Roberts and Allison 1), but a poetry of experience is best when it is complicated rather than "natural," if "natural" signifies simply and transparently representative of lived experience. Using personal experience in poetry is often seen as problematic and as a potential limit to creativity and innovation. In a recent article in *Poetry*, former U.S. Poet

Laureate (2001–2003) Billy Collins, who is often criticized for writing light verse, traces the limits of what he calls "memory-driven" poetry (281). He suggests that a poem based on past events must convey an awareness of its own unfolding in time in the present tense and an awareness of its own language if it is to be successful as more than a narrative of events (283). Memory, he insists, should serve as a springboard or a departure point for a poem rather than an end unto itself. He continues by claiming that "it is impossible to view the past" without implicating the remembering agent in the present remembering; for Collins, "the observer is an ingredient in the observed" (285).

Poems of experiential agency often foreground both personal experience *and* the perception, retelling, and aestheticizing of personal experience, thereby preemptively acknowledging and tackling concerns like Collins's and avoiding what Jed Rasula, in borrowing from Jonathan Raban and Northrop Frye, calls "low mimetic realism" (318). Political poems of experiential agency usually employ self-reflexive narrators who consider the implications of poeticizing experience. Chapter 1 therefore also explores the complexities of embodying experience and testimony in poetry, as this abiding self-consciousness is a major part of the figures of voice utilized in *experiential agency*, and to a lesser extent, in *authoritative agency*.

Some critics go so far as to claim that a first-person narrator who proclaims and stages the self as speaker is indispensable for political poetry. Alicia Ostriker, in her 2001 essay "Beyond Confession: The Poetics of Postmodern Witness," claims that any poetics that denies a self is useless; furthermore, she writes that poetry of witness needs a consciousness that suffers and chooses in order to stage an ethical and political model for readers. Indeed, she points out a major difference in socially and politically engaged postmodern poetry compared to high modernism—the poet must be present and located in the poem (35). Chapter 1 tracks how the poet inscribes the speaker-poet (the one with the experiences) into poems and the effects it has on the political nature of them. In doing so, I try to tease out the ways that experience *works* politically in poetry and how its representation can *make* poetry political.

In the first half of the chapter on experiential agency I mostly consider first-person, lyric-narrative, free verse poems. Personal experience provides the power, justification, and a great deal of integrity to poems by Levine, Forché, Michael S. Harper, Komunyakaa, Gary Snyder, Sylvia Plath, Anne Sexton, Lowell, and countless other poets I do not discuss in this book. For example, Komunyakaa's Vietnam War poems have an added integrity derived not from aesthetic dexterity (of which they have plenty), but from the reader's knowledge of Komunyakaa's history as a soldier in Vietnam. His most anthologized poem, "Facing It," in which the speaker visits the Vietnam War Memorial, is inseparable from the facts of the war and its nearly 60,000 American dead. The reader knows that the poet is staging a voice, but one that speaks of the lived experiences that mark it. Instead, even if, as Roland Barthes, Paul de Man, and others have pointed out, the "I" in the text is different from the person who writes the text, an added level of poetic agency may be derived from Komunyakaa's experience itself.[14] Even so, this poetic strategy has been criticized by scholars and poets for being romantic, simplistic, and for glorifying witness or participation in events of extremity. Rasula, for instance, hints that many of Forché's and Rich's poems are "grounded in methods of emotional manipulation" (319). When a voice has too much of this kind of integrity there is always a risk of reader nausea, of being overwhelmed with the accomplishments and courage of the speaking "I." Many of my colleagues refuse to read or teach Whitman because they dislike his constant (and often grandiose) repetition of the first-person pronoun and of his range of (real or imagined) experiences. Much Language Poetry works to decenter the self for this very reason, so that the speaking "I" remains in the peripheries, rather than being the proverbial center of attention, even if, I would argue, Whitman's "I" is much more complex, versatile, and democratic than these colleagues consider it.

In the second half of chapter 1 I explore the second subset of embodied agency—authoritative agency. These poems draw on the Whitmanian tradition in embracing the poet's assumed cultural authority and role as a people's representative. The speaker-poets of these poems insist on their abilities to know the conditions of others, and they command the corresponding right to inscribe a type of enjoining authoritative voice that demands action from readers. Many of these poems, moreover, protest social injustice in exhortatory tones and implicitly assert poetry's didactic functions. Adrienne Rich's use of apostrophe to call forth a community of readers to action—which Mary K. DeShazer has pointed out is common amongst women "resistance poets" from South Africa to El Salvador to the United States—symbolizes the rigorous, relentless spirit of these poems. Many are activist poems at heart. They demand action, and they insist that readers use their *own* experiences to create change. Along those lines, Anne Herzog calls Rich's poetry a "poetry of shame [that] readies for revolution," evoking community, guilt, and shame in order to bring about change (267); Roger Gilbert also points out her insistence on the "power to know the other's pain and the injustices that produced it" (155).

Much the same can be said (often minus the shame) for confrontational poems, which few poets working in print still write. That mantle has been taken over by many hip-hop artists. Amiri Baraka, Sonia Sanchez, Audre Lorde, June Jordan, and Nikki Giovanni have all written great confrontational poems that challenge their readers to act and to redefine their consciousnesses. Authoritative poetry, whether of Rich's variety or like that which came out of the Black Arts Movement and the Chicano Movement, does not necessarily rely on empirical experience, events, happenings, or referents, which is not to imply that the poetry of experiential agency relies exclusively on a staunch model of factual history. As Goodman says in her discussion of a Harjo poem, "poetic evidence" is the only type of validation necessary for political poetry (45). Finally, authoritative agency often circumvents the usual channels of compromise and negotiation in social and political space, a strategy that has provoked the sensibilities of many critics, one of whom I write about briefly in this section of chapter 1. At the end of the chapter, I discuss at length a poem that successfully joins the strategies of both experiential and authoritative agency.

Poems of *equivocal agency*, which I analyze in chapter 2, challenge poems of experience while maintaining a strategic political engagement, showing that political poetry need not rely exclusively on referentiality or experience. Whereas the problems of memory are complicated by the poems in chapter 1, those in chapter 2 rely on a different model of agency. Often influenced by surrealism, magic realism, and Native American traditions, the poems I examine here problematize notions of direct experience, while foregrounding equivocation, paradox, strangeness, irony, and parodic voices. This indirection can lead to a ghostly sense of absence in many poems. These poems, moreover, often articulate utopian or dystopian visions that depart from identifiable contexts, speakers, and human presence, thereby asserting the primary agency of the imagination. These poems suggest that persuasion and the representation of realistic lived experience are unnecessary for political poetry, while their eerie, parodic, and prophetic voices are able to make more global claims than poems of experience can.

Poems such as Simic's "Cameo Appearance," as well as poems from Merwin's *The Lice* and Forché's *The Angel of History*, as well as others by Harjo, Sherman Alexie, Charles Wright, and Marcos McPeek Villatoro rely not on first-person speakers poeticizing personal experience, but on transpersonal experiences of loss and oppression, often evoked via multiple voices, discontinuous sequencing, and staged voices (often composite, ironic, or parodic). Other poems, such as Derek Walcott's "The Season of Phantasmal Peace," augur an imaginary strangeness, an alternative visionary moment nearly devoid of human presence more in the vein of Blake's and Duncan's preferences for "visionary" poetry. This kind of poetry separates the speaker in some capacity from the limitations of personal experience and the conventions that implicitly govern poems of memory, witness, and interiority. Jane Frazier's essay on Merwin's "disembodied narrators" points to how the poems in this chapter "lack a particular self so that they may make their quests without the burdens of the ego"; as such, the speakers' actions "remain part of a journey or process" rather than discrete end points (341). In much the same way, many of the speakers in the poems of this chapter are "disembodied narrators" who often move through their lines like ghosts.

In chapter 3 I discuss a way of being political that foregrounds language itself and the linguistic and cultural differences between English and Spanish and its speakers. Bilingual poems that switch between languages and cultural codes demonstrate the agency of the linguistic and transnational migrant; their code switching enacts a figurative migration across national borders, contesting American identity and the primacy of English in U.S. literature. The primary source of agency in these poems is the multilingual and multicultural voice and the ways that it crosses a variety of borders between nations and between English- and Spanish-speaking cultures. Poems of *migratory agency* thus have bilingual textures that challenge English's position as the approved language for poetic, social, and political expression in the United States. In these poems language comprises a contestatory public sphere redolent with political ramifications. Though the primary site of production for these poems is North America, their visions tend toward Latin America, the marginalized spaces of "American" culture, and the Spanish language. As Stephen Tapscott notes, the status of poetry in Latin America is vastly different than in the United States and the poet's standing in many Latin American countries is more public and revered. He writes that Latin American countries often "nominate their writers to be diplomats, international attachés, or makers and administrators of public policy," which "surprises" North Americans, whose poets are often marginalized (1). Gibbons points out the same dynamic in Cardenal's commitment to revolutionary solidarity with the people of Nicaragua as it is a social responsibility he has inherited from the "Latin American tradition" (286), and Nicaraguan novelist and poet Claribel

Alegría once commented that she would refuse to shake the hand of any Nicaraguan writer who did not address the revolution and U.S. intervention in the 1980s (Jaffe 3).

Consequently, the bilingual and transcultural Latino/a poems I discuss in chapter 3 are emblematic of the heightened possibilities for poetry as public discourse and as a way to create community, to call disparate languages and experiences into communion—a type of accord through discord—even though many of these poems are laments for the difficulties of living in the United States. English alone is insufficient for the kinds of political and social work these poems attempt. Rather than serve as a supplement to English, Spanish is a crucial partner in remaking "America," where most people speak Spanish, not English. Moreover, in poems such as Jimmy Santiago Baca's "Mi Tío Baca el Poeta de Socorro," poetry itself has a palpable agency tied directly to being Chicano, to speaking Spanish—the speaker's uncle's "poems roused *la gente* / to demand their land rights back." Poems of migratory agency, therefore, traverse geographical and linguistic boundaries and make apparent the political character of language, migration/immigration, and community.

In chapter 4, I argue that hip-hop, especially when performed live at small clubs, has the most political power of any contemporary poetry because it can activate a powerful collective agency and a participatory political experience. Some readers only familiar with the hip-hop culture they see and hear on MTV and BET and in McDonalds commercials may be tempted to dismiss this claim off-hand. My claim, indeed, requires qualification. Not all hip-hop is politically progressive or resistant to corporate, governmental, and societal structures of oppression, poverty, violence, racism, and injustice. Much commercial hip-hop, especially the multi-platinum pop variety, could be said to embody an individualistic, hypermaterialistic, and consumptive agency. It no longer scares politicians, pundits, or parents because it can seem ludicrous on its surface and because it implicitly supports many dominant American values concerning consumption and the pursuit of individual wealth. However, hip-hop culture is richer, more varied, and much more complex than mainstream radio and cable television suggest. Many hip-hop artists make incisive, creative, and sociopolitically conscious music; these artists, I would argue, have their fingers on the pulse of the nation's multicultural urban spaces more so than poets who work in print. Many of these artists' lyrics and live performances display a powerful type of community-based agency, what I call a *contestatory urban agency*.[15] These artists, moreover, challenge not only the injustices of the larger

American culture, but also what they perceive as the vacuity, ignorance, and greed of mainstream hip-hop. Even though KRS-One's 1989 proclamation in my introduction's epigraph that "the age of the ignorant rapper is done" has sadly not come to pass, much hip-hop retains the promise of a dynamic art with resistant political power.

The impact of hip-hop on generations of young people in the United States is palpable. Poetry, whether written by Emily Dickinson, Elizabeth Bishop, Langston Hughes, or Lucille Clifton, may be a beneficiary. Houston A. Baker, Jr., writes that hip-hop has revised the current generation's expectations of poetry, which suggests the need for further work on hip-hop as a dynamic, popular form of poetry. If printed poetry is to flourish in secondary schools and colleges, where many students listen to hip-hop everyday, instructors could exploit students' knowledge of hip-hop as an entry way to teaching other types of poetry. Baker's understanding of poetry as "disruptive performance" and as a "sounding space of opposition" also opens up space for hip-hop lyrics to be read as poems. Poetry, for Baker, is an "alternative space of the conditional," a notion important in many formulations of political poetry (94–96), especially in the ways that poems can create imaginary visions of justice and injustice. Mark Costello and David Foster Wallace, too, claim that hip-hop is "serious poetry" and that it was the first music to begin creative work on the "threat of economic inequality to American ideals" (98–100).

Joseph Harrington opens up further space for the study of hip-hop as poetry when he writes that "poetry" overdetermines poems. He claims there is no a priori essence to poetry; it is important, he insists, to look at noninstitutional forms of poetry that "decenter and decentralize art-writing from the norms and sites of literary authority" (10–11). Of course, however, much hip-hop is thoroughly institutional—the commanding roles that corporate conglomerates MTV (owned by Disney), Viacom, Clear Channel,[16] Sony, and others play in producing, promoting, commodifying, and controlling much hip-hop music co-opt large swaths of its cultural landscape. Moreover, Harrington writes that the cultural uses of poetry in the 1990s shifted as radically as they did in the Romantic period, an important point for a study that charts the strategies of political poetry, especially as I consider the ways hip-hop has emerged as political poetry. He also notes that critics and poets tend to define poetry with reference to "the public"—"either as an alternative to or refuge from the public, as a vehicle or mode for participating in and engaging with the public, or as a way of negotiating or problematizing the separation of public and private spheres" (168). Much of the hip-hop that I discuss can be seen as a counterinstitutional poetics as well as a poetic strategy for engaging the public.

In chapter 4 I focus on hip-hop's thoroughly countercultural *contestatory urban agency*. In the first half of the chapter I establish the parameters for this agency and closely examine some lyrics in order to elucidate how its primary rhetorical figures operate. I stay cognizant here of Baker's discussion of "positive sites of rap" (59–60) and Michael Eric Dyson's "enabling, productive rap messages" (7), where hip-hop is oppositional cultural criticism. I imply then that many of the songs I discuss are "positive sites of rap" that exist as alternatives to much politically acquiescent commercial hip-hop. As in the previous chapters, I select songs that I feel best represent the various aspects of contestatory urban agency. Tricia Rose points out that one of the most compelling struggles in hip-hop music is the "discursive tension" between individual agency and structural oppression; she claims that they must be "joined at the hip" in order to show how so called self-destructive behavior is much more complex (142). The lyrics I discuss often try to work out this tension while making sharp sociopolitical commentary. To reiterate, my choices of artists and songs are subjective and aligned with my knowledge base and aesthetics, preferring hip-hop that is politically and socially progressive over the hedonist and wealth-obsessed varieties.

In the second half of chapter 4 I explore what some hip-hop artists are currently accomplishing that other poets are not. I discuss live hip-hop shows as participatory spaces of potential collective agency and change. Dyson suggests that the rap concert "creates space for cultural resistance and personal agency" (5–6). Maria Damon makes a similar gesture in her claim that poetry slams comprise a "contestatory" public sphere capable of community-building (327), and Rose calls rap the "contemporary stage for the theater of the powerless," claiming that rap groups use shows to address social and political issues (125, 134). I use these critics' claims as departure points to argue that live hip-hop shows at small clubs can carve out a space of interactive engagement, where dominant cultural values are contested and collective agency is created. The hip-hop show, therefore, is an apt space for exploring the successes of a political poetry in the United States. To make this argument, I use Arendt's theory of "acting in concert" and the work of other public space theorists. I also draw from my personal experiences at hip-hop shows and on conversations with a close friend, a Brooklyn-based freelance hip-hop journalist, DJ, and the owner/operator of an independent hip-hop record label.

Moving Forward

As I often tell my students, all writing is about choice. The choices I made in writing this book reveal much about my biases, aesthetic preferences, and political commitments. In the conclusion of this book I consider some notable exclusions—Language Poetry, spoken word, and poetry with other primary forms of agency—I made in writing about the landscape of contemporary American poetry. Further, my basic categories of political poetry are not exhaustive nor are their borders hermetically sealed against the influences of other literary figures of voice. As such, in the conclusion I give a reading of a poem that spans strategies—Dove's "The House Slave"—and of one that uses humor as its primary form of poetic agency.

The most obvious choice I made was in terms of my theoretical framework. In this book I put forth a new model for understanding the varieties of American political poetry from the mid-1960s to the present. Most critical studies of American poetry are organized by theme (Vietnam War poetry, for instance), by writer identity (that is, Chicana/o poetry, African American poetry), or by conceptual category (that is, poetry of "witness"). These frames are limiting, often leading us away from the language itself and into ever-narrowing thematic concerns and/or identity categories. I argue that political poetry overflows these boundaries and settles more dynamically into a collection of distinct, but overlapping, rhetorical strategies. These strategies foreground various kinds of poetic agency that have unique ways of acting politically. Analyzing the ways that political agency is actualized in poems' rhetorical strategies, specifically in their figures of voice, allows for the contingencies of identity positions and thematic concerns while emphasizing how poems address social, economic, and political issues. Most importantly, I believe, it allows us to talk about poetry in a more expansive manner, and it move us away from arguments that poetry "makes nothing happen" to conversations about *how* poems *themselves* happen.

I hope, then, that this book illustrates successfully the various poetic strategies and types of agency contemporary American poets use to give their poems political life. I believe that hip-hop music and printed poetry are vibrant and exciting aspects of contemporary American culture. By placing these various forms of contemporary American poetry in conversation with each other, this project contends that poetry grapples ably and in myriad ways with the complexities of geopolitics, social injustices, and politics writ large. In juxtaposition they can tell us much about each other's vulnerabilities and competencies. However, I do not want to establish a binary between printed poetry and hip-hop, especially because I look at hip-hop lyrics on paper, where, unfortunately, they lose much of their power. They have many similarities as well that bind them together under the heading of "poetry." I know, though, that some readers will find the juxtaposition of "high" culture with supposedly "low" popular culture disagreeable. Yet others may find that in the juxtaposition that a "counterdiscourse has become institutionalized" as Georg M. Gugelberger has written about the academy's recent fascination with testimonio texts by Latin American peasants (3). Whether *I* write about it or not, however, there will be a vibrant part of hip-hop (and printed poetry as well) that will remain countercultural and contestatory as it must if it is to continue to challenge dominant discourses. Poets—whether they are Chinese T'ang dynasty exiles, English Romantics, Nicaraguans in the midst of coups and revolutions, Americans writing about Vietnam, women's rights, and the World Trade Centers, or hip-hop artists—have long tried to make their verse do political work. The following chapters attempt to explain *how* they do so in the multicultural, multilingual United States.

CHAPTER 1

Embodied Agency

INTRODUCTION

In his book about globalization, capitalism, and the failure of developing countries to integrate the extralegal poor into their economic and legal structures, Peruvian economist Hernando de Soto explains a legal theory that responds to the ways that people organize their lives outside of the law. He writes, "It is 'experience' that gives life to the law demonstrating . . . that the law must be compatible with how people actually arrange their lives. The way law stays alive is by keeping in touch with social contracts pieced together among real people on the ground" (108). I begin this chapter with de Soto because of his words' striking parallels with the modus operandi of the poems of *embodied agency*. One need only substitute "poetry" for "the law" to make de Soto's claim about on-the-ground experience a perfect gateway into the poetry of this chapter. The poems I discuss demand that we see that experience "gives life" to poetry. Poetry, moreover, "must be compatible with how people actually arrange their lives." Most dramatically, poetry "stays alive" by "keeping in touch" with the dynamic, confusing, and sometimes horrifying ways that "real people on the ground" experience the world. Poetry, for the poets of this chapter, is not only about imagination and creativity, nor is it a calculated retreat from the empirical world. It is an engagement with lived experiences, their own and that of other people and the communities to which they belong (and to which they imagine they belong). Poetry is political, these poems insist, when it "keeps in touch" with experience; poetry, like "the law" for de Soto, works best when it is organic, when it responds to the ways that people live their lives in the world, to their needs, and to their experiences.

I want to return briefly to the working definition of experience I advanced in this book's introduction. As I stated there, the poems in chapter 1 portray the lived experiences of quasi-historical actors, of people living in history. Walter Benjamin believed that personal experience is the content and "source" of traditional storytelling because it can be "passed on from mouth to mouth" (83). Poems of embodied agency figuratively enact the exchange—and thereby the transformation—of experience with readers. My understanding of experience is also influenced by Latin American *testimonio* scholars.[1] Although he claims that any attempt to define testimonio is "at best provisional, at worst repressive" because it is "by nature a protean and demotic form," John Beverley defines testimonio as a "novel or novella-length narrative" that is "told in the first person by a narrator who is also the real protagonist or witness of the events he or she recounts" (24). Most testimonios, moreover, are narratives of struggles against oppression that chronicle a fight on behalf of a group of people.

I return to this primarily Latin American form in chapter 3, but for now I want to make clear that the poems of chapter 1 are *not* testimonios. The testimonio, for the poems in this chapter, helps outline the importance of narrative, a first-person speaker, experience, and collective struggle. Beverley notes that testimonio "is not so much concerned with the life of a 'problematic hero,' " but "with a problematic social situation that the narrator lives with or alongside others" (27). His point suggests a movement away from the speaker-poet's experience as an end unto itself and toward the collective context for that experience. Many poems I write about in this chapter suggest that the speaker-poet's experiences are part of a larger collective experience. Experience, then, is not merely personal; it is a metonym for a larger group of other people's experiences. However, as Giorgio Agamben notes in his work on experience in the twentieth century, "nobody would be inclined to accept the validity of an authority whose sole claim to legitimation was experience" (14). Thus, poems of embodied agency are *poems* that gain authority from what Goodman calls "poetic evidence" (45), which is really a way of saying that poems have authority as poems first, testaments to experience second. They do not have experience as a "sole claim to legitimation"; if they did, they would function better as memoirs.

Experience is crucial to poems of embodied agency, but imagination is also a key component of this poetry's understanding of events in the world. Spanish poet Federico García Lorca knew all too well the bitter twists and turns of the world. Nevertheless, he once wrote that "visible reality, the facts of the world and of the human body, are much more full of subtle nuances, and are much more poetic than what imagination discovers" (28). Lorca, it appears, believed that the visible world and the world of human experience are the greatest wellsprings for poetry even if for him the ultimate "facts of the world" were harsh, unkind, and sinister. He seemingly rejoiced in them up to his assassination in 1936 at the beginning of the Spanish Civil War, murdered before he was able to write poetry during a war that would dramatically transform Spain into a fascist state. He was martyred, then, before he was forced either to make poetry out of the context of war, or, in the words of Wallace Stevens, to evade the "pressure of reality" on the imagination by ignoring the environment around him. Stevens styles the question this way: retreat inward or take on the world's horrors? His lectures on poetry and politics suggest the early modernist's estimation of the poet's zero–sum game. According to Stevens, when the "pressure of reality" is great, such as it was throughout Europe before and during WWI and II, the poet must turn either to "resistance" or "evasion" (cited in Des Pres *Praises* 18).[2]

In this view, then, the role of the referential world of social and political events, conditions, and observable realities is paramount in the writing process, even if the poet chooses to evade that world. The context in which a poet finds himself or herself living, writing, and observing both precedes the production of poetry and exists concurrently with poetic creation. Imagination, under such a formulation, is a reactionary force that responds to events, and this responsorial impulse is a critical aspect of political poetry of embodied agency. However, the force of events in the world on the writing process does not prevent poets' political imaginations from being preemptive, transformative forces of discovery. Poetic agency, in other words, is first a response to living conditions, but it can also transform perceptions of those conditions.

Much of the twentieth-century's best (and worst) political poetry has been influenced by experiences of war or by perceptions of war from the home front. War, though, is neither the primary arbiter of nor the sole realm for political poetry; it must be considered just one ground of, one impetus for it. In this book, though I am careful not to elide poems' contexts, my primary interest is poets' rhetorical strategies for making context *present* as a political tool. However, many critics have customarily focused on war as a way of understanding and categorizing political poetry, and for sound reasons. A war can provide a relatively contained framework for approaching poetry, especially if the war has pervasive and far-reaching cultural, political, economic, and humanitarian impacts. For these reasons, I begin this chapter on *embodied agency* with an illustration of *how* two poets have foregrounded their experiences of war. War, for all its complexities and paradoxes, can be a simple, boundaried context for explaining some key features of embodied agency and how lived experience and poetic creation can work together.

Carolyn Forché's *The Country Between Us* (1981) and Yusef Komunyakaa's *Dien Cai Dau* (1988) are two seminal volumes that deal intimately with poets' first-person experiences of war: Forché as an Amnesty International aid worker in El Salvador, Komunyakaa as a soldier in Vietnam. Despite some critical differences, especially in their poetic gestation processes—Komunyakaa did not publish poetry dealing explicitly with his Vietnam experiences until thirteen years after the war officially ended, whereas Forché spent 1978 to 1980 in El Salvador and then published the book in 1981—the poems of the two volumes establish the speaking voice of first-person lived experience in similar ways. Two poems illustrate a principal manner in which individual experiences anchor a poem's meaning, context, language, and strategies for making political poetry. They both depict these experiences as illuminating as well as confounding.

Forché's "The Colonel" and Komunyakaa's "We Never Know" are dramatically different poems formally, the first a prose poem, the second a brief imagist poem. Though both poems turn on dramatic, visceral images, the self-conscious first-person speaker is the key component of both poems, as it is for many poems discussed in this chapter. Both poems, moreover, echo the observations of Samuel Beckett's Molloy, a character whose internal monologue is inseparable from his interaction with the world and with other people. Molloy says, "I speak in the present tense, it is so easy to speak in the present tense, when speaking of the past. It is the mythological present" (34). Based upon past experience, Forché's and Komunyakaa's poems relate the details of experience in past tense verbs, but personal experience and the experience of writing about it are both foregrounded via the present tense, "the mythological present" of the poem's production. This technique foregrounds the retelling and poeticizing of experience, as if highlighting any slippage or fissure the poet sees between the original event and the event of the poem's making.

"The Colonel," which relates the speaker's experience of eating dinner at a Salvadoran general's house, begins with a blunt assertion of first-person experience and a demand for the reader to see the poem as "true": "What you have heard is true. I was in his house." The lines that follow include a selective, detailed description of the evening's events and the house in which they occurred. The lines that anchor the self-conscious strategy move auspiciously from the poem's most shocking images and its past tense verbs to the present tense: "He *spilled* many human ears on the table. They *were* like / dried peach halves. *There is no other way to say this*" (16; my emphasis). Here, the speaker-poet recounts her experience in the past tense verbs typically used to describe past events; however, the speaker then enters the poem in the present to highlight the event of retelling. As a result, the poet is doubly present—as the person in the poem and as the person writing the poem. As Joann Gardner writes, the "journalistic matter-of-factness of Forché's style acknowledges the primacy of event over verbalization" (412). Similarly, Sharon Doubiago points out that it is not the speaker who is confused or hesitant, but "the poet with the burden of her U.S. aesthetics" and the poetics "of the isolated, private self" that struggles to turn experience into poetry (35–36). Experience, then, in "The Colonel," is primary, and the verbalization of that event is secondary. The speaker's agency, therefore, is a product both of her experience and of the way she recounts that experience. She makes explicit that the telling of experience— Benjamin's "storytelling"—is a conscious, stylized rhetorical strategy that is purposefully transparent and confessional.

In "We Never Know," Komunyakaa makes a similar move. He has said that poems are most effective when they are "formed from a composite of meaningful images" and that he remembers the war mostly as "internalized" imagery (Baer 6–7). Like "The Colonel," his poem moves through a series of images that retell an experience with past tense verbs—a Viet Cong soldier "danced" in the "tall grass" after being shot, gun barrels "glowed white-hot," and a "blue halo of flies" "claimed" the body. The middle of the short poem heralds the change in voice. After finding a photograph in the dead soldier's fingers, the speaker says, "*There's no other way / to say this*: I fell in love" (26; my emphasis). Other than the contraction Komunyakaa uses *exactly* the same line as Forché does and with similar results. The speaker seeks not to report events, but a way to accentuate his *current* struggle to verbalize the experience appropriately. Also, whereas the speakers' experiences are the primary forces of these poems, their statements of presence *inside* the poems as well as *inside* the experiences anchor both.[3]

I view these two poets, who overall at these points in their careers had dissimilar aesthetics, as utilizing an intentional strategy to politicize experience, thereby giving it agency, while also complicating its place in poetry. Their two poems clarify some significant points about political poems with *embodied agency*. Brian Massumi's *Parables for the Virtual* indirectly illuminates the role of first-person agency and experience; he connects perceptions to actions, so that a perception *is* an action in its "latent state." Drawing from Henri Bergson, he claims that "perceptions are possible actions" (91), just as poems *as* perceptions, I argue, represent possible worlds, actions, and communities. In the above poems, perceptions of experience reinvest past actions with new imaginative possibility even as the poems themselves become *new* actions. Massumi's suggestion that an action must "produce" an "outward effect" and "disengage possibilities" (106) is highlighted in these poems as they catalog both their speakers' interiority and the "outward effects" of both their actions and the actions of others. Additionally, according to Massumi, an agent's movement is always primary and the positions in the social world he or she assumes are always secondary to movement. Any agent's subject position, he says, "is an emergent quality of movement" (7–8). This notion allows for the primacy of experience in poems of embodied agency: poems can be thought of as "emergent qualities" of the speaker-poet's experiences. As Massumi foregrounds the body in motion, so these poems foreground the speaker-poet in motion through the empirical world.

Although both Forché's and Komunyakaa's poems are based upon their experiences (albeit experiences they re-imagine in verse), the political poems discussed in this chapter—both of *experiential* and *authoritative* agency—do not necessarily assume that all experiences must be fully verifiable. In the introduction to her anthology of poetry of witness, *Against Forgetting*, Forché writes that poems of witness to events of extremity must be evaluated differently. She says that they should not be submitted to any test of "accuracy" or "truth to life." Such poems, she reminds us, are de facto "evidence" of what has happened, and they may be "the sole trace of an occurrence" so that there might not be an independent account with which to verify whether or not the poem is "true" (31). In the case of "We Never Know," where a Vietnamese man dies at the hands of an American soldier, it matters little if the speaker-poet's *own* experience is verifiable because millions of Vietnamese were killed by American soldiers.[4] Further, Forché's formulation also rightly suggests that imagination, metaphor, indirection, and figurative language play key roles in poems of *embodied agency*; after all, both Forché and Komunyakaa create *figures* of voice that emphasize their experiences. Experience may be the prime mover of a poem, the greeting that extends outward into the world of complicated socioeconomic and political conditions, but it is only one tool at the disposal of poets. Poems, most importantly, are not newspaper articles; they are not by convention bound to accuracy, truth, or empirical verification.

EXPERIENTIAL AGENCY

Hélène Cixous has long stumped for the primacy of experience both in literary texts and in our reading of them. Because experiences of the same event "leave different marks" and "different memories" on individuals, she claims that what texts *do* primarily is transmit perceptions of experiences to readers (230). She argues that readers should read texts to gain insight into the experiences of others. She believes that texts should "establish an ethical relation to reality" since it is important that texts have both a message and "a relationship to humanity" (231). Consequently, poets who inscribe their experiences into poems as a primary strategy for making political poetry are implicitly establishing an "ethical relation" to their realities, their memories, (their) history, and to the humanity of their audiences. As Charles Altieri has claimed, lyric poetry is capable of creating a bond between the speaking self and readers in that the speaking "I" can implicitly claim that his/her experience is representative of others' experiences (*Self* 22). Altieri's claim dovetails with the basic assertion of the testimonio (and with a relatively fundamental tenet of some hip-hop), but lyric poetry creates that bond partly through figures of voice that foreground the "different marks" of moving experiences.

Michael S. Harper's "Deathwatch" represents poems that embody first-person experience even as they connect that intimate experience to a more expansive social context. Poems such as this one in Harper's oeuvre emphasize personal experience as both the focus of the poem and as a departure point within the poem to do greater political work. Like many other poems that have the poetic agency of personal experience, this poem is an elegy. One in a series of wrenching elegies in *Dear John, Dear Coltrane* (1970) in which the poet deals with the deaths of two infant sons, "Deathwatch" is probably the most political of these elegies, and because the anger the father feels over the death of his infant son is so understandable, the visionary leap he makes from one death to a broader American context is lucid and efficacious.

Though each of the poems in this part of chapter 1 have first-person viewpoints, the speaker in "Deathwatch" never refers to himself using the first-person pronoun "I," but the poem remains in the first-person throughout. In the first stanza,[5] the speaker retells the words of his wife, who has just given birth to a premature son. These two lines are structurally simple—both start with "she tells me how" and end with his wife's testimony about surgery and their baby (65–66). In both cases, the speaker is in an object position, and so uses the first-person object pronoun "me."[6] Further, when the speaker refers to himself elsewhere in the poem, he does so formally. When the wife refers to their son, she says that he is "strong, / like his father." In the second stanza, when directly addressing his dead son, the speaker says that the infant had "the face / of your black father," which is an especially important assertion of blackness given that Harper's wife is white. In these cases, the speaker's experiences are heard from the voices of two perspectives, both as individual father and as archetypal father, a tactic that serves to create a collective space of shared experience with readers as (black) fathers and parents.

Joseph A. Brown once wrote that for Harper "no moment or matter is too private to be exorcised in a healing song" (215). Though "Deathwatch" elegizes a sad private event, it also indicts and exorcises U.S. racist history. The first two stanzas combine the poet as father's experience with the poet's knowledge of medical terminology learned as a premedical student. The cold, impersonal terms "episiotomy," "placenta," "adrenalin holes," "autopsy," and "disposal papers" convey a measured distance from their human implications. Jahan Ramazani, discussing another Harper elegy, writes that Harper's interaction with his son "has been mediated and mutilated by the impersonal, objectifying discourse of the hospital" (*Poetry of Mourning* 257), and so it is here. When the poem connects discrete personal experience to broader sociocultural contexts, it is subtle but pragmatic. The leap is necessitated by events—when the speaker and his wife "sign the autopsy / and disposal papers," the event is symbolically framed by the implications of dying black in a white-controlled country. The papers are "in black ink / on white paper / like the country" in which the speaker's son was born. For Harper, personal experience is inseparable from politics and, as Ramazani points out, "death and mourning are bound to a grid of blackness and whiteness," which gives the speaker no choice but to view the loss "through the lens of his racial experience" (258–259). Harper also explores an idea interrogated in depth by Leslie Catherine Sanders in her book on the development of African American drama (*The Development of Black Theater in America: From Shadows to Selves* 1988): African American artists and citizens exist largely on white cultural ground. Although this condition may be changing with the popularity of African American cultural forms such as hip-hop and with the increasing Latina/o population, Harper's lines suggest that this country has been *written* by, *built* by, and *made visible* by the arts, lives, deaths, labor, and blood of African Americans, with little official, institutional recognition for their efforts apart from death certificates and disposal papers. The implication is a lament that African Americans are most visible in their deaths, which has certainly been true for rap stars Tupac Shakur and the Notorious B.I.G., both of whom gained in celebrity after their murders.

The speaker-poet contextualizes his son's death within the landscape of what Harper has called Americans' "psychic weight of discovery" of racism's horrors in a country ironically founded upon a supposedly egalitarian Bill of Rights (Antonucci 507). In the third stanza, the speaker connects his experience to W.E.B. Du Bois's, specifically to a letter Du Bois received from a student presumably after Du Bois's own son died. In linking his personal experience to a specific historical incident, Harper avoids the faults Robert von Hallberg finds with much Vietnam-era political poetry by Bly, Duncan, James Wright, and others. When von Hallberg criticizes the techniques of what he calls "visionary political poetry," he does so because it leaps from observation to visionary prophecy; he finds that its excessive oracularity does not "permit the exercise of analytical intelligence." He also writes that rapid juxtapositions do not allow for concessions, qualifications, and "rational virtues" (*American Poetry* 139). Even if Harper's technique did not circumvent such criticism in its specificity, the speaker-poet is uninterested in concessions, qualifications, analytical intelligence, or other "rational virtues." The death of infant sons and the brutalities of racism are difficult to make the subjects of concession and rationality, especially in the context of a letter that denies African Americans their essential humanity and "a collective history of mourning" (Ramazani 259).

The voice of the speaker is full of rage rather than qualification or concession. In Harper's poetry, according to Niccolò N. Donzella, this rage works to "to introduce sleepwalking natives" to their lives as citizens ignorant of the complexities and paradoxes of America (806). This rage, an emergent quality of lived experience, is evident in the poem's final stanza and three-line coda, where the poem is styled as an elegy: "This is a dedication / to our memory." Because the speaker's memories remind him of the letter Du Bois received at Cornell, Harper ends the stanza with the question asked of Du Bois: " 'Will you please tell us / whether or not it is true / that negroes / are not able to cry?' " The question is depraved and disturbing, but elusive, for even Du Bois is not "sure of the answer."

The speaker, though, provides a de facto answer in the coda, which has a marked change in tone: "America needs a killing. / America needs a killing. / *Survivors will be human*" (original emphasis). These lines call for an exorcism that destroys the conditions and systems of thought that enable racism and help prevent people from seeing others as fundamentally human, capable of feeling pain and sorrow. This extrapolation from individual experience to a social conclusion based on that experience is both intensely personal and intensely political.

It distills the speaker's rage into a repetitive chant. However, as Ramazani suggests, Harper also "risks merely reversing the very scapegoating he condemns" (259) as his strategy refuses concession or qualification. For the speaker, infant death and racism deserve no concessions. Harper's strategy makes individual experience political and gives that experience poetic agency. Even so, though the poem foregrounds individual experience, it veers dangerously close to an axiomatic refusal to see personal tragedy as in some ways distinct from collective tragedy.

Whereas Harper's techniques in "Deathwatch" force readers to view a personal experience in broad political and cultural terms and to see how the voice of lived experience can contest a discriminatory ideology, Galway Kinnell's "When the Towers Fell" derives its experiential agency from the witness to a communal, shared happening. The poem was published one year after 9/11, and it directly explores the experience of watching the terror attacks. For some critics, the poem's publication in *The New Yorker* creates substantial problems of reception. Marjorie Perloff, who notoriously doubted that poems in *The New Yorker* are capable of political force, once pointed out that W.S. Merwin's eerie Vietnam poem "The Asians Dying" (1967), which I discuss in chapter 2, originally appeared "on a glossy page between those gorgeous ads for fur coats and diamonds and resorts in St. Croix" ("Apocalypse" 130). Cary Nelson disagrees with Perloff's assessment that the poem's placement obviates its political impact. He suggests that magazines such as *The New Yorker* have always been rife with contradiction (120–121). It is also possible that political poems are even more conspicuous and jarring when juxtaposed with luxury advertisements. After all, what media does not contain mixed messages? These often disconcerting contradictions abound in hip-hop, where some rappers often celebrate a variety of contrasting values. The context for Kinnell's poem is also unique in that it speaks to New Yorkers about a New York event. It is difficult to find fault with its appearance in the quintessential New York periodical, even if it reaches a largely white, cultural elite.

In his discussion of Wallace Stevens and the Greek poet Constantine Cavafy, Terrence Des Pres argues that both saw poets as "*outside* observer(s) distressed by the march of events" but not "*inside* participant(s) overwhelmed and mute in the face of events themselves" (23; original emphasis). His formulation applies to Kinnell's speaker-poet. In "When the Towers Fell," the speaker is both an outside observer of the event and an inside participant (but not one literally *inside* the towers), as many New Yorkers would likely describe themselves. Des Pres goes on to say that the position of outside observer is the same position most readers occupy as distant from disaster "but well within reach of its shock waves" (23). Kinnell's speaker struggles to give voice to the event, its aftermath, and his experiences of them. He makes clear that he is both apart from and a part of the scene, both an insider and outsider.

When the poem opens with the line "From our high window we saw the towers / with their bands and blocks of light," the speaker immediately establishes his role as a witness, and thus an outside observer. But he also inscribes the experience as collective ("*our* high window" and "*we* saw"), so in some ways he is an inside observer as well. Though it is possible that Kinnell refers to himself and his partner/wife in this line, there is no question that millions of New Yorkers could view the towers from their windows. Yet this lofty vantage point also gives the poem a stigma of wealth. Despite the fact that many housing project apartments had views of the towers, Kinnell's speaker's view seems from the penthouse. He attempts to reconcile—with mixed results—this vantage point with populist principles later in the poem. After setting up the towers as a visible entity, he suggests the haunting surreality of their loss, of the observer's inability to see them again: "we grew so used to them / often we didn't see them, and now, / not seeing them, we see them." These lines construct a world in which disorder reigns and the senses are unreliable perceptors of experience. The loss of the towers, the opening stanza implies, challenges our ways of experiencing the world, especially our ways of *seeing* it.

After the opening ten-line stanza in which the speaker sets up the vantage point of his experience, the second stanza takes two strange turns. It shows a poet struggling with, and succumbing to, the difficulty of writing about a widely viewed event. The speaker contends with questions that challenge the existential status of an artist faced with disaster. What does a poet do when his experience is so drastically different from the experiences of New Yorkers who lost loved ones? Especially now that occasional poetry is an artifact of the past, how does a poet respond to such a tragic public event? Maurice Blanchot suggests that disaster makes writing a difficult if not impossible enterprise. According to Blanchot, the disaster is an experience of being rendered completely passive. The disaster, moreover, is a pervasive and general experience of calamity that redefines the limits of human experience and what are signified as "disasters": "disaster . . . does not have the ultimate for a limit: it bears the ultimate away" (28). Kinnell's response to the terrorist attacks reveals both the difficulty of his task and the ways that disaster utterly redefines personal and collective experience.

In the second stanza, Kinnell tests his populist, inclusive, democratic mettle. He begins with four listless, bathetic lines that show "The banker," "Humberto," "The trader," and "The mail sorter" at their tasks in the towers. Kinnell makes the intention of these simple sentences transparent in the next eight lines, which alternate between French and their English translations. They show in a transparent way that the attacks killed "poor and rich" and "wise and foolish," amongst other classes and types of people. The message is simple, undeniable: death was indiscriminate. Two aspects of Kinnell's strategy stand out. First, the technique is heavy-handed, unnecessary, and a bit contrived, although it is interesting that the only named person in the poem is a wage worker with a Romance language name. Second, the use of French is perplexing. Perhaps Kinnell was thinking of *The New Yorker* audience (if indeed he composed it for that audience), but the immediate translations negate the need to read French. The French, however, is less appropriate than Spanish, which was spoken by countless thousands in the World Trade Center, especially by its wage workers. Spanish would have been more realistic and more true to life than French, and to this reader at least, less contrived. Kinnell, though, may have been bound by his knowledge and experience. If knowledgeable in French but not in Spanish, he may have felt more comfortable with using the former to suggest the hundreds of foreign nationals who lost their lives in the attacks. The use of French may also resonate more given the conflict with the French about the war in Iraq. Though the conflict was not yet astir in September 2002, the poem's French could be seen now by supporters of the Iraq War as denigrating the French for refusing to be part of the U.S. coalition, which would be a serious misreading of the poem.

If Blanchot believes that writing about disaster is an impossible task, Cixous provides a better, although disheartening, strategy for writing about disaster. For her, "things which are unspeakable" and that "take our breath away" should be addressed by "inscribing the question, signifying our impotence, our obligation, our memory of what is happening" (232). Kinnell does precisely this when he uses a deflated, hopeless voice to catalog the varieties of death in the towers. The syntactical parallelism is striking:

> Some died while calling home to say they were O.K.
> Some died after over an hour spent learning they would die.
> Some died so abruptly they may have seen death from within it.
> Some broke windows and leaned out and waited for rescue.

The eighth in the series is the most abstract and lyrical and seemingly the most painful for the speaker: "Some leapt hand in hand, the elasticity in last bits of love-time letting—*I wish I could say*—their vertical streaks down the sky happen more lightly" (my emphasis). This line is markedly different from the four above, which are matter-of-fact and concrete (with the exception of the third one, which is more lyrical and abstract). These four lines assert the speaker's impotence and tortured memory, but in different ways. In the more concrete, distant lines the speaker speaks calmly, coolly, without emotion, whereas in the eighth line the speaker interrupts himself with "I wish I could say." Strangely, though, the speaker does *say* in the poem what he is unable to say in a reality based on his experience. As such, he signifies the feeling of passivity the experience gives him; the poem is thus an intervention in the city's memory of the event, but a failed one. Though the line is the most lyrical of the eight, it is interrupted by dashes—"I wish I could say"—that signal a failure to transform memories and experiences into poetry, a strategy that is similar to Forché's and Komunyakaa's discussed earlier. The repetitive lines make the deaths vivid, but they also suggest the difficulty poets face when the attacks have been seen hundreds of times on television and in memory.

The problem Kinnell faces in making poetry out of 9/11 is best understood by considering connections between artistic and historical accounts of an event. In *Private Poets, Worldly Acts: Public and Private History in Contemporary American Poetry*, Kevin Stein discusses the differences between "a poem about an event and an historical account of the same event" (6). He points out that objectivity is not the province of either form, especially in light of the debunking of the notion of historical "objectivity" and the "official story" done in much poststructural and postcolonial theory.[7] Stein points out that Barthes's "The Discourse of History" shows that historical accounts are similar to novels, stories, and poems that deal with history—each are "constructed from fragments of experience" and pasted together to make "a unified 'whole' " (6). "When the Towers Fell" is certainly "constructed from fragments of experience" (as are many poems of embodied agency), both the speaker's and others' experiences told by the speaker. But it is not a unified whole unless one considers a poem itself a unified whole, even when it pastes together perceptions, memories, images, and a frantic monologue. The poem thus enacts the fragmented nature of the event proper and the ways that the event disrupted the clean narratives of many lives.

Kinnell's poem is different from historical accounts that purport to objectivity in that the experiences the poem includes are consciously subjective, disjointed, and fragmented. He does not attempt to create a unifying or objective narrative. Are poems about events such as this one always political though? The answer must be yes in that they encourage readers to understand an event in a certain way. An affirmative answer does not denigrate those who lost their lives, nor does it necessarily suggest that Kinnell is using the event for political ends. It merely suggests that perceptions of the event and works about the event will always be political. There are, however, differences in strategy and political commitment in poems about events, as will be obvious in Amiri Baraka's poem about 9/11 and in two hip-hop artists' responses I discuss in chapter 4.

Finally, when the speaker of "When the Towers Fell," alludes to a searchlight looking for bodies that "always goes on / somewhere, now in New York and Kabul," Kinnell takes the greatest risk of the poem. He moves from a confused lament for and witness of those who died in the World Trade Centers to those who die in what he implies are needless and meaningless wars and terrorist attacks the world over. More specifically, his implicit condemnation of the war in Afghanistan suggests that there are thousands of innocent dying there as well. However, it seems a risky strategy in that Americans roundly supported the effort to oust the Taliban. Kinnell does not flinch in his lament for those who suffer in tragedy, whether they are Afghanis or New Yorkers, and his strategy reveals a willingness to run the risk of alienating part of his audience.

Kinnell has won many prestigious awards, including the Pulitzer Prize (1983); the next poet I discuss is less visible. Luis J. Rodríguez, a Los Angeles-born Chicano, brilliantly uses personal experience to give poetic agency to the Latina/o community. "Then Comes A Day" (1989), a reflection on Rodríguez's youth as a gang member, portrays experience a bit differently than do the poems discussed thus far. The poem's speaker holds the memories of past experience up to the light of present experience and explores the ramifications of the two juxtaposed. The speaker of "Then Comes A Day" appears to live by William James's pragmatist credo: "I live, to be sure, by the practical faith that we must go on experiencing and thinking over our experience, for only thus can our opinions grow more true; but to hold any one of them—I absolutely do not care which—as if it never could be reinterpretable or corrigible, I believe to be a tremendously mistaken attitude" (207). For James, all principles are potentially revisable based upon new experience, and everything about our experiences and our understanding of the world is subject to change. As James might have said, nothing outside the flux secures the issue of it.

In Rodríguez's poem, the speaker's present experiences force him to revise his perceptions of both past and present. Even though white, upper-class Brahmin James's experiences were much different than a poverty-bound Chicano's, their ways of (re)organizing and understanding experience are strikingly similar. In "Then Comes A Day," the speaker returns twenty years later to the neighborhood of his youth to face his violence-filled past. The primary political voice of the poem comes in the speaker's perceptions of the collision of his past with his present experience. Rodríguez opens the poem with the speaker's observations from within a confined, decaying space. His voice and its poetic agency are bounded, limited, narrow, and impoverished: "The Resurrection Cemetery is an oasis of green, / encircled by the rising structures of the Edison / Utility Company and new roads interwoven through / the felled homes that once flowered with families" (cited in *Poetry Like Bread* 183–184). The poem begins then from within a calm center, an oasis, the Resurrection Cemetery, which implies that death is the only place where peace can be had amid such decay. The two proper names, the only two in the poem, are also important in that they render the space knowable, local. The speaker's reference to a specific community makes the poem not a general political poem about poverty and injustice, but a particular political commentary. Further, the use of proper names can be understood as a strategic use of Ernesto Cardenal's *exteriorismo* (exteriorism), which included the use of proper names and places and concrete diction in response to the abstract romanticism of much Latin American poetry.[8] In "Then Comes A Day," the use of concrete diction and proper names locates the poem and the speaker's experiences in a specific space so that its politics work "glocally"—on *local* issues impacted by *global* forces, such as economic "progress" and migration/immigration.

The first stanza shows the poem's abiding concern with experiences of loss and decay and their effects on community, a concern akin to the community-based aesthetic I explore in independent hip-hop music in chapter 4. Rodríguez's words for the "old neighborhood" are full of decay: "sprinkled," "remains," and "splinters" describe the "wood-frame shacks." The speaker implies that in this context the issue of community fits under the larger official discourse of "progress," a largely unquestioned principle often used to quell dissent about urban development projects in American cities. The Nobel-winning economist Joseph Stiglitz suggests that this discourse is used to show that the "growing divide between the haves and the have-nots" "*is* progress" that poor communities and countries "must accept" (Stiglitz 5; original emphasis). Rather than improve this poem's community, "progress" and "gentrification" have "discolored" the neighborhood. The community's new " 'immigrants' "—a term the poet puts in quotation marks to question its meaning—are not poor blacks, Latinas/os, or foreign nationals; these "immigrants" are presumably wealthy, gentrified, white people. These wealthy "immigrants" suggest an urban renewal project prominent in city centers that often evicts poor, actual immigrants to make room for wealthy people who have no desire to live in mixed communities. Rodríguez's clever play on the terms "progress" and "immigrants" calls into question the American doctrine of progress as a means to prosperity for all.

The manner in which the speaking "I" first appears anchors the poem's experiential agency and its attack on "progress." In the third stanza, the speaker points to the rift between his past experience and his current identity: "It has been twenty years since I roamed these / earthen streets. Coming back, I am as new, alien, / except in the old cemetery where many of my / friends are buried." Here we see the prominence of the speaking "I," a marker of many poems of experiential agency. Two decades later, Rodríguez's version of this speaker is the walking dead as well as an "alien" whose community is found only amongst headstones. His memories are also primarily of loss, as they call forth "so many funerals" and "revenge, / as thick as mud." Further, none of his friends died of natural causes, but rather by drugs, gangs, police, suicide, car crashes, and "diseases / science conquered long ago." The speaker's experience is marked by loss, displacement, and isolation, but how the speaker contextualizes these memories matters most.

In the final four stanzas, the speaker struggles with memories of dead friends and with rage produced by justice long-denied. When he says self-consciously, as if to himself, "I have carried the obligation to these names. / I have honored their voices / still reverberating through me," the speaker is "not simply a phantom manipulator of words but a confused actual person, caught in a world of catastrophe that the poem must somehow mirror and transcend" (Ostriker "Beyond Confession" 35). This "confused actual person" is then a composite of the lost voices of his fallen friends that course through his body; the speaker seeks both to reflect these voices and to use them to fight for justice for the dead. When Forché explains her reasons for writing poetry about what she witnessed in El Salvador, I hear the speaker of "Then Comes A Day": "In my own life, the memory of certain of those who have died remains in very few hands. I can't let go of that work if I am of that number." For Forché, this process stems from memories that "arise from the exigencies of conscience" (Montenegro 36) and demand resolute action. While Forché is uncertain of the redemptive value of remembering, Rodríguez's speaker implies that redemption, though difficult to achieve, is possible, not simply an irony of being buried in "*Resurrection* Cemetery" (my emphasis).

Ultimately the speaker of "Then Comes A Day" searches for justice and redemption even as the poem questions whether redemption is possible amid such decay. Natural processes suggest that redemption is indeed possible: the earth has the speaker's dead friends' fingers, "but not what they touched"; each death is "new life"; from wombs "revolution is birthed / through an open-mouth scream"; and in the final stanza, dawn breaks, bringing "first light" to the cemetery. Yet these flickers of redemption occur only on the path of a constant search for justice, a "long, crevice-filled road / I've been stranded on all this time, / trying to reach a destination that climbs / uneasy over the horizon." The speaker's search for justice is uncertain, dangerous, and partly successful in isolating him in a fight against poverty and community dissolution.

For the speaker, however, this lengthy fight for justice can be redemptive if and when the "revolution" is fulfilled. This realization emanates from his personal memories of loss. Near the end of the poem, the speaker discovers that "Twenty years come / that don't make a day, / then comes a day / that makes up / for twenty years." Two decades of defeat can therefore be redeemed in a single day in which revolution and justice become realities instead of distant possibilities. This revolution is both personal and collective; it facilitates a leap from individual experience to communal experience and from memory to present reality. In this process, the speaker "leaps from the narrative to the visionary levels," a "dominant" strategy of much 1980s poetry pointed out by Charles Altieri.[9] For Altieri, this "scenic style" is firmly entrenched in the Romantic tradition where poems often "achieve closure" by a visionary leap. He criticizes this mode because it implies that the speaker's discoveries are contingent upon events; thus, the self is "created rather than creative" (*Self* 15). For "Then Comes A Day," where the speaker's active experiential agency literally moves the poem and the voice of experience actively creates the poem's perceptions, avoiding Altieri's objections is important. Whereas the poem "achieves" a semblance of closure in the speaker's leap, "Then Comes A Day" is based on events in the speaker's life; declining to use these experiences in order to achieve some type of closure would necessarily discount the primacy of the speaker's experience and the ways that events shape lives. The speaker's creative agency is after all an impassioned response to the very conditions of a collective experience of poverty.

The preceding examples of *experiential agency* suggest that there are complex social frameworks for agency. Poets who write using experience elucidate these complex conditions in part by using figures of voice that place poems in social space. Experience, for these poets, is a political force and a useful tool for writing poetry. Further, the conceptions of agency in these poems are evolving, shifting, and constantly in play, which make any poem's conception of agency difficult to capture. Pierre Bourdieu's practice theory shows that the reproduction of social practices, both positive and negative, occurs through agents rather than through laws, institutions, structures, or principles; as such, because agents can be unpredictable and precocious and because their experiences can be confusing, this broad framework is always in motion.

Finally, like poems of *authoritative agency*, which often directly confront readers, poems of experiential agency do not recount a limited range of American experiences. Rather, they are exemplars of a strategy unconfined to a type of experience or to a certain set of political and social engagements. I could have chosen Mark Doty's "Homo Will Not Inherit" (*Atlantis* 1995), which abstracts somewhat the poetic agency derived from experience, or one of numerous Philip Levine poems in lieu of "Then Comes A Day," as Levine often employs similar strategies and time frames in his speakers' experiences. Also, many recent and visible poems, such as Eliza Griswold's "Buying Rations in Kabul" (*The New Yorker* June 27, 2005) and Billy Collins's "Statues in the Park" (*The New Yorker* July 25, 2005) employ voices with poetic agency similar to those of experiential agency.[10] These two poems rightly imply that political poems that use experience and a recognizable first-person speaker are the most prominent of political poems in the literary establishment and appear with some frequency in magazines such as *The New Yorker* and in journals such as *The Virginia Quarterly Review*. Experience, however, also has a prominent place in poems of migratory agency and in much hip-hop, but as secondary factors. Many poems in the next section are similar to ones discussed thus far, but with important differences in tone, attitude, and the ways that speaker-poets represent their relationships to their communities.

AUTHORITATIVE AGENCY

Political poems of *authoritative agency* are usually confrontational and often didactic; they are insistent, demanding, and unrelenting.

Frequently grounded in their speakers' experiences, they often claim a more encompassing sense of authority from experience than do poems of experiential agency. They challenge their audiences and often condemn the social and political conditions that make such poems necessary actions in the documentation of and resistance to those conditions. These poems, like many politically charged hip-hop songs, seldom offer compromise or qualification. For this issue I want to return briefly to Robert von Hallberg, who claims that many poets in the Vietnam era wanted to "speak for the country, even at the risk of rhetorical rotundity." He imagines that these poets eschewed "gradual change" and compromise because these virtues "involve taking seriously differences that can be measured only with patience and discrimination." Not only does he imply that poets who write authoritative poems and who use the Whitmanian voice lack patience and discrimination, he also claims that their poems "encourage a lack of proportion in political thought" (*American Poetry* 142). He is partly right, for the following poems *are* impatient and resolute.

Yet authoritative poems also support a view that von Hallberg's approach is dangerous, even absurd, in the contexts of unjust war, the civil rights movement, and environmental destruction. In these situations, concessions and accommodations are ways to say "just wait," "be patient," and "stay in your place," admonitions long heard by African American civil rights leaders and cataloged in the stories of Richard Wright's *Uncle Tom's Children* and most powerfully in Nina Simone's "Mississippi Goddamn."[11] The Black Panthers and the civil disobedience of the Student Non-Violent Coordinating Committee's (SNCC) and the Southern Christian Leadership Conference's sit-ins and freedom marches *were* about a certain kind of patience but not about concessions, nor are these poems. Von Hallberg's admiration for poets who "register fine distinctions where other poets and people see none" and for poetry that speaks of "accommodation rather than opposition" (*American Poetry* 228) clearly did not include many poems by Nikki Giovanni, Sonia Sanchez, Amiri Baraka, June Jordan, Carolyn Rodgers, Robert Bly, Denise Levertov, Thomas McGrath, Edwin Rolfe, Gary Snyder, and Adrienne Rich, whose poems often view accommodation as acquiescence to a status-quo that perpetuates racism, misogyny, imperialism, and corporate power. Yet poems of authoritative agency do not simply catalog speakers' perceptions and feelings. They are often explicit calls to act, to revolt, to protest, but they are not solely protest poems that are protest tools first and poems second.

The first poem I discuss is relentless and confrontational, unyielding and controversial. Nikki Giovanni's first two books of poetry,

Black Feeling Black Talk and *Black Judgment*, both published in 1968, contain many political poems of authoritative agency. After numerous readings, "The True Import of Present Dialogue, Black vs. Negro" (*The Collected Poetry* 19–20) stands out as a premier example of an authoritative political poem, although not as her most successful. Its authoritative voice is a primary product of how the poem values life. Reginald Gibbons has noted that political poems must take a stand on the value of life itself; he writes, "It is no surprise when a great and political poem like Neruda's 'Alturas de Macchu Picchu' prizes life over death, but a political (and especially a revolutionary) poem must also begin to say *whose* life" (288; original emphasis). In "The True Import" and other poems in Giovanni's 1968 books, black life is infinitely more valuable than white life, and her poems protest white racism and the institutional structures that support it. Giovanni's political position in these poems—in many ways representative of the Black Arts Movement—has created contentious debate, some of which I outline in order to contextualize the confrontational and authoritative voice of Giovanni's poem.

There are two primary schools of thought with regard to the inflammatory rhetoric of the Black Arts Movement. On one hand, critics such as J. Saunders Redding attack the 1960s Black Aesthetic for what he considers its hate and reverse racism (cited in P. Harper 239). This group would likely view "The True Import" as an unequivocal document of racism and anti-Semitism. This understanding allows—perhaps rightly so—no room for strategic rhetorical intent and generally offers no further depth. On the other hand, critics such as David L. Smith, though they do not apologize for anti-Semitic lines like those in Amiri Baraka's "Black Art" or in "The True Import," find a cogent social and political framework for the controversial rhetoric of the Black Arts aesthetic. Smith suggests that Baraka uses the term "Jew" in part because American culture "provides us with an effective language of oppression" but not one of liberation, and that "Jew" brings "emotional force" to the poem. This type of poetic strategy is an example of what Smith calls "an art which outrages by being outrageous" ("Amiri" 243–244). In the same vein, Phillip Brian Harper suggests the primary reason for the use of racist language in the late 1960s: the "enemy" of the Black Arts Movement was the white "establishment" (238) without differentiation and without apology. Smith's approach provides a de facto consensus point I take from here on: "too often the work is marred by the swaggering rhetoric of ethnic and gender chauvinism" ("The Black" 93), which emblemizes an uncompromising rhetorical strategy pledged to revolution by any means.

The rhetorical strategy of "The True Import" falls squarely within this debate. The poem fails as anything beyond an example of a poem of authoritative agency not because of its refusal to compromise in a way that would please von Hallberg, nor because the poem is unequivocally racist as Redding would have it, but precisely because of the poem's unyielding authoritative voice. This particular figure of voice makes the poem appear as a *literal* appeal for blacks to kill whites rather than the figurative injunction pointed out by Jennifer Walters in her essay on Giovanni and Dove. Walters implies that the notion of killing in the poem is both symbolic and literal such that the poem can be understood as advocating " 'killing' the white *values* imposed on Black America" (214; my emphasis) rather than as indiscriminately killing white *people*. However, her claim is more wishful thinking than rigorous reading, as a brief exposition reveals.

The inflammatory rhetoric of "The True Import" includes short, repetitive lines devoid of punctuation but for two resonant question marks. The fifty-line poem includes "nigger" twelve times, "kill" twenty-four times, "you" twenty-five times, and "can" thirty times, rhetoric that clearly diverges from most poems of experiential agency. Giovanni's experiences as an African American woman presumably authorize her to address with vitriol her black male audience,[12] and she has claimed that her "vitality" (rather than "role") as a poet is based on a "trust" borne of personal experience. According to Giovanni, a poem says of its author " 'I saw this through my eyes' " (Elder 71), which is a claim that resonates with (and justifies) poems of experiential agency. But, importantly, her experience does not appear in the poem, just the authority borne of her experience as a black woman. The first three lines have provocative voice: "Nigger / Can you kill / Can you kill." Because the poem has no punctuation and it relies for its rhythm on the impatient, fast-paced spoken voice, these lines repeatedly challenge the audience. The repeated "Can you" creates an insistent oral demand within a "vernacular performance" as an "immediate, communal form to be experienced in public" (Smith "The Black" 101). Here, the provocation twice reaches a spoken climax with a powerful "huh?," not as markers of confusion but as demands for an answer as in a fast-paced game of the dozens that encourages immediate responsive action. These techniques seem to create a demand to act against white people rather than a figurative injunction to "kill" white institutions.

This claim is fulfilled by Giovanni's own comments. She has said that this poem concerns her distaste for hearing "talk of going out to die for our rights." Dying, she says, "is not the hardest thing to do. It's harder to go out and kill for your rights." She claims that

"The True Import" was written as "a protest against [any] attitude" (Giovanni 374) that puts a premium on dying for civil rights, as in these lines: "We ain't got to prove we can die / We got to prove we can kill." According to the poem's speaker, her audience must learn "to kill WHITE for BLACK." For many in the Civil Rights Movement in the 1960s, compromise was not an option.[13] Malcolm X's famous declaration "By any means necessary" is the implied framework for many of Giovanni's 1968 poems, including "The True Import." But to reiterate, it is not this attitude that makes the poem less successful than the following Giovanni poem; the poem's very insistence on direct action makes it incapable of discriminating between action against oppressive white institutions and action against white people in general.

Phillip Brian Harper has shown that "The True Import" "expose(s) the logic of the Black Arts ethic that governs work from the movement generally" in its use of the second-person pronoun and in its complex address to two audiences—one black and one white (240, 247). But Giovanni's "My Poem" (*The Collected Poetry* 86–87), from *Black Judgment*, is a better example of *authoritative agency* even if it is less confrontational than "The True Import" and less representative of the Black Arts Movement. If the speaker's voice in "The True Import" sounds like an insistent but insecure bully peer-pressuring her friends to act, the speaker of "My Poem" is a confident, convincing revolutionary proclaiming an inspiring belief in her cause. The repetition, orality, and fundamentally oppositional character remain but largely absent is the assaultive voice. As such, the first-person singular speaker plays a major role in "My Poem," unlike in "The True Import," which contains not a single "I." Here is the first stanza:

> i am 25 years old
> black female poet
> wrote a poem asking
> nigger can you kill
> if they kill me
> it won't stop
> the revolution

It is important that the speaker names herself and asserts her identity immediately; the lowercase "i" remains so throughout the poem, a technique that suggests the speaker's identity is secondary to the revolution, to black lives in general. The poem gains a large part of its political vibrancy from the strategy of selflessness, itself a vital element of revolutionary thought. The simultaneous assertion and denial of individual experience makes the repetition throughout the poem of the first stanza's final three lines powerful rather than redundant. For the speaker, revolution needs personal experience to give it identity, but it needs more a willingness to sacrifice all that is personal.

The primary rhetorical strategy of "My Poem" gives authority to collective agency and action rather than to personal experience. Even the speaker's poetry is expendable because *her* voice is subsumed by the voice of the movement: if she "never write(s) / another poem" the revolution will continue. Yet poetry in general is not expendable just as black lives in general are not expendable. The poem's authority comes from the individual's role as a single cog in a collective action, in which the individual could die but the movement would not. This notion emphasizes not the willingness to kill for the cause, but the willingness to be subsumed by the cause. The revolution, after all, "is in the streets" where people meet and move in unison, not in fifth floor apartments that isolate people from others.

The next poem of authoritative agency has a substantial shift in subject matter, but not one in the poet's strategy for making a revolutionary political poem. Based solely upon subject matter, political engagements, and disparate personal backgrounds, poems by Nikki Giovanni and Gary Snyder make for an odd juxtaposition. However, "Front Lines" (from Pulitzer Prize–winning *Turtle Island* 1974) has a great deal in common with the above Giovanni poems. It is confrontational, albeit more subtle than many poems of the Black Arts Movement, oppositional, and full of violent images. Like "My Poem," "Front Lines" foregrounds collective agency, here in the service of environmental activism. And, like "The True Import," Snyder's poem uses visceral imagery, a bellicose tone, and an enemy figure in order to mark the "front lines" in a war on the environment. This authoritative and oppositional tone likely led Charles Molesworth, a champion of Snyder's work, to dismiss the poem because poems *like* "Front Lines" had been written "better" by Snyder earlier in his career. Molesworth implies that the poem should *only* be read as an urgent message of environmental doom because it appears among the "primarily celebratory poems" of *Turtle Island* (151).

"Front Lines" is better understood, in part, as an example of what Leonard M. Scigaj calls "ecopoetry": poetry that engages environmental concerns, considers the environment an equal partner in the sustenance of human societies, and refuses to use nature as a benign backdrop for human actions, emotions, and thoughts. In ecopoetry, "the preverbal experience is primary," which results in poems that are the "verbal record" of the "poet's originary experience in nature" (28–29, 80). As such, the poet's experiences with the environment are the driving force of a poem's creation. Experience, therefore, is primary, and language is a "flexible tool" used to represent and transform these experiences into poetry (80). Whereas Scigaj's focus on the "referential base of all language" (5) would seem to take some of the creation out of poem-making, Snyder's "Front Lines" employs both micro-level metaphors and an extended metaphor. This figurative language has the rhetorical effect of heightening the stakes for the environment. Also, though the poem does not explicitly refer to the speaker's experiences, many readers are likely familiar with Snyder's history as a logger, fire lookout, and environmental activist.

Snyder begins "Front Lines" by personifying those who harm the environment as rapists and the environment itself as a woman practicing self-defense. The first line depicts succinctly what these rapists cause: "cancer" (18). He thus creates a strangely powerful mixed metaphor of rape and cancer. Like a metastasizing cancer, rapists spread across the land and destroy it. The depictions that follow of the rapists' actions and their effects on the earth are unequivocal. In the second stanza, their actions are perverse: the "Realty Company" and its clients "say / To the land / Spread your legs." Here, Snyder compares the depraved abuse of a woman with the greedy abuse of the land for profit. In the fourth stanza the rape imagery is more visceral and figurative. The speaker imagines the bulldozer as a man raping a woman; it "grind(s)," "slobber(s)," "sideslip(s)," and "belch(s)" "*on top of*" the earth and its bushes, which Snyder pictures as having "skinned-up bodies" (my emphasis here and below). Snyder paints the wanton siege of the environment by greedy men and their machines as a stomach-turning rape scene.

All rapes are brutal, but they are doubly so when both men and machines are the perpetrators. The angry and intrusive machines in "Front Lines" point to a disturbingly problematic relationship between humans and the environment. The pathetic fallacies show how much agency humans have ceded to conscienceless machines and further suggest that humans have become *like* machines in their unthinking (and programmed) abuse of the earth. "A chainsaw *growls*" like a predatory animal and "jets *crack* sound" overhead as if disturbing the basic senses of the natural world. Under the influences of such predatory machines there can only be "foul" breezes. The poem suggests that such a proprietary and destructive relationship with the land leads to or is symbolic of the overall "sickness" of America. As Katsunori Yamazato has claimed, Snyder "indicts" an entire civilization "devoid of sensibility of and respect for other life forms, mindlessly engulfed in its own destructiveness" (235).

The poem is most encompassing and oppositional when Snyder draws a parallel between environmental destruction and sick country. When the "jets crack sound overhead," the speaker responds with the startling "it's OK here" as if the jets represented a sustainable natural order. The remainder of this stanza, though, shows a much different reality: "Every pulse of the rot at the heart / In the sick fat veins of Amerika / Pushes the edge up closer." This "edge" is the cancer that "swells" across the land in the first line of the poem; America is rotting due to its disregard for the earth. This "rot" is not only visible on the earth's scarred surface; it is also an internal condition that makes sick the earth's circulation, its ability to sustain itself. Here, Snyder is prescient in his claim that America's development is not *sustainable*, currently the buzz-word and development strategy par excellence among environmental studies scholars and planners. "Front Lines" suggests that America's reckless development practices are unsustainable, violent.

The speaking voice in this poem is obviously confrontational, especially in its visceral, unforgiving imagery and in its extended metaphors of rape and war. But the way that Snyder frames this opposition in terms of political agency is his most effective technique. Rather than simply outrage readers, many of whom are probably already environmentally conscious, Snyder opens and closes the poem with the voice of collective experience and agency. In the first stanza, "*we* feel / a foul breeze" from the cancer. This outrage and the agency needed to oppose it are collective rather than individual. As most environmental organizers claim, a single individual modifying her behavior, consumer decisions, or practices will not impact environmental issues. If I refrain from driving a car it will have no discernible effect on global climate change. Any such effect would result only from macro policy decisions and enforcement.

Snyder concludes the final stanza with a call to collective action in the front lines of environmental activism. On one side of this well-marked "line" is "a forest that goes to the Arctic / And a desert that still belongs to the Piute." On the other side, bulldozers, chainsaws, and realty companies rape the land. The line that must be drawn is obvious. The speaker imagines a collective of environmental defenders standing with the forest and desert behind them. According to the speaker, it is "here" that "*we* must draw / *Our* line." Snyder's "we" creates both an authority more powerful than a single speaking "I" and a collective and mobilizing framework for environmental action in opposition to rapists who do not allow the "trees [to] breathe." This rhetorical voice foregrounds collective action, and, in the words of Scigaj, it works "to revise perceptions and coax sustainable actions in readers" (277). If the poem is successful in equating those who harm the environment with rapists, then it suggests a potential shift in how we think about humans' relationships with the environment. Snyder's collective "we," moreover, and the presumptions he makes in speaking for his constituents, as it were, engages the sensibilities of the Whitmanian tradition in a line extending through Neruda and Ginsberg.

Like "Front Lines," Adrienne Rich's "For the Record" (*Your Native Land, Your Life*) employs an authoritative, confrontational voice. Rich, unlike Snyder, is well-known for politically and ideologically charged poems that have displeased a variety of critics and reviewers, some of whom Anne Herzog discusses in her article on Rich (258–261) and to whom I refer readers in search of sources critical of her work. Whereas "Front Lines" implicitly challenges readers to act as a collective to protect the environment and to revise their perceptions of its destruction, "For the Record" challenges readers to account for their actions and to revise perceptions of inaction. In both poems, an authoritative tone not directly derived from experience shows that readers cannot blame the environment they live in for their problems. Instead, both poems challenge readers to see themselves as sources of the world's problems.

The authoritative voice of "For the Record" is generative of Rich's insistence on "her power to know the other's pain and the injustices that produced it" (Gilbert 155), a hallmark of poems of authoritative agency and, most famously, of Whitman's "Song of Myself." The poem's speaker, therefore, does not hesitate to call forth those injustices and blame readers for them, nor does she flinch in spanning the globe to catalog horrors, injustices, and apocalyptic upheavals. The first five stanzas interrogate the human tendency to project anger upon the visible manifestations of problems rather than the ultimate source of injustice: ourselves. In doing so, the poem gives no hint of qualification or excuse. Rich shows that attributing poverty, war, riots, environmental devastation, suffering, and oppression to neutral things, such as clouds, stars, mountains, trees, houses, buildings, and barbed wire, is absurd. The poem further suggests that the natural environment is subject to and secondary to human agency: "if the mountains spewed stones of fire into the river / it was not taking sides / the raindrop faintly swaying under the leaf / had no political opinions" (31–32). Natural resources are also innocent, but not the people who manipulate them for violent means: "The trees didn't volunteer to be cut into boards / nor the thorns for tearing flesh." For Rich, built structures are incidental to social injustice as well. By showing that "things" are forcedly involved in terror as instruments of human cruelty, the poem places blame directly on each human "whose signature / is stamped on the orders, traced / in the corner of the building plans." The evocation of the South African homelands of Apartheid ("barbed-wire / stretched around crouching contemporary huts") suggests that terror is often systematically conducted under the auspices of convention and order. In its totality, this epic catalog of injustices is a streaming sequence unbroken by a period, a strategy used to overwhelm the reader with a sense of injustice. However, it also makes the problems global; as an unintentional side-effect, individual action seems futile in light of pervasive, global suffering, which is a shortcoming of this type of poetic agency and voice. In attempting to show the prevalence of social injustice, they often style it as so pervasive that human agency seems futile to affect change.

For Rich, attributing injustice to human conventions, material creations, the environment, and social and political practices instead of to human actions and decisions, is cowardly and dangerous. "For the Record"—the title gives her claim rubber-stamped (and ironically, institutional) authority—insists that all individuals are responsible, including those who do not act. It is unacceptable, according to the poem, for any person to respond to human atrocity with a dismissive *that's just the way the world is and there's nothing I can do about it*. In this poem, the issues are decidedly *not* too big for people to do something about them, which somewhat belies the lengthy catalog of problems the speaker outlines. The poem implies that even those who cause no harm but do nothing about these horrors are as worthy of blame as those who commit the acts. The final seven lines of the poem make clear this strategy, its authoritative agency, and Rich's desire to provoke readers to act:

> Look around at all of it
> and ask whose signature
> is stamped on the orders, traced
> in the corner of the building plans
> Ask where the illiterate, big-bellied
> women were, the drunks and crazies,
> the ones you fear most of all: ask where you were.

Here Rich directly challenges readers to ask who is responsible for the suffering cataloged in the poem. "Look around at all of it" commands readers to act by refusing to ignore suffering. This command reaches its pinnacle in Rich's use of apostrophe ("you"), which is the crucial cog in the poem's rhetorical strategy even though it does not appear until the final line. Two critics help to understand how apostrophe operates in Rich's work. For Terrence Des Pres, Rich uses apostrophe to subvert the humanistic "we," which he says has been "one of the more successful illusions of high culture" when used to refer to "all of us or 'man' in general." He points out that this " 'we' has always been the property of an educated elite, male, white, and eurocentric" (357–358). Unlike Snyder, who uses "we" in "Front Lines" even though the poem works against "man's" destruction of the environment, Rich uses "you" as a direct injunction to readers and to challenge the ways we speak of the collective and of community. For Alicia Ostriker, on the other hand, feminist poets use apostrophe "to challenge the neutrality of the reader" and to address "a 'you' who is perceived as an antagonist" ("Dancing" 215). In "For the Record," Rich claims that no individual is neutral in the suffering of others; further, "you" are an antagonist if you do not act against injustice.

By grouping "you," the reader,[14] with the marginalized and stereotypically destructive elements of society, the poem styles all people as responsible for fighting social ills. As such, the poem attempts to create feelings of guilt. Herzog suggests that "For the Record" evokes shame and guilt in the last seven lines, but not in a "self-righteously accusatory or self-flagellating" manner. Instead, she claims that "they are spoken in a communal context" (267). Though the final lines are a communal call to action by means of an individual recognition of complicity, they are undoubtedly accusatory and self-righteous. The speaker does not ask herself *where was I?* and thus remains above contempt. Nick Halpern explains that Rich's "prophetic mission" places her *in* but mostly *above* her poems: "She writes poems in which she imagines herself as a solitary figure in the sky." Though she does write poems in which she "represents herself as a figure in the city, in the streets," Halpern notes, "too often" she is "not like someone who is leading an everyday life but someone who is walking the earth" (184–185). This seems to me exactly the dynamics of "For the Record." The speaker-poet simultaneously walks the earth and hovers above it in the sky, seeing all and demanding that those who lead "everyday" lives take responsibility for what they do. Her blistering, authoritative tone attempts to spur readers to forgo indifference for socially motivated action. This didactic voice is present in many poems of authoritative agency and may seem heavy-handed to some readers. Yet Rich's strategy makes it difficult for even these readers to extricate themselves from certain implications—the juxtaposition of "the ones you fear most of all" with "you" forces readers to reconsider their actions as indistinct from the villainous.

If "For the Record" is provocative and righteous, Amiri Baraka's "Somebody Blew Up America" has added doses of aggressiveness, defiance, and many would argue, offensive language. Most readers are likely aware of the controversy surrounding the poem, so it is unnecessary to review in depth Baraka's career as a "persistent chronical of controversies, most of them having been provoked by Baraka's own deliberately incendiary polemics" (Smith "Amiri Baraka" 235). The poem, written in response to 9/11, was first delivered to the public on September 20, 2002, at the Dodge Poetry Festival in Waterloo, New Jersey, where it created a maelstrom of complaints, most of which focused on the poem's commentary on Israel. At the time of the reading, Baraka was Poet Laureate of New Jersey, and Governor Jim McGreevey, two years prior to his own controversy, asked Baraka to resign. Baraka refused. It would be disingenuous to ignore the poem's criticism of Israel or its lament for the genocide of European Jews during the Holocaust; therefore, I focus on its rhetorical strategy and authoritative agency. Though such an approach could be seen as ignoring, overriding, or even exacerbating the anti-Semitism, it is important to look at a poem that ignited such controversy due to its rhetoric in a study of the rhetorical strategies of political poetry. Inflammatory rhetoric, after all, is a crucial element of many political poems of authoritative agency and many in the Black Arts Movement, although it is folly to ascribe to what James Smethurst calls a "great-man theory in which Baraka's work becomes a metonymy for all Black Arts literature" (261). This poem, moreover, is meant to incite, to be an uncompromising, authoritative utterance.

Overtly confrontational poems such as "Somebody Blew Up America" are unusual in contemporary American poetry. Politically engaged hip-hop and spoken-word artists have taken up the mantle assumed in the 1960s by G.I. poets opposing the Vietnam War, and by Black Arts Movement and Chicano Movement poets opposing the institutionalized racism of the United States. Not only is the poem's strategy anomalous in printed poetry, its length (233 lines) departs significantly from many contemporary political poems, unless it is considered as a spoken-word performance piece or a hip-hop song, which are usually longer than written poems. Further, in the United States, unlike in many countries in Latin America, where poetry is a "fugitive means of expression" and offers the practical advantage of being easier to copy, distribute, memorize, and chant or perform publicly than fiction (DeShazer 13), Baraka's poem, especially given its use of African-American Vernacular English (AAVE), has more in common with many hip-hop songs, the American "fugitive means of expression" par excellence.[15] Even so, its form, length, and rhetorical strategies make it a sprawling litany of accusations, collapsed historical contexts, and conspiracy theories, all of which combine to make it a fascinating, provocative mess.

"Somebody Blew Up America" does not open with a defiant voice. The first seven lines, which differ in tone and voice from the rest of the poem, serve as prologue and de facto justification for its oppositional perspective. In prosaic English the speaker says matter-of-factly that "All thinking people / oppose terrorism / both domestic / & international," but that "one should not / be used / To cover the other." These flat, calm, measured lines are enclosed in parentheses to separate them from the invective that follows; they seem a strange prefatory apology for that invective. Cleverly, though, they proclaim the speaker's opposition to the terrorist attacks, but also set up his opposition to "domestic" terrorism, which alludes to the coming attacks on corporate and imperial power.

After these prefatory remarks, Baraka's speaker confronts the official public discourse about 9/11. He creates a somewhat abstruse enemy whose claims he questions throughout the poem: "*They* say it's some terrorist" (my emphasis). This relatively ambiguous enemy oddly, and perhaps appropriately, echoes the ambiguity concerning the identity of the terrorist enemy in the "War on Terror." Even though "they" is difficult to parse because Baraka collapses centuries of global, historical, and geopolitical contexts in order to assume a far-reaching purview of oppression, it certainly refers to the white, Euro-American imperial power the poem rebels against—more specifically the military–industrial–corporate complex. One aspect of "they" is pointed out explicitly by rap group dead prez—currently the only overtly revolutionary, political hip-hop group with a major label record deal (the rest record on independent labels)—in the song " 'they' schools," which addresses the abuses of the American public school system (*lets get free* 2000). Dead prez notes that the "same people" who run the school system run the prison system; it is no wonder, they suggest, that more African Americans find a home in the latter than in the former. For Baraka's speaker as for dead prez, it is dangerous to trust anything "they" say or do.

Beginning in line 25, after the speaker doubts that "American terrorists" such as the Ku Klux Klan, Skin heads, "the them that blows up nigger Churches," Trent Lott, David Duke, Rudy Giuliani, and

Jesse Helms were not responsible in some way for the attacks, Baraka begins the major rhetorical strategy of the poem. Here's the line: "They say (who say? Who do the saying." This parenthesis remains open for the entire poem and structures nearly every line thereafter. All but 44 of the final 207 lines of the poem begin with the word "who."[16] These lines combine relative clauses and questions that simultaneously refine the actions and history of "they" while also questioning them. Some are very specific, such as "Who genocided Indians," "Who invaded Grenada," and "Who blew up the Maine," even as others are general, such as "Who tell the lies," "Who the biggest executioner," and "Who make money from war." It is important not to read each "who" as *either* an interrogative pronoun that introduces a question *or* as a relative pronoun that introduces a subordinate clause. Baraka brilliantly does both at once—defining "them" also questions "them." The repetition of "who" clauses creates an owl sound that mimics a night owl keeping watch on events that pass under her perch. Baraka's voice is thus a revelatory one that functions to expose injustices on its watch.

The repeated "who" phrases feature historical figures, most of whom are revolutionaries, civil rights activists, assassinated leaders, leftist freedom fighters, *and* the pariah figures who oppress them. The huge number of names—both heroes and enemies—is overwhelming, but it give the poem a strange texture of both historical particularity and undirected rant. David L. Smith claims that Baraka's poems are best as political art when they are "grounded in historical particulars" and worst "when based on abstractions, generalized attacks, and broad exhortations" ("Amiri Baraka" 236). "Somebody Blew Up America" fulfills both poles on a large scale. 9/11 gives the poem particularity whereas the preponderance of historical and geopolitical contexts realize Smith's claims about Baraka's least successful political poems and, for some, compromise his credibility as a rational voice. However, the numerous historical and geopolitical contexts are strategically convincing in one important manner: to show the global reach and influence of American power. The poem's implied text suggests that the world's disastrous events over the last century contain American fingerprints. When the speaker simultaneously asks and declares "Who killed" Malcolm X, the Kennedys, Martin Luther King, Jr., Steve Biko, Salvador Allende, Che Guevara, Laurent Kabila, Patrice Lumumba, Huey Newton, Medgar Evers, and Rosa Luxembourg, it sounds like conspiracy theory, but also like the result of a white capitalist global power structure that destroys progressive voices. Even if Baraka cannot claim that the CIA was directly responsible for the assassinations of these figures, he can safely declare that American policy, influence, and fingerprints were on the weapons that killed them.

Baraka's sweeping indictment of American actions covers slavery, reconstruction, Jim Crow, the infamous incident at Tuskegee, and also more generally American corporate and cultural imperialism. This scathing critique includes a functional rejection of a capitalist concept of ownership, especially as it concerns natural and human resources. For the speaker, there seems to be little difference between the ownership of slaves and the ownership and exploitation of natural resources for the benefit of the rich. Lines such as "Who own the oil," "Who own the soil," "Who own the air / Who own the water," and "Who own the ocean" suggest a malicious intention to commodify the very materials that sustain life and to control every citizen's fundamental ability to breathe and eat. Further, lines such as "Who define art / Who define science," "Who own this city," and "Who make the laws" imply that American corporate powers control the structures that define the world and determine right from wrong. Further, "they" "make money from war" and "want the world" to be "ruled by imperialism and national / oppression and terror / violence, and hunger and poverty." These lines sum up Baraka's strategy—to subvert the official public discourse in a war on terrorism that America fights to bring freedom, democracy, and peace to the oppressed places of the world. Instead of a "war on terror" and "war on poverty" the poem claims that there are wars to *maintain* terror, poverty, oppression, and the vast power inequalities they enable.

The sound effects of "Somebody Blew Up America," especially its AAVE, repetition, and rhyme, oppose the authority of elitist, commodified corporate language. (Unless of course one claims that hip-hop language has been thoroughly commodified, a claim that I hope to dispel in chapter 4.) Three lines near the end of the poem illustrate these features; here the speaker ridicules three prominent black conservatives for their support of these imperial power structures: "Who do Tom Ass Clarence Work for / Who doo doo come out the Colon's mouth / Who know what kind of Skeeza is a Condoleeza." First, "Who do" and "Who know" highlight one prominent feature of many AAVE varieties, including those used in hip-hop culture—the absence of the third singular suffix -*s*. In Standard American English (SAE), these lines would read "Who *does*" and "Who *knows*." By eliding these suffixes, Baraka not only implicitly challenges public discourse delivered in "proper"[17] English, he also uses the dialect of many young African Americans in the hip-hop community. Additionally, in using "Who do" and "Who know" instead of SAE Baraka increases the poem's orality. "Who do" creates a fluid rhyme whereas "Who does" sounds stilted; "Who know" combines with other similar structures to create a fast-paced invective meant to be read aloud. Baraka is also unafraid to employ simple—although here he regretfully taps into hip-hop culture's relatively pervasive misogyny—internal rhymes such as the one between "Skeeza" and "Condoleeza" in order to increase aural effects. AAVE, rhyme, repetition, and syntactic parallelism anchor the poem, elements that have long structured black political speeches, sermons, and revolutionary pronouncements. Finally, however, Baraka uses all of these techniques almost as ends unto themselves rather than to engage his audience initially in order to turn their attention to some greater conclusion.

Baraka erases historical, cultural, and geopolitical differences and speaks of events about which he does not have intimate experience in order to create a sweeping indictment of American misdeeds. His authority is partly borne of his experiences as a member of a minority group, but it is more a product of his refusal to compromise or to fear retribution. As such, his voice draws on and displays a trust in the poet's role as a populist spokesperson, who is able to articulate people's experiences, and the events that mark them, in unique ways. The differences between this poem and Kinnell's 9/11 poem are obvious and need no further explanation, as will be its differences from the hip-hop songs about 9/11 in chapter 4. The differences between Kinnell's poem of experiential agency and Baraka's poem of authoritative agency beg a question: Are there poems that fruitfully combine experiential and authoritative agencies?

SYNTHESIZING EXPERIENTIAL AND AUTHORITATIVE AGENCIES

Carolyn Forché's "Return" (1981) successfully combines the strategies of experiential and authoritative agency. This first-person, lyric-narrative, free verse poem is an exemplar of embodied agency. It synthesizes first-person experience, memory, and poetic authority via an interplay of voices that Michael Greer calls a "dialogue in verse" showcasing "the poet's self consciousness about her own political role" (172). The primary rhetorical strategy of "Return" is a staged dialogue interrogating experience, authority, and their consequences on an individual's political ideals. These dual figures of voice incarnate agency derived from experience and from authority respectively.[18]

"Return" (17–20) and the other poems in *The Country Between Us*, which was the Lamont Poetry Selection for 1981, have been written about by a number of critics. I depart from critics interested in the poem's content, politics, and insight into war's effects on its observers. I am concerned with the poem's rhetorical strategy and embodied agency. Some background is necessary, though, to introduce the poem. As mentioned earlier, Forché worked for Amnesty International in El Salvador during its civil war. The U.S. government provided aid, intelligence, and funding to El Salvador and its paramilitary death squads, who were responsible for tens of thousands of *desaparecidos* (disappeared persons), most of whom were innocent peasant farmers sympathetic to the leftist guerillas. The United States intervened in support of their right-wing dictatorship in the fear that the populist, *campesino* rebels were communists. The backdrop for "Return"[19] is the speaker-poet's re-entrance into life in the United States after her two years in El Salvador.

These two disparate worlds give rise to the two disparate experiences and voices that mark the poem, thereby calling into question strict boundaries between time and space. The poem radically disorders these two worlds, so that they vector into and out of utter difference and utter sameness. Forché's sophisticated figures of voice and authority in the poem make this suspension possible. The poem thus has two alternating first-person speakers—one the poet, the other her friend, Josephine Crum, to whom the poem is dedicated. The speakers directly address each other using the second person "you" so that their conversation appears somewhat staged and exaggerated. This strategy styles the dialogue as a quiet interchange between two old friends rather than as a piece of moralizing public discourse. When Josephine first speaks, in line thirteen, she says, "So *you* know / now, *you*" (my emphasis). In the next four lines, she repeats "you" five times, each phrased in order to repeat what the reader has not heard the speaker-poet say. Phrases such as "you know," "You've seen," and "You've heard" show Josephine speaking for the poet about her experiences in El Salvador. This technique allows Forché to avoid demagoguery, the arrogance of bragging about hardships survived, and the sensationalization of violence. When the conversation is between friends, readers overhear instead of being the subjects of preaching.

This dialogic strategy allows the poet to maintain authority without proselytizing or presuming to speak for others. Forché is acutely aware of the questionable ground of authority she trod in writing about El Salvador. She has spoken at length about the creation of a quasi-fictional, first-person voice. This voice, she says, stages a "self" that speaks of "its own sensitivity," which may be "an inappropriate act, if the self derives its authority from its privilege over the 'other,' whether this be the privilege of knowledge or experience, and whether the 'other' be the implied reader or the one to whom the poem is addressed" (Montenegro 35). For Forché, rejecting a hierarchical relationship between a poem's speaker and its audience and subject allows the poet to write of what she has seen and experienced. Also, she creates a poetic self that exists on an equal basis with those she writes for and about—the poem does not disclose a "privilege of knowledge or experience." The voices in "Return" reveal their fragilities and obsequiousness when they reject the privilege of speaking to an audience; they assume that there is *no* audience. Instead, the two voices speak to each other, which gives each of these voices the authority of friendship. After all, it is easier to be frank, condemnatory, and demanding with a friend than with the public.

Despite Forché's claims, this conversation *between* friends is inequitable. Of the poem's 125 lines, the speaker-poet has 47 lines whereas Josephine has 78. On the surface, Josephine's perspective as an American greatly outflanks Forché's perspective influenced by her years in El Salvador. However, many of Josephine's lines restate what the poet has presumably told her about the time she spent there. Thus, the poet's experiences in Salvador give the poem its primary agency, even if that agency is first passed through the prism of a conversation in which the friend, and not the speaker-poet, takes on an authoritative agency.

The speaker-poet's and Josephine's speaking voices vary greatly even though they both speak of the poet's experiences. The speaker-poet attempts to reconcile her experiences in El Salvador with her life in the United States, and she struggles to make compatible the fear of driving "those streets with a gun in [her] lap" with the order, cleanliness, and comfort of "the Safeway" and the "fine white / hands" of American men. The stark contrast between the two worlds leaves the speaker unable to talk about her experiences—"all manner of speaking has / failed"—and seemingly unable to "keep going." The rift between order ("clean toilets" and "iced drinks") and disorder gives the speaker vertigo and makes her view her suffering as inextricably linked with the suffering of Salvadorans rather than North Americans. Unable to rest, to speak, to feign normality in a supermarket, or to connect with other Americans, the speaker-poet is overwhelmed by guilt. Guilt and grief create a hyper-responsibility that extends to mundane realities, such as a trip to the supermarket and simple conversations with North Americans: "I cannot, Josephine, talk to them."

Despite the speaker-poet's inability to talk to other North Americans, the poem speaks when the poet cannot. The speaker-poet's inability to speak belies the material reality of the poem itself because the poet's personal experience in both worlds forms a bridge between the people of El Salvador and the people of the United States. Like the oppressed Salvadorans, the "remnants" of the speaker's life "continue onward" despite her inability to give sufficient voice to her experiences. In associating the speaker-poet's plight with that of Salvadorans, the poem collapses the gap between two worlds. Poetry, then, creates *The Country Between Us*—the poem as bridge brings together two countries, two friends, and two divergent experiences. I expand implicitly on this notion of joining different Americas—south and north, poor and rich, Spanish-speaking and English-speaking—in chapter 3.

Whereas the speaker-poet's voice is uncertain and timid, Josephine's is authoritative. She speaks directly of the brutal events in Salvador that the speaker-poet witnessed but largely refrains from speaking of in "Return." Josephine mediates between the poet's experience and the audience. She speaks of two irreconcilable worlds, not between the United States and El Salvador, but within El Salvador that the poet saw first-hand: "the pits where men and women / are kept the few days it takes without / food and water" and the "cocktail / conversations on which their release depends." These contrasting experiences reveal the violent detachment of those in power from the people who are the subjects of "torture reports." The conspicuous repetition of "men and women"—once in the body pits and once in the position of detached observers who "read / torture reports with fascination"—makes explicit the connection between the suffering and the comfortable, even while those in power imagine themselves as apart. This strategy makes reading "torture reports with fascination" grotesque, as if the "men and women" were reading their own torture reports.

Here the poem explores what Greer calls "the re-representation of world as spectacle" in the American media. He argues that images of violence from distant places allow viewers to remain detached from injustices. Josephine's later lines interrogate what Greer calls the "conversion of history into a domestic spectacle" (175). When Josephine addresses the speaker-poet about North Americans' taste for violence, she says to her: "Go try on / Americans your long, dull story / of corruption, but better to give / them what they want." Josephine does not hesitate to tell the speaker-poet in harsh detail what Americans want, sensational stories and images: "Lil Milagro

Ramirez, / who after years of confinement did not / know what year it was, how she walked / with help and was forced to shit in public"; "Jose . . . waving his stumps / in your face, his hands cut off by his / captors and thrown to the many acres / of cotton"; and "a labor leader . . . cut to pieces and buried." The cunning strategy in these lines simultaneously denounces sensational, ungrounded violence as perverse entertainment even as Josephine gives readers exactly what she denounces.

Because these disturbing lines are given to Josephine, Forché is able to deflect accusations that she has succumbed to sensationalism. But if the speaker-poet is able to escape blame, Josephine's authoritative, condemnatory voice does not allow other Americans to do so. Josephine's condemnation suggests a similarity to Rich's "For the Record"—that all Americans are complicit in the suffering of Salvadorans and that a superficial interest in their misfortune is disgraceful. In his essay on Forché, Larry Levis claims that when art shames its readers, it makes them "more conscious, more human, more capable of bearing pain and perceiving the beauty of bearing it" (11). Yet are shame and guilt unsustainable short-sighted ways of pursuing social change and justice?

Josephine indirectly chastises North Americans and reserves her direct attacks for the speaker-poet's insularity and arrogance. In her first lines, Josephine tells the poet not to "flatter" herself because *all* people suffer. In the last thirty-one lines of the poem—Josephine, it is important to note, gets the final word—her attack on the speaker-poet deconstructs American complacency and privilege. Here, Josephine's authoritative voice is its most tenacious. She says to the speaker-poet:

> Your problem is not your life as it is
> in America, not that your hands, as you
> tell me, are tied to do something. It is
> that you were born to an island of greed
> and grace where you have this sense
> of yourself as apart from others. It is
> not your right to feel powerless.

Privilege, according to Josephine, is a cultural convention that makes Americans believe they have the capacity to live as though any individual is capable of insulating herself from the well-being of others. For Josephine, rugged individualism is a myth built on fear and selfishness. Lee Zimmerman writes that "overcoming" disconnection and helplessness in this poem requires "opening to voices and visions that, rather than substantiating the self, threaten to demolish it" (96), which is exactly what Josephine does here. She demolishes the speaker-poet's sense of an isolated self "apart from others"; she also crushes the speaker-poet's self-indulgent lamentations of her difficulties after returning home. The speaker-poet's earlier complaints pale to Josephine's incisive remarks about the poet's "hands," which connect to Jose's hands "cut off by his / captors and thrown to the many acres / of cotton." Unlike Jose and other Salvadorans, the poet and other Americans still have hands with which to fight injustice. For Josephine, people with "hands" have no "right to feel powerless"; this right is reserved for those who are actually powerless.

Forché's rhetorical strategy in "Return" is sophisticated and artful. The poem's experiential agency resonates with the credibility of blood, agony, and hardship in El Salvador, but without romanticization. She utilizes a clever conceit in her willingness to give authority and control to Josephine, who admonishes the speaker-poet for her arrogance and complacency. These techniques circumvent what Charles Altieri suggests is the transparency of lyric poetry. For Altieri, a poem can claim that its speaking "I's" experience represents human experience in general, but the speaking "I" is always on a "constructed stage" that reveals its status as an imaginative creation. Consequently, poetic authority is always provisional (*Self* 22). In "Return," Forché's strategy implies that the poet does not have this authority, but her friend does, and in abundance. Whereas the speaker-poet's agency is derived from her experiences of extremity, the poem's agency is largely derived from the authority embodied in Josephine's powerful recriminations and recontextualizations of the poet's experiences. Alicia Ostriker's essay on postmodern poetry of witness best sums up the crisis Forché deals with in "Return": "the simultaneous impossibility of *objective* witness and of *subjective* wholeness" ("Beyond Confession" 39; original emphasis). Forché's rhetorical strategy makes this point resound as she needs Josephine's struggle for "objective witness" and a speaker-poet's struggle for "subjective wholeness."

Summary and Conclusions

When I was defending my M.A. thesis many years ago on the political poetry of Forché and Rich, one of my committee members asked me how I would respond to the notion that poets such as Rich and Forché often unintentionally subscribe to a romantic heroism that makes the poet brave, unyielding, and risk-averse in her pursuit of justice. These poets, he suggested, tacitly support a conception of romantic individualism that their poetry largely works against. I responded naively with Forché's justification for writing about events she witnessed in El Salvador: "If I did not wish to make poetry of what I had seen, what is it I thought poetry was?" ("El Salvador" 257). Though Forché certainly justifies a political poetry of experiential agency, does she also reductively justify the appropriation of others' suffering, the poeticizing of the horrific, and the romanticization of the poet's role as dramatic witness? While she gives authority to personal experience and a justification to poetic agency borne of experience, she also suggests that poetry is a type of referential reportage. But most crucially, for present purposes, her quote points to a conservative, reactionary element present in much contemporary political poetry, especially poetry of embodied agency—many political poets want the self back. After the doubts poststructuralism and postmodernism have cast on the "self" and the work poets such as John Ashbery, Jorie Graham, and the Language poets have done to fracture, question, and disorder the "self," many political poets want to make sure that individual identity and personal experience—and the agency and authority derived from them and the sense of community they are part of—remain vibrant elements of poetry. The poems discussed in chapter 1 (and numerous others that share their strategies) insist that using the self's experience is a primary strategy for making poetry political.

Martín Espada's "The Meaning of the Shovel" (135–137), for instance, showcases the difficulties engaged poets such as Forché face when negotiating the pursuit of justice and the parameters of appropriation for poetic gain. In Espada's poem, the speaker-poet attempts to find the language—as well as the justification for his practice as aid worker and creative writer—for representing the poor and oppressed and for bridging the gap between US poet and poor Nicaraguan. Here are the opening lines, in order of stanza (per the subtitle, the speaker-poet speaks from within *Barrio René Cisneros* in Managua), that see the speaker-poet engaging in standard practice aid work: (1) "Here I dig latrines. I dig *because* last week / *I saw* a funeral in the streets of Managua"; (2) "I dig *because* yesterday / *I saw* four walls of photographs"; (3) "I dig *because* today, in this barrio / without plumbing, *I saw* a woman"; (4) "I dig *because* today I stopped digging / to drink an orange soda. In a country / with no glass"; (5) "I dig *because* today my shovel / struck a clay bowl centuries old"; and (6) "I dig *because* I have hauled garbage / and pumped gas and cut paper" (my emphasis). In each of these stanzas describing some hardship, murder, or oppression in anecdotal detail, Espada links his justification and representation to his witness, to what he has seen, which suggests a distance between himself and those he represents—*seeing* something is fundamentally different from *experiencing* something. The witness, even one working and living amongst a community, is separate; though he may not be a tourist, he can still *leave* when the others cannot. He tries to mitigate this distance with work, charity, and poetry. Espada works to close the gap inherent in representation by implying: *I am here working with and among the people; I am not a tourist and my advocacy is authentic.*

In John Beverley's and Georg Lukacs's terms, where Beverley discusses the testimonio tradition, Espada and Forché create "problematic heroes" in which the speaker-poet "lives with or alongside others" in a difficult socioeconomic situation (27). "The Meaning of the Shovel" includes both: the "problematic hero" foregrounds his own agency and selfless dedication to uplifting (whether it is efficacious or not) an impoverished community in which the narrator lives and works, even if temporarily. More problematically, however, is the notion of the poet as a professional writer who represents the poor as a form of "class privilege" the poor do not have (Beverley 29). The poem ends with the speaker-poet "digging until the *passport* / in [his] back pocket saturates with dirt, / because here [he] work(s) for nothing / and for everything" (my emphasis). The U.S. passport, Espada suggests, is a silver bullet, a ticket out of this neighborhood of extreme poverty; even though it is permeated with the dirt of Nicaragua, on some level joining his identity with that of the poor there, it reveals his status as an outsider who *represents* these people in an international forum specifically *as a writer* and aid worker, not as a Nicaraguan living in solidarity with the poor. In my reading, then, Espada's "shovel" and Forché's "*Country Between Us*" ultimately *represent* or symbolize international aid, which is always complicated (and compromised) by the privilege of the aid givers. As such, its "meaning" is mediated by those who give aid, but through the lens of what they witness and by their attempt—at least in the cases of progressive international aid organizations—at solidarity with the poor and the pursuit of justice for them.

Esapda's and Forché's justifications, finally, with all their bravado and swagger, are bettered by Robert Hass's response to a similar question; if I were to redo my thesis defense, I would use his qualified claim for a political poetry of witness in lieu of Forché's.[20] Hass has often said that presenting images of justice is the best way for poetry to be political. In an interview with *The Iowa Review*, Hass said that the task of poetry is to "make images of a livable common life" and "to make images of justice," "ideal images," "outraged images" or, he continues haltingly, to "just do witness." Hass implies that the poet has a choice—much like Wallace Stevens said is the choice between resistance and evasion—between discomfort and silence. Hass says, "It's [witness] part of the job of being a poet, but you'll always feel a little bit like a voyeur and a tourist writing those poems. And a little uneasy reading them. But the choice is that or silence, and so you do it." For Hass, who perhaps takes on a more subtle embattled stance, poems that engage sociopolitical issues and that deal with injustice will make both poet and reader "uneasy." There is the rub: we are uncomfortable when we read or write about disturbing injustices. As long as the poet understands that and inscribes it in her poem, it will be difficult to suggest that the poet is assuming an embattled, heroic stance. However, as I hope chapter 2 shows, poetry does *not* need the self for it to be political. The poems I write about in chapter 2 are not poems of witness and often not of outrage, but they are definitely not the province of silence or evasion.

CHAPTER 2

Equivocal Agency

Seems, madam? Nay, it is. I know not "seems."
'Tis not alone my inky cloak, good mother,
Nor customary suits of solemn black,
Nor windy suspiration of forced breath,
No, nor the fruitful river in the eye,
Nor the dejected havior of the visage,
Together with all forms, moods, shapes of grief,
That can denote me truly. These indeed seem,
For they are actions that a man might play,
But I have that within which passes show;
These but the trappings and the suits of woe.

—Shakespeare, *Hamlet* 1.2.76–86

INTRODUCTION

If the poems of *embodied agency* in chapter 1 foreground models of
agency that style personal and communal experience as politically and
poetically viable, the poems in chapter 2 largely bypass questions of specific experience. Political poems of *equivocal agency* do not focus on the
first-person experience of an event or on the retelling or memory of an
experience. Nor do they focus on the authoritative voice that comes
from faith in one's knowledge, experience, or righteousness. Instead
they generally center on a speakerless scene, create a fantastic picture, or
imagine a world that may or may not exist referentially. They exaggerate,
stretch, invent, and play with the world as it is in order to create worlds
as they may be in the future or as they *seem* in the present. In *Hamlet*,
Shakespeare creates a dialectic between appearance and reality, between
"seeming" and "being." In his response to Gertrude, Hamlet expresses
discomfort with her refusal to acknowledge that his grief is authentic

rather than staged. However, Hamlet's words also reveal a certain irony as he consciously takes on and performs an antic disposition throughout the opening acts of the play even though he claims that he has "that within which passes show." The infinitives that define the play—"to be" and "to seem/appear"—are useful for beginning to understand how political poems of equivocal agency work. In these poems there is no strict "to be"; instead, they have something akin to what Tim O'Brien calls a "surreal seemingness." In *The Things They Carried*, O'Brien writes that "there is always that surreal seemingness, which makes the story seem untrue, but which in fact represents the hard and exact truth as it *seemed*" (78; original emphasis). Poems of equivocal agency stage the power of the imagination, thereby calling into question any strict divide between truth and falsity, being and seeming.

The poems I discuss in this chapter problematize direct notions of experience, while utilizing equivocation, paradox, strangeness, irony, and rhetorical guises. The strategies of these poems show the importance of the speakerless scene, abstract language, nonspecific diction, and nonconcrete references. These are often the poems that intimidate students looking for definitive answers to questions such as *What does this poem mean?* and *What is this poem about?* These poems often defy simple interpretation and pose challenges to critics attempting to tease out patterns of rhetorical strategies between poems. Further, though these poems are clearly political, their content, especially for a poem such as Harjo's "A Postcolonial Tale," may require a more focused interpretative endeavor, a deeper engagement from readers, and a willingness to suspend disbelief and strict notions of referentiality. As such, the subject may be injustice or poverty writ large rather than small.

In the introduction to *Against Forgetting*, Forché points out that poetry of witness often uses paradox and equivocation. She suggests that the language of the everyday is inadequate for poems of witness in the violent and repressive contexts in which they are produced. She writes that when the "quotidian has been appropriated by oppressive powers" so that language becomes unusable for protest, poets must pursue truth through indirection (41), a claim that connects subtly with Mutlu Konuk Blasing's notion that poems that highlight their differences from normal speech can be the most politically adroit. So, too, poems of equivocal agency generally rely not on first-person speakers poeticizing experience, but on indirection, utopian/dystopian visions, and transpersonal experiences, sometimes evoked via parodic, staged, distant, and fragmented voices.

Whereas poems such as Harper's "Deathwatch" and Kinnell's "When the Towers Fell" refer to verifiable personal and historical events, the poems in chapter 2 may not refer directly to a discrete event or to a historical period. For example, the Charles Simic war poems I discuss do not refer to a particular war or sociopolitical context; in contrast, most of Yusef Komunyakaa's Vietnam poems are bounded by that war and a soldier's experience of it. Further, Robert Bly's poems about the Vietnam War do not rely on poetic agency from experience. Instead, his protest poems are surreal, imagistic pieces with startling juxtapositions and strange disconnections from the referential world.

There is also a sharp divide *within* political poems of equivocal agency. Whereas many have a referential context discernable from the poem's content, subject, title, or strategic placement in a volume of poetry, others do not have a specific context or subject. To utilize the above examples, Komunyakaa's Vietnam poems appear in a volume of exclusively Vietnam poems, *Dien Cai Dau*, where the title is in Vietnamese. Further, the front cover features photographs of soldiers, the back cover a photograph of Komunyakaa in uniform, the epigraph is dedicated to his brother "who saw The Nam before" Komunyakaa did, and the first line in the volume is "We tied branches to our helmets" ("Camouflaging the Chimera"). In contrast, even though many readers may know that Simic grew up in German-occupied Belgrade during the 1940s, "Paradise Motel" (*A Wedding in Hell* 1994) and "Cameo Appearance" (*Walking the Black Cat* 1996) do not have specific contexts as part of their rhetorical strategies. The architecture of these poems is designed to suspend time, place, and experience in favor of imaginative breadth.[1]

There are two primary rhetorical strategies in poems of equivocal agency. The first strategy is *comprehensive*, in which the poem is divested of identifiable context in order to create a more encompassing and inclusive vision of a socioeconomic reality. These poems are largely unbounded by the limitations of strict context-formed discourse. To continue with the war example, these comprehensive poems are about war in general or some aspect, result, or effect of contemporary warfare. The second strategy is *particular*. These poems are directed at and comment on a specific context, situation, or dynamic. They are not about war or about poverty; they are about *a* war in Vietnam or poverty *in* Detroit. There is, however, a substantial area of overlap between the two types of equivocal agency. Both types employ similar strategies, but their intended interventions diverge. A poem that speaks to racism in general uses a different strategy and perhaps has potentially different effects than one that speaks to racism *in* South Africa. I do not intend to create a strict global/local dichotomy, but it is useful to differentiate between poems that aspire to general political insight and ones that comment on specific contexts.

For both types of equivocal agency, the speaker is usually removed from the limitations of personal experience and the conventions that implicitly govern poems of memory, witness, and interiority. Unlike political poems of personal experience, these poems often employ what Jane Frazier and Charles Molesworth call "disembodied" narrators. In an essay on W.S. Merwin, Frazier writes that "Merwin's narrators betray little or no personal identity and often seem as if they are voices speaking free of the body" (341). Although the rhetorical effects of Merwin's strategy differ from those of the poems in this chapter—Frazier suggests Merwin's narrators evince a desire "to join the self with the universal" (342)—the concept of the disembodied narrator illuminates the ways that poems of equivocal agency move away from the readily identifiable, prominent, involved, fully embodied, and mostly first-person narrators in poems of experiential agency. Poems of equivocal agency move away from the realistic narrative impulse that forms much of—though not all of—the shape and logic of experiential agency.

In addition to a move away from the narratives of first-person experience by an identifiable speaker, poems of equivocal agency also move away from the readily recognizable world. Robert Pinsky suggests that such a move might be part of the poet's "responsibility," to re-present the world from a unique angle, one that does not square with simplistic views propagated in various media and widely accepted as accurate and unimpeachable. Pinsky claims that "before an artist can see a subject" she must first "transform it" in order to "answer the received cultural imagination of the subject with something utterly different." Pinsky believes that transformation "comes before everything else" in the writing process ("Responsibilities" 9). It is debatable whether or not this step is first; however, utterly transforming the referential world is a key rhetorical strategy in poems of equivocal agency as well as a key element of poetry as countercultural discourse.

Poems of equivocal agency can be seen as part of a larger movement in scholarship and literature since the 1960s. "Transforming" traditional referential history and "the received cultural imagination" became imperative for many writers beginning in 1960s. Since the decade that saw the assassinations of the Kennedys, Martin Luther King, Jr., and Malcolm X, many postmodern fiction writers and post-structural theorists have scrutinized the validity of previously unquestioned historical accounts and the role of language in not only reflecting but in creating history. A key philosophical underpinning of much postmodern theory and literature—a suspicion of the "official story" and its master narratives, especially those that emerged out of enlightenment reason and narratives of "progress"—helped to shape an environment in which academics, journalists, novelists, and poets began to reexamine history and narrative in their works. The "break-down of the 'official story' created space for other stories and other voices" (Geyh et al. xiii) in texts as diverse as Gloria Anzaldúa's revision of the myths that have informed understandings of "America" and Joseph Heller's *Catch-22* (1961). In *Borderlands/La Frontera: The New Mestiza* (1987), Anzaldúa suggests that a new oppositional consciousness develops only by revising received historical traditions and rewriting religious and cultural myths that subjugate women and indigenous people.

One of the most powerful results of the questioning of the "official story" has been the advent of nuanced, creative models of history and memory that diverge from appeals to models of experience and logic. These models assume that historical prototypes omit (or simplify) important factors and forces, whether it is marginalized and oppressed voices or geopolitical complexities. In Latin America, "el boom," which includes the fiction of Gabriel García Márquez in Colombia, Julio Cortázar in Argentina, and later Cristina Peri Rossi in Uruguay, among others, focused international attention on *realismo mágico* (magic realism).[2] Magic realism combines elements of literary realism with elements of the supernatural. The fiction of magic realism favors the "truth of sensation" over the "truth of fact" and stresses the supernatural ties of the past to the present,[3] both of which suggest that history is never really past and that people often feel historical forces such as racism and colonialism as sensations as much as "facts." Their alternative visions of historical forces countered the oppression, dictatorial power, disappearances, and skewed histories promoted by Latin American governments.

Many poems of equivocal agency take the motives and ideals (if often not the style) of magic realism as their implicit baseline. For them, the truth of sensation is more compelling and powerful than the often co-opted and erased facts of experience and event. As such, their rhetorical strategies often (but not always) merge with those of novels such as Leslie Marmon Silko's *Ceremony* (1977), Toni Morrison's *Beloved* (1986), and Sherman Alexie's *Reservation Blues* (1995). These fictional works utilize techniques similar to Latin American magic realism to "thematize the fragmentary, disjunctive, and often contradictory nature of historical evidence . . . rather than presenting history as a continuous, unified story" (Geyh et al. xxiv). Similarly, the narrator of O'Brien's *The Things They Carried* (1990) distinguishes between "story-truth" and "happening-truth," where a story about an event that includes the sensations and feelings of its participants can be more truthful and insightful than the rote retelling of what happened during an event. The "what happened," O'Brien implies, always misses the spirit of events and the marks they leave on participants.

In addition to these alternative literary models of history and experience, theoretical accounts of history such as Benjamin's "Theses on the Philosophy of History" (in *Illuminations*) appeal not to experience but to a prevailing mood about history and the wide-ranging human consequences of historical events. These alternative approaches to history have generally been the province of fiction and theory. However, such techniques are not simply within their purview; many political poems, especially those in chapter 2, forgo unified narratives and traditional historical perspectives, preferring instead surrealism, magic realism, equivocation, visionary strangeness, and parodic rather than sincere voices. The poems in this chapter, moreover, reveal the limitations of traditional historical approaches. In *Private Poets, Worldly Acts: Public and Private History in Contemporary American Poetry*, Kevin Stein discusses poetry that "acknowledges the inadequacy of 'official' or 'objective' histories" and that "juxtaposes its own in opposition" (19) to those histories. Though poems of equivocal agency sometimes utilize their "own" histories, they usually implicitly claim that "official" histories inaccurately represent actual events in the service of dominant social, economic, and political interests.

These poems loosen the strictures of historical narrative, and they also move away from the potential limitations and pitfalls of lived experience as the decisive arbiter of knowledge, creative vision, and political power. Experience, they suggest, must never bind poetry if it is to remain independent from fact-based reporting. Poststructuralism reveals flaws in Western logic, and a brief digression into the claims and failures of trauma theory helps illuminate some important techniques in poems of equivocal agency. According to trauma theory, traumatic events are not remembered in the ways that normal events are. A traumatic experience, the theory goes, is a "missed" experience inaccessible to normal memory and thought processes. Cathy Caruth defines trauma as an "overwhelming experience of sudden or catastrophic events in which the response to the event occurs in the often delayed, uncontrolled repetitive appearance of hallucinations and other intrusive phenomena" (11). I do not intend to belabor the intricacies of trauma theory, but I want to suggest that a possible factor in some critics' aversion to poetry of witness and experience is partly due to the suspicion of experience and memory caused by the prominence of Post-Traumatic Stress Disorder (PTSD), trauma theory, and the issues surrounding recovered memory. In addition to critics' explicitly stated concerns about poetry of experience as a mere mimetic exercise in which the poet is a simple recorder of the world, trauma theory suggests that "experience" itself is a questionable signifier.

Trauma theory, though, is rife with problems.[4] In "The Trauma Trap," in the March 2004 *New York Review of Books*, Frederick Crews outlines some major difficulties with trauma theory that challenge its central claims. For instance, the problems with recovered memory: How is it possible that some memories (those recovered during regression) are more legitimate than others? How is it that the memory of trauma does not stand apart neurologically from normal memory? Crews points out that there is no evidence of memory repression in any study of holocaust survivors. He shows that memories of traumatic events are actually *better* remembered than ordinary ones. The idea, I believe, that an agent cannot know her experience must be abandoned. Our experiences must not be thought inaccessible to us; in poems of equivocal agency that depart from strict models of experience, for example, we must first know our experiences before we consciously (and strategically) depart from them.

Although it is imperative to discount any notion of trauma as a "missed" experience unknowable by an agent except through recovered memory therapy, the connections between trauma theory and the rhetorical strategies and figures of voice in poems of equivocal agency are instructive. Cassie Premo Steele argues that trauma is not recorded in the usual, narrative way we remember experiences; instead, they are "encoded" in images that give us "insight into the questions of 'experience,' so often deadlocked between praise from humanist feminists and rejection from poststructuralists" (3–4). Like the memory of a traumatic experience, which may be disjointed and disordered, the poems in chapter 2 often shift and displace any simple narrative of experience. They often fracture—or refuse to use—the humanistic, unified, singular speaking voice and opt instead for the primacy of images, sensations, and sounds, or for voices that expose the limitations of "experience" narrowly understood as *what can be turned into an accessible, realistic narrative*. As Steele claims, poems can be like memories in that they comprise images, feelings, rhythms, sounds, and physical sensations of the body as "evidence" that transforms experience into poetry (5). Poems of equivocal agency highlight and cut short that transformation, refusing to move completely from image into narrative coherence or closure, preferring instead to leave images open and ungrounded by experience.

Poems of equivocal agency, therefore, are usually indirect; they tend to approach a subject—indeed, the very notion of a subject—indirectly, from oblique angles. In contrast to Forché's "The Colonel," Kinnell's "After the Towers Fell," Snyder's "Front Lines," and other poems of experiential and authoritative agency in which the speaker approaches the subject directly and transparently, the poems in chapter 2 approach their subjects with a set of different lenses. Whether in the surreal space of a Simic cityscape, or in the haunted, ubiquitous presence of ghosts on the reservations of Alexie, these poems forgo certainty for atmospheres redolent with indescribable presences.

These poems, finally, are often unbounded by strict temporal and spatial considerations, and they are removed in part from any conception of agency that explains experience. Any account of human agency, for Anthony Giddens, has two imperatives. It must be "connected to a theory of the acting subject" and it must "situate action in *time and space* as a continuous flow of conduct" (2; my emphasis). Giddens outlines precisely why and how poems in chapter 2 challenge the frameworks for agency. In these poems there is often not a singular, identifiable acting subject with the characteristics of a real person in the world. They do not contain a continuous flow of actions in time and space. Because they are freed from the constraints of human agency, which must always operate in time and space not in discrete moments but continuously in response to conditions, situations, and other agents, these poems have grander, more spectacular (and often more imaginative) political voices and visions.

COMPREHENSIVE EQUIVOCAL AGENCY

Charles Simic's poems best represent the voices of comprehensive equivocal agency. The prevailing critical sentiment about his voice centers on its enigmatic, minimalist, riddling, and surreal character. Poet and critic Bruce Weigl has written that Simic "remains an enigma, even within the eclectic tradition of postmodern American poetry." His poems, moreover, differentiate him from other contemporary poets because of their "particularly inclusive and worldly vision" (1), a quality key to poems of comprehensive equivocal agency. The speaker in many Simic poems is "oddly anonymous, a self without a self—a passerby, comfortable in his self-imposed exile"

(Engelmann 46). And Simic, who grew up in Belgrade during WWII, does not "assault" readers with his "personal history" (Sack 134) by heroicizing his childhood experiences of war. His experiences likely inform his poetic sensibility, but indirectly rather than in concrete details; Lisa Sack points out that Simic is "a master of indirection" who "selects and juxtaposes a few striking images" (134) to create mysterious, anguished atmospheres. In the poems discussed here these atmospheres are sustained through indirection, surreal images, and a detached, parodic voice rarely used in poems of embodied agency, where the tone is grave, urgent.

The first line of "Paradise Motel" depicts a world where no one is spared torment. Two simple declarative phrases separated by a semi-colon join utterly violent, demented, and irreconcilable spheres: "Millions were dead; everybody was innocent" (75). In a world without accountability marked by hyperbolic absolutes, the speaker is a distant, unreal, cloistered figure. He says calmly: "I stayed in my room." This juxtaposition suggests that "paradise" is a suspended pur-gatory, an illusion of disinterested, bourgeois individualism and that denouncing responsibility for the world is cowardly. These three terse, clipped phrases are hallmarks of Simic's minimalism, elision, and refusal to supply a geopolitical context. The poet provides no details that render the scene local, knowable, and thereby less frightening. Helen Vendler claims that a Simic poem often creates "an unbearable tension [that] darkens the air" and turns readers into "prisoner(s) within its uncompromising and irremediable world" ("Totemic Sifting" 119–21). And so it is in the first line and a half of "Paradise Motel."

Another figure—the de facto foil to the speaker—enters the poem in the latter half of line two. Even though the poem is without specific context, "*The* president / Spoke of war as of a magic love potion" (my emphasis). As Vendler points out, Simic tends to use "menacing" def-inite articles ("Totemic Sifting" 119), and this one here cedes all paro-dic and ironic authority to this president. If the speaker is without identity, without use (in a mirror his face appears to him as "a twice-canceled postage stamp"), *the* president evokes the merged identity of every president who has spoken of war as a transformative solution. The president's "magic love potion" is seemingly able only to make the "refugees crowding the roads" "vanish / With a touch of the hand." The most unnerving aspect of this disappearance is the speaker's parodic voice—not only do the refugees vanish, but it happens "naturally." Does this voice manifest the depraved wish-fulfillment of countless presidents who see refugees as thorns in their sides? Even more menacing than this implication is one that "History" is a carnivorous predator that has eaten the refugees: "History licks" "the corners of its bloody mouth." Simic's vision of this horrifying world of "paradise" is so expansive that it includes the lens of history through which we understand that world.

"Paradise Motel" has a biting, parodic voice that renders absurd war, isolated individualism, and the idea of "paradise." After all, every paradise requires large swaths of disaster and horror elsewhere in order to make it identifiable as a paradise, each of which is necessarily apart from less-desirable places. Further, entering paradise requires an individual to isolate oneself from those parts of the world where refugees suffer and presidents make them disappear. Finally, a paradise such as a postcolonial island in the Caribbean is only paradise to visitors, not to impoverished residents who drive taxis, clean hotel bathrooms, and live in shacks.

"Cameo Appearance" also has a sardonic voice, but a desperate one. Its first-person speaker plays a more prominent role, but he is an unreal amalgamation of war refugees the world over. The speaking "I" does not rely on experience, but on a depressingly comic and surreal displacement characteristic of refugee experiences *in general*. Vendler's assertion that Simic is "the best political poet, in a large sense, on the American scene" is borne out in this poem. For her, Simic's poems are "more terrifying in their human implications than explicit political documentation" ("Totemic Sifting" 131–132) based on experience, ideological commitment, or the direct protest of sociopolitical ills. Simic's grand vision is haunting precisely because it is not grounded in experience or context.

"Cameo Appearance" bears many similarities to "Paradise Motel"— a conspicuous absence of geopolitical context, a war-torn world, a caricatured leader, and refugees—but it has a more prominent first-person speaker. However, this speaker is again a nonentity who cannot recognize himself in the world of the poem. "Cameo Appearance" takes its cue from a Theater of the Absurd as practiced in the mid-twentieth century by, among others, Antonin Artaud in France, Edward Albee and Amiri Baraka (LeRoi Jones) in the United States, and Osvaldo Dragún in Argentina.[5] The poem shows the speaker playing a typecast role as "one of the / Bombed and fleeing humanity" from a war-torn "burning city" (97). The speaker, moreover, quite literally performs this role. The poem begins with the self-consciously absurd assertion: "I had a small, nonspeaking part / In a bloody epic." Immediately, Simic creates a remarkably expansive context; the speaker laconically confuses any divide between reality and fiction, dramatic actors and real-life agents. In the process, Simic suggests an aspect of all social relations. Giddens writes: "All social reproduction is grounded in the knowledgeable application and reapplication of rules and resources by actors in situated social contexts . . . social systems are chronically produced and reproduced by their constituent participants" (114). In Simic's poem, the speaker disturbingly applies the rules of the refugee in the "situated social context" of a burning city, and he ironically and sadly reproduces the refugee's nameless, placeless suffering. Within this "epic" the speaker's place is so miniscule and insignificant that he vanishes before his *own* eyes.

The overarching conceit of the poem, over and above the speaker's role as refugee, is the speaker's viewing of the fleeing refugees on videotape. He is showing the videotape of the incident "to the kiddies," but even after rewinding the tape a "hundred times" the kids cannot "catch sight" of the speaker/refugee. Despite the speaker's certainty ("I know I was there"), in the words of "honest" Iago, the villain of *Othello*, there is no "ocular proof" to confirm that the speaker was actually present. Throughout the poem Simic parodies the American media's tendency to play and replay film clips of distant disasters. In his criticism of the media's "re-representation of world as spectacle"—as discussed earlier with regard to Forché's "Return"— Michael Greer suggests that the American media's penchant for continually broadcasting sensational images of violence desensitizes viewers (175). In "Cameo Appearance" these disturbing, violent images are archetypes of poor, suffering indigenous people; refugees and victims of war or famine, they plead to the camera, to their god, or to a rich country halfway across the world. In looking for himself on the videotape, the speaker thinks he is "squeezed between the man / With two bandaged hands raised / And the old woman with her mouth open / As if she were showing us a tooth / That hurts badly." Everyone who watches network news in the United States has seen these two people. Their poses and ministrations are well known, but the people themselves are not. They are simply images of suffering, abstractions in services of an idea: compassion for residents of East Timor, Rwanda, Niger, Guatemala, or Bangladesh, people whom Americans will never see face-to-face.[6]

In the final calculation, for all of its disturbing strangeness, the poem's Theater of the Absurd stages a world not unlike our own. The "great leader" may or may not be who he purports to be. When the speaker sees the great leader "in the distance," he wonders if it is indeed the great leader, or "a great actor / Impersonating our great leader." As in the referential world, it is difficult to sort out what is real from what is fabrication, especially in a country in which one of our most revered presidents was a Hollywood actor.

The speaker's question also shows a keen understanding of Shakespeare's most pliable conceit: the *Theatrum Mundi* (Theater of the World) trope, in which "All the world's a stage / And all the men and women merely players" (*As You Like It*). Shakespeare put this notion to great use and so does Simic; in "Cameo Appearance" the world of suffering is a stage viewed from afar. Tragically, however, in the final stanza the speaker points out that disaster is not within the purview of this trope. In this burning city "one take / Is all they had time for." What is really absurd, according to "Cameo Appearance," is that after the planes leave the burning city, the cameras leave as well. The refugees stand "dazed in the burning city, / But of course, they didn't film that." When the sensational events are over and the requisite images captured, those wielding cameras leave and the suffering continues unabated, unnoticed.

Simic's rhetorical strategy in these two poems is inclusive. He elides context and specificity for a rounder, ironic indictment of the ravages of and justifications for contemporary warfare. If either of these poems had a definite geopolitical context—if the president of "Paradise Motel" were Pinochet, Mugabe, or Milosevic—they would forfeit a large amount of their power to unsettle and disturb. As such, these poems rely on the *reader's* experiences and on her ability to imagine a context, rather than on the speaker-poet's experiences. In her seminal work on closure in poetry, Barbara Herrnstein-Smith asserts that a poem "cannot be regarded as totally independent" of the "reader's extrinsic experiences," which include experiences of "*language itself.*" She continues, "It is upon our past linguistic experiences that poetry depends for its most characteristic effects" (97; original emphasis). Therefore, a reader brings her experiences to a reading, thus making the lack of specific leaders in Simic's poems encompassing ways to reference readers' experiences. Further, a reader's experience of language allows the poets in this chapter to approach subjects elliptically because they assume that readers have imaginations with which to leap and bound alongside the poems. In other words, Simic's poems show the benefits of equivocal agency vis-à-vis embodied agency—poems in chapter 2 can be more flexible and less strident.

In "A Postcolonial Tale" (*The Woman Who Fell from the Sky* 1994), Joy Harjo *imagines* imagination as a primary tool for social change. In her customary form—the prose poem—Harjo's first-person plural speaker delivers platitudes about creation and imagination. Unlike

Simic's terse, laconic lines, Harjo's long, prophetic lines style imagination as capable of creating change. One critic calls Harjo's "highly political imagination" a "weapon in an anticolonial national struggle" that works to "decolonize our very spirit otherwise hegemonized" (Hussain 52). Harjo uses imagination as—in the words of Frantz Fanon—"a historical process of becoming" (28) and the postcolonial tale she writes describes the process of recreating community not through television and guns but through dreams and imagination. As such, "A Postcolonial Tale" re-imagines myths—first the creation story and second the colonial encounter, presumably between white settlers and Native Americans.

As in other poems of comprehensive equivocal agency, Harjo opens her poem with an immense, global horizon, but with a difference; she makes it commonplace *and* grandiloquent: "Every day is a reenactment of the creation story" (104–105).[7] Because the "creation story" happens daily, it is a source of knowable community, but it also remains a source of mystery. In the poem's second sentence, "We emerge from / dense unspeakable material, through the shimmering power of / dreaming stuff." The language here is elusive, fantastic, and consciously enchanted, but not haunted as in Simic. We know immediately that the speaker, who remains a "we" throughout, is concerned with community, collective experience, and imagination. Yet this story or "tale" is not the key to unlocking another world as "This is the first world, and the last." In the poem's cosmology, the stakes are high because there is no redemption in a world beyond.

Whereas imagination may be highly compartmentalized in a white Euro-American worldview, in many Native American traditions it is closer to boundless. Jenny Goodman, amongst other critics, claims that Harjo, a Muskogee Creek Indian, uses traditions "that expand narrow definitions of political poems" (49). As part of her mythopoeic ethos she uses iconic figures such as the trickster crow; indeed, in the imaginative construct of "A Postcolonial Tale," "we" are never "far from the trickster's bag of tricks." The trickster, most importantly, is seemingly able to restore order to the postcolonial world by freeing it from Enlightenment reason. Thus freed, the community is at liberty to imagine itself anew.[8]

Before there is a possibility of redemption via the imagination, there has to be a fall, not from original sin, but from the sin of colonization. In "A Postcolonial Tale," the colonial encounter is itself a creation story. During colonization a new world is created and cultures are transformed. Indigenous people, Harjo suggests, were "stolen" and "put / into a bag carried on the back of a white man who pretends to own / the earth and sky." Trapped in the postcolonial world ("the bag"), they fight until they make a hole, then fall to the earth though they are "not aware of falling." Once they have punctured the "bag" of colonial rule, they land "somewhere near the diminishing point of civilization" where schoolchildren are "learning subtraction with guns." When the speaker imagines creation and created world this way, she does not—as Goodman points out about another Harjo poem—show "nostalgia for a mythic Native American past before the Europeans stepped onto the continent" (50). The poem does not simply reject Western culture and *its* creation myths; instead, Harjo re-imagines the colonial encounter as one that can be reinvented and redeemable through imagination. Moreover, "every day" the creation of the world is "reenacted" by us and is thus ameliorable by us because "we" are not captive agents incapable of acting outside the "bag."

The final third of the poem has a critical change in voice similar to the sestet of an Elizabethan sonnet. This three-stanza resolution gives a "solution" for the problems of colonialism and the world created by it. The poem's chantlike repetition suggests a building optimism. The two lines that signal the change indicate that imagination is both divine force and human product: "The imagining needs praise as does any living thing. / We are evidence of this praise." Even though imagination is a transformative force that helps children shun violence ("children put down their guns") and all people take on a compassionate community-based ethos ("We imagined tables of food for everyone"), imagination's products ("story" and "song") are unable to "translate" either "the full impact of falling" or "the power of rising up." Imagination, then, is the primary means to developing and sustaining community, but imagination must be acted upon, set in motion by people who have the potential to fall and to rise up— imagination requires *acting agents*. The poem thus carves out space in the world where imagination can flourish. Even though imagination can be transformative, it alone does not comprise the world in which we live. Stories and songs cannot describe the "full impact" of colonization. Without this void, this undefined space, imagination is a nonstarter. There has to be some space that is always undetermined, even by imagination; this is the space in which imagination must operate.

The poem ends with the notion that "the imagination"—notably a collectively held single imagination—"speaks with / us," "sings with us," and "loves us." The community's relationship with "imagination" is reciprocal; people give to imagination *and* receive from it acceptance and compassion. "A Postcolonial Tale" thus sets in motion what Hannah Arendt discusses in her work on public policy formation. She claims that any agent is capable of forming her opinions in consideration of others' interests; as such, a policymaker must negotiate the differences between her interests and "the interests of the group." She implies that the failure to account for others' interests is partly due to a "lack of imagination" (*Between Past* 241–242). When extended from policy formation to the formation of opinions in the social world, this notion suggests the possibility that racism, misogyny, xenophobia, and any difference constituted as conflict (rather than merely as difference) is partly due to a lack of imagination. The violence of the colonial encounter, then, is a failure of a powerful group of people to imagine themselves as another group of people. Imagination bridges cultural and political gaps, in much the same way that Eliza Rodriguez y Gibson says that Harjo's poetics "create a rich sense of historical and spatial interconnection across tribal and cultural lines" (107).

Harjo's poem can be understood via the implied context of colonial encounters the world over (especially in the Americas), and her prophetic, optimistic voice is an apt transition to Derek Walcott's "The Season of Phantasmal Peace" (*The Fortunate Traveller* 1981), where the context is more global. It is the most strategically and politically comprehensive of all the poems in this chapter, and its voice the least recognizable as human. Although Walcott was awarded the Nobel Prize for Literature in 1992, two iconic critics, Harold Bloom and Helen Vendler, have been skeptical of his poetic voice and rhetorical strategies. Their comments are appropriate starting points for reading "The Season of Phantasmal Peace" as a premier example of the strategy of equivocal agency. Bloom claims "bafflement" over whether Walcott has "developed a voice altogether his own, the mark of a major poet," or has adopted a "composite voice of post-Yeatsian poetry in English" (1). Vendler expressed a similar sentiment about the originality of Walcott's voice shortly after the publication of *The Fortunate Traveller*. His voice, she wrote, "was for a long time a derivative one;" his "place," she continued, is not a poem, "but rather an essay in pentameters" ("Poet of Two Worlds" 25–26), presumably about colonialism. "The Season of Phantasmal Peace" renders these criticisms, which are born from a simplified notion of individual genius isolated from the sociocultural and historical contexts in which a poet works, void. The poem, after all, does not utilize a recognizable first-person speaking voice, nor does that voice hold forth as an essayist but as a visionary creating potential beauty from tatters.

In *Derek Walcott: Politics and Poetics* (2000), Paula Burnett argues that Walcott's poetic "impetus has been to devise an inclusive solution" (8) to problems stemming from colonialism, racism, and political conflict. Walcott, she claims, is "an idealist" who "believes in the openendedness of possibilities" (9). Part of this idealism and pro-clivity for inclusion, she points out, "repudiates the tragic view of the human condition that sees it as unable to transcend the patterns evinced by the past." As such, Walcott "recognizes that the dream can lead the reality into amelioration" (8–9). As Burnett's claim makes clear, Walcott's vision is not piecemeal but holistic; his aesthetic is not exclusionary but encompassing. For Walcott as for Harjo, the imagination can do political work; in it inheres the possibility for positive, transformative change. In the words of Paul Breslin, then, "The Season of Phantasmal Peace" is an "affirmation of the transcen-dent" (320). It supplies the ultimate in "inclusive" solutions and "open-ended" possibilities.

As is true of the previous poems in chapter 2, the first line of Walcott's poem is a relatively abstract and mysterious comprehensive vision. However, Walcott begins with a "then" statement that sug-gests an absent antecedent: "*Then* all the nations of birds lifted together" (464–465 my emphasis). In conjunction with "all," "Then" immediately gives the poem an epic scale, as if the events detailed therein are the culmination of (or response to) centuries of oppressive violence and division. Finally, the lines insinuate, *all* the *human* nations of the world are united in a moment of peace. Line one also initiates the poem's main symbol—"nations of birds" sym-bolizes *nations of people*. The use of birds in lieu of people is more indirect, which is in keeping with the disembodied voice of equivocal agency; birds, moreover, have the ability to fly, and indeed, when many birds fly, they fly in flocks. This extended conceit is perhaps the primary reason that Vendler calls it the "best" poem in *The Fortunate Traveller*, as she worries about any poet who is invested in a certain "subject" that may result in his use of language simply as "ornament to his message, the rhetoric for his sermon" ("Poet of Two Worlds" 32, 26). This poem is light not heavy-handed, visionary not directive, beneficent not exculpatory, and its speakerless voice is transparent rather than histrionic. A sermon, after all, needs a sermonizer, which is something that this poem lacks.

Walcott's united birds miraculously lift what normally cannot be lifted but by the rotation of the earth around the sun: "the huge net of shadows of this earth." These shadows, which appear in different form throughout the poem, are "in multitudinous dialects, twittering tongues." The conceit is apropos: like birds, the human nations of the world speak "multitudinous" languages. This unified action is a "lifting together" in which speakers of different languages do not have to compete with each other for space, resources, and power. Because shadows are obscuring agents, once they are removed from the earth, everything is clear; there is no "dusk, or season, decline, or weather." All that is left from the vantage point of the "wingless" earth dweller for this moment is a passing "phantasmal light" that no shadow "dared to sever." Burnett points out that this "lifting movement is an extraordinarily physical evocation of flight, and of transformation to weightlessness, figuring a visionary translation from body to spirit" (204). Burnett's keen reading of the poem focuses on its "roots" in Revelation, its "remaking [of] the apocalyptic story," and its commentaries on the title poem of *The Fortunate Traveller* (204). For my purposes here the biblical symbolism of dark and light and the juxtaposition to "The Fortunate Traveller" are of less concern than Walcott's prophetic voice.

Not everything in "The Season of Phantasmal Peace" manifests unmitigated hopefulness and cooperation. According to Breslin, Burnett paints Walcott's aesthetic as "open and forgiving towards all" as well as "immune to the callow temptations of racial or political anger" (324). Breslin argues that Walcott's "polystylistic language" is not acquiescent, but an ongoing struggle to coalesce anger to inclusion, something we see on display in "The Season." Breslin seems right, especially when Burnett points out that the poem "models a benign paradisal vision" (204). Her claim does not plumb with either Walcott's description of the birds as warriors ("battalions . . . waging peaceful cries"), or with the final vision of the poem in which the "season" of love and light lasts only "one moment." Burnett rightly claims that the poem "offers only a glimpse" (204) of a transformed, peaceful world, but there is also a subtle insinuation that the people of the earth simply do not get it. The second stanza begins with "And men could not see" and continues with "they could not hear." Perhaps there is something other than flying that humans cannot do that birds can: seeing and hearing the beauty and peace that is possible by working together.

Ultimately, the language of Walcott's poem is lyrical, melodious. Phrases such as "betrayals of falling suns" and "the pause / between dusk and darkness" are stylized and beautiful. Walcott's rhetorical strategy foregrounds the ephemeral, transitory beauty and abiding mystery inherent in this miraculous moment of "phantasmal peace." There is nothing certain about a moment of absolute peace in a world wracked by war, famine, greed, genocide, intolerance, and terrorism. This moment is almost necessarily carried across the earth by those things that inhabit the skies, not by those who live in "dark holes in windows and in houses," but by those things that pass in and out of our lines of sight with ease and speed. Despite the almost totally disembodied visionary moment of the poem and the lack of palpable human presence, especially that of an identifiable speaker, the poem ends with an "exquisitely judged note of balance, between the depressing truth of degenerate human nature and the hopeful, encompassing truth of a greater compassion" (Burnett 205). In the final line, Walcott explains why the peace lasts only "one moment": because "for such as our earth is now, it lasted long." His strategy, then, at the end, re-dramatizes the comprehensive, global context. He keeps his voice and vision hovering above the earth, rather than on the earth in a specific city or country.

Walcott's poem represents how political poems might, at first, have no recognizable political *content*. The poems discussed in the first half of chapter 2 demonstrate, then, why it is misleading to determine and classify political poetry strictly on the basis of content, subject matter, or identity position. Imaginative visions can in themselves be political. Michael Palmer's "Sun" (*Sun* 1988), though, points to potential problems with poems that may be unrecognizable as political. Reading Palmer's poetry is challenging even for experienced readers; he has said that it is "a lifelong proposition" for him to "understand" his *own* work. In explaining this enigmatic comment, he cites Robert Browning's comment on one of his own poems: "When I wrote it only God and I knew what it meant; now only God knows" (cited in Bartlett 129).

Palmer's poetry threatens what he calls the "Anglo-American empirical tradition" in which a poem is "a place in which you tell a little story, the conclusion of which is at the bottom of the page just where it is supposed to be." Like the Language poets, with whom Palmer shares an "attempt to bring into question surfaces of language [and] normative syntax," he works against dominant strains of American poetry, especially poems of experiential agency (those poems with first-person speakers, clear narratives, and embodied experience). Further, he dislikes poems that "posit" a self, inadvertently creating "a poetry of personality"; instead, the "self" must be "transformed through language" in order to hold onto the "mysteries of reference" (Bartlett 126, 129, 130–131, 127). Despite his desire to move away from narrative and represented experience, Palmer remains interested in politics. As Eric Murphy Selinger points out, Palmer is "interested in the way politics might inhabit poetry as *something more than subject matter*, particularly when by 'politics' we mean something like 'atrocity' " (7; my emphasis). All of this suggests that if politics are to enter Palmer's work, it will be in an equivocal, shifting, and indirect manner, all of which are characteristic of equivocal agency. Palmer's poetry, though, stretches the limits of this type of poetic agency, thereby testing its effectiveness.

Palmer's comments about how narrative works in his poetry—it "shimmers at the edge of the page" in "scraps" (Bartlett 132)—can be applied to his poetry's political voice. It too is elusive, appearing only in "scraps." Even so, "Sun" is one of his most obviously political poems, but it is not immediately obvious *how* it is political because Palmer wants to frustrate any simple correlation between poetry and politics. More so, he wants to avoid romanticizing any artistic or political representation of atrocity. As pointed out in chapter 1, there is an inherent risk in foregrounding one's witness to and experience of extremity. Palmer has derided "poets' shuttle down to Nicaragua and so on to get material," which he says is "a betrayal of what is to be meant by the political." One of the many problems with these "shuttles," he says, is that poets "appropriate" what they have witnessed as subject matter to proclaim "in stale poetic language" something that implies " 'Look how much human feeling and fellow feeling I have.' " For Palmer, such poetry is "self-congratulatory" ("Dear" 12, 26), a criticism that echoes those cataloged at the end of chapter 1. Selinger suggests that Palmer's *Sun* can then be understood as a "counterpoint" to Forché's *The Country Between Us*, which he says "soothes" readers with its "familiar grammar, forms of reference, and moral compass" (7). Putting aside the specious claim that Forché's Salvador poems are comforting (which belies any engaged reading of them), it is clear that "Sun" is neither soothing nor familiar, and that its rhetorical strategy, poetic agency, and figures of voice diverge dramatically from Forché's "Return."

"Sun" begins with four statements that foreground the acts of writing about and representing atrocity. Each begins with a command: "Write this." In the first two lines, brief phrases depicting military/imperial violence follow the command to record: "We have burned all their villages" and "We have burned all the villages and the people in them" (233–235). The remainder of the poem frustrates any attempt to summarize its political voice/perspective. It is dotted with "scraps" of references to state-sanctioned violence in WWII Germany and in the Vietnam War: "Darmstadt," "Plain of Jars," "Plain of Reeds," "Neak Luong," and "Goebbels." These allusions, however, are relatively obscure, and Palmer chooses not to footnote them; the poem's political reference points are buried in disconnected allusions, syntactical dislocations, nonreferential pronouns, nonlinear trajectories, and isolated, verbless sentence fragments such as "Pages which accept no ink." Selinger writes that Palmer is unwilling to "indict, or witness to" American atrocities because "to name them, would be both to 'mis-appropriate' them for the poet's purposes and to collaborate in a mode of representation in which naming and power are uncomfortably allied." Yet Selinger also suggests that Palmer risks "evasiveness" (15), and it is this claim that I find most illuminating.

Whether or not "Sun" evades some greater engagement with politics is debatable, but it is clear that poems that utilize techniques and strategies like the ones outlined above are difficult to recognize as political. As a public discourse politics must be accessible to citizens, not just those citizens who have the patience, theoretical background, and intellectual capacity to understand philosophical inquiries into the nature of language, knowledge, and representation. Further, Palmer's claims (and those of many Language poets) about the political content of much contemporary poetry suggests that writers should *not* address directly anything remotely resembling "politics" or "atrocity." Such a claim is dangerous; it discloses a longing for a purity of language, of discourse, of politics, and an exclusion of "politics" from literature. This position inadvertently makes politics strictly the province of the elite, as any nontheoretical, linear poem about politics or disaster always borders on appropriation and commodified pomp. Indeed, only certain readers need apply.

Moreover, by opening the poem with obvious political work then obscuring it and refusing to engage it throughout, Palmer too romanticizes his own refusal, saying in effect *look at me, my refusal to appropriate atrocity is heroic and honorable.* When asked about the Language poets, Philip Levine said as much: "in the long run they will undoubtedly enrich our poetry, but I dislike that heroic, embattled stance" in which they style themselves as fighting a "war in which they represent experiment" and other poets represent institutional staidness ("Staying Power" 28–29). Palmer implies that atrocities should not be discussed—in a mainstream media that Palmer and the Language poets explicitly work against, or in a poetry that directly addresses global events. To be fair, though, Palmer *and* Forché foreground the act of writing about political issues and humanitarian disasters and the difficulties inherent in it, albeit in dramatically different voices. But unlike Palmer, Forché experienced first-hand the atrocities she writes about. Even so, Forché's stylistic transition between *The Country Between Us* (1981) and *The Angel of History* (1994)[9] suggests that Forché understood the shortcomings of the former volume's first-person, lyric narratives depicting her experience.

In the endnotes to *The Angel of History*, Forché writes that the poems therein are "not about experiences," but a "gathering of utterances" that "issue from my own encounter with the events of the century but do not represent 'it.' " Her earlier style, moreover, has "given way" to a poetry that is "polyphonic, broken, haunted, and in ruins, with no possibility of restoration" (81). These endnotes suggest that Forché was likely affected by criticisms like Palmer's in the years after the publication of her El Salvador poems. Further, her explicit concern with the representation of experience and the use of multiple voices and fragments points to an abiding problem with her agency as poet. When she writes that her previous style has "given way" to this new one, it is easy to notice the lack of linguistic agency in the shift. She has effectively given up control over events as well as her primary voice of experience; in doing so, her aesthetic begins to dovetail with Palmer's. In his review of *The Angel of History*, Jon Thompson asks a question that plagues "Sun," Forché's work,[10] and many political poets and their critics: "at what point does the witnessing of witnessed—and unwitnessed—human catastrophe pass from poetic and political necessity to the exploitation of the horror for dramatic effect?" (7). This question is important to ask, but the level of discomfort matters more. If a work of art makes us uncomfortable, it may be due to its exploitation of horror, but it also may simply mean that images of violence and atrocity *should* make us uncomfortable regardless of how they are presented. They *should* make us question our roles—as citizens, as consumers, as voters—in the policies and power structures that enable poverty, war, and violence. They also force us to question the voices, strategies, and effectiveness of political poetry. I believe that poems of experiential *and* equivocal agency are important, if divergent, types of engaged writing; *both* kinds of poetic agency, moreover, can be viewed as romanticizing the poet's role, and *both* can be seen as interrogating that very role, but in starkly different voices.

PARTICULAR EQUIVOCAL AGENCY

The differences between *comprehensive* and *particular* strategies of equivocal agency are subtle and will be teased out in the following examples. The primary difference is context. While poems with comprehensive strategies have vast, global contexts, those with particular strategies have specific, focused (but expansive imaginative) contexts. However, their similarities are more instructive than their differences, so the divide here is a fine one used to suggest that the over-arching context within a political poem can have dramatic effects on our readings of them. The poems discussed hereafter in chapter 2 have explicit contexts, several of which are dependent upon additional knowledge about the contexts for their production and publication. For instance, Levine's "They Feed They Lion" does not refer specifi-cally to the 1967 Detroit riots, but Levine has repeatedly said that he wrote it in response to them. Similarly, Bly's "Counting Small-Boned Bodies" does not expressly refer to Vietnam, but given his public pro-nouncements about the war, daily Pentagon body counts, and the sec-tion title of *The Light Around the Body* (1967) in which the poem appears, the context is obvious. Poems of particular equivocal agency, finally, usually speak to public issues that do not need direct reference in the poem. The issues are either urgent or the historical moment makes the context demonstrable.

The first three poems considered here all emerged from one of the most tumultuous decades in American history. The Vietnam War, the Civil Rights Movement, high-profile assassinations, and widespread antiwar protests and urban riots marked the 1960s as a decade of out-rage and dissension. Poets entered the center of the maelstrom, so much so that American culture was "lyricized" during the Vietnam era as citizens began to view poetry "as an inherently anti-establishment vehicle for their political expressions" (Bibby 7). In his study of Vietnam resistance poetry, Michael Bibby argues that American poetry from 1965 to 1975 should be periodized as "Vietnam-era Poetry" and that any categorization of 1950s, 1960s, and 1970s poetry as "Postwar Poetry" obscures the true nature of our national and literary history (23–24). Robert von Hallberg also argues that 1965 heralded a critical shift in the nation's poetic sensibilities. After 1965, he laments, poets stopped using concessions, qualifications, adversatives, and "reasonable language" such as "even," "is needful," "neverthe-less," "not that," "none as Yet" "let us only"[11] that was appropriate in the 1950s (*American Poetry* 129–130), a decade that some argue was characterized by a cultural consensus, at least among the middle and upper classes.

Bly, W.S. Merwin, and Levine all entered these public conversa-tions, and all three wrote remarkable poems of equivocal agency. Bly was one of the most politically active writers of his generation. In 1966, he and David Ray founded American Writers against the

Vietnam War—the more visible forerunner to Sam Hamill's *Poets against the War*, which so angered Laura Bush—that organized protest readings and public demonstrations. In 1968, Bly won a National Book Award for *The Light Around the Body*, a volume replete with poems critical of U.S. actions in Vietnam; he used his acceptance speech to encourage draft resistance. Bly's polemics led James F. Mersmann to call him "one of the most annoying and most exciting poets of his time" (113). Von Hallberg falls on the "annoying" side of the critical fence, reserving his utmost scorn for "The Teeth Mother Naked at Last" (1970), which he calls the most "ambitious" of Vietnam-era "period poems" that are marked by an absence of qualifications and "reasonable language" (*American Poetry* 142). Mersmann also opines that Bly's Vietnam magnum opus has "prose opinions and not poetic insights," a fact that has led critics to "misread" his work (124).

In "Counting Small-Boned Bodies," Bly's political voice is on full display. Though not lengthy and bombastic like "The Teeth Mother" and not directly confrontational like "Somebody Blew up America," the poem's staged, perverse, and disembodied speaker indirectly challenges the official bureaucratic propaganda of the U.S. military. Walter Kalaidjian calls the poem a "burlesque performance" and suggests that the poem employs Bly's surrealism in a "subversive tone" that "flouts the half truths and windy abstractions of bureaucratic propaganda." There is a lot to discuss with regard to this poem, but the best place to begin is with Kalaidjian's note about its tone. The poem obviously has a subversive tone and "black humor" ("From Silence" 198–201), but stopping there is insufficient. How exactly does that voice work? First, Bly's much discussed use of the "deep image," which William V. Davis points out "has never been clearly or fully defined" (7), is nonetheless helpful for understanding this poem. Deep image poems generally employ images that work "below the level" of "rational thought"; further, these poems generally have a "fluid, dreamlike construction" and an "intense subjectivity" (Mills 211–212, 217). In "Counting Small-Boned Bodies," the images are horridly dreamlike and irrational. The speaker imagines in a strange progression all of the dead Vietnamese bodies first as the "size of skulls," then as small enough to fit "a whole year's kill" on a desk, and finally, as small enough to fit into a "finger ring" (*Selected Poems* 73). The reader must forgo "rational thought" in order to accept Bly's parodic voice. The increasing smallness of the bodies fluidly distills the perversity of daily body counts in the hundreds or thousands into the size of a "finger ring."

Victoria Frenkel Harris claims that the tone of this poem can "never be confused." Despite its "sarcastic presentation," she writes that Bly "exudes naked emotion, rage" (22). However, the tone *can* be confused, and Harris herself misreads it. The poem does not have a trace of emotion or rage; the voice is calm, cool, calculated, and slow. The first line is matter-of-fact, distant: "Let's count the bodies over again." Of the poem's seventy-four words, fifty-six are monosyllables. These monosyllables greatly slow down the lines. As in Pound's "In a Station of the Metro," the second and final line of which ends with three consecutive stressed monosyllabics—"petals on a wet, black bough"—that stand in stark contrast to the first iambic line, Bly's poem relies on monosyllables both for sound and sense, with the former echoing the latter. When the speaker says "we could fit / a whole year's kill in front of us on a desk," the tone is slow, measured, and, most of all, deadpan. There is no melody or rhythm or rage. The parodic voice would not work if it were not detached and emotionless, dystopian rather than enraged. This is not a protest poem with authoritative agency; it is a satiric poem with a disengaged voice.

Further, Bly's poem, the previous lines especially, proliferates prepositions. In his assessment of his own political poetry,[12] he explains that he uses a "Smart-Blake-Whitman" line, which is "additive" and "monotonous" with an abundance of prepositions, often becoming "swollen by them" (*Selected Poems* 196). Not only do these prepositions extend lines while slowing them, they add to the absurdity of the speaker's vision. With each additional prepositional phrase, the image grows more preposterous. The final line would be sufficient with the image of fitting "a body into a finger ring," but the addition of "for a keepsake forever" makes it doubly absurd and stinging. Similarly, the image of making a "whole plain white with skulls" becomes *more* depraved with the consciously poetic phrase "in the moonlight" added gratuitously.

In much the same way, Bly's heavy use of repetition and conditional statements, which grammatically signal the hypothetical, make the tone calmer, more measured. "If we could only make the bodies smaller" is repeated three times in the brief poem; this perverse desire is nonetheless expressed in a hypothetical, betraying the speaker's rationality in the face of such absurdity. He *knows* that it is impossible to fit a year of dead Vietnamese on a desk. As such, it is not the vision itself that is grotesque, but the speaker's *wish* that such a world were possible. This twist is Bly's brilliant move in the poem. It is relatively simple to create a grotesque vision of a brutal war; it is another thing altogether to get into the psyche and hopes of a military machine.

This move is possible only with a calm, detached voice that does not "exude rage" but an irrational rationality depraved in its demeanor as well as in its desire. Bly's use of the "Smart-Blake-Whitman" line, even for all its monotony, is perfect for such a venture. As Bly says, this line is given to "declaration rather than inquiry" and to "rhetoric rather than exchange of feelings" (*Selected Poems* 197). In "Counting Small-Boned Bodies" the speaker declares his desire, but evinces no feelings that buttress it. This empty rhetorical voice echoes the horrifying, detached language of daily kill counts during the late 1960s. In this poem, then, equivocal agency's dystopian voice is a counterpoint to the utopian one present in Walcott's poem.

Whereas "Counting Small-Boned Bodies" is perhaps the finest of Bly's Vietnam-era political poems—not least because it is concise, restrained, clever, and because its voice is a parodic absurdity, unlike some of his longer meditations on the effects of Vietnam on the American psyche—"The Asians Dying" is the most noticeably political poem in Merwin's brilliant *The Lice* (1967). In poems devoid of punctuation and marked by disconnected, surreal images, ambiguous syntax, elusive meditative phrasing, and an abiding sense of absence and death, Merwin considers the aspects of experience and consciousness that defy narrative expression. The political poems in the volume move more by haunting strangeness than by specific ideological platform. Each poem can be seen paradoxically as both a self-contained unit as there are no smaller syntactical units within the poem—no sentences and few unequivocal phrases—and as an experience that cannot be expressed effectively in language. These poems portray the world as better understood as a mysterious place than as a rational, logical one governed by scientific and human laws.

"The Asians Dying" is thus a model example of particular equivocal agency. There is no readily identifiable, realistic speaker. There is no punctuation to help the reader sort out the haunting, surreal images or to sequence them logically. The only quasi-human agents in the poem are odd abstractions from decay and absence, without breath, color, or immanence. The four primary movers in the poem, the ones that act or are acted upon, are symbolic images: "The ash the great walker"; "the possessors"; "the ghosts of the villages"; and "the open eyes of the dead" (118–119). However, the reader knows that the poem refers to the atrocities of the Vietnam War because the title demands this interpretation. However, Merwin's aesthetics are not given to overt political statements or representations of the "real" world. Instead of speaking of empire, soldiers, or the Pentagon, he creates visionary personifications that make U.S. actions in Vietnam more omnipresent and disturbing. The battle then takes place not in "the poisoned farmlands" and "watercourses" of Vietnam but in an imaginary, mythological space where the stakes are cosmic as well as human. "Possessors" sounds much more forbidding than soldiers and "ash the great walker" is a more unsettling image than smoldering villages.

In contrast to Marjorie Perloff's claim that "The Asians Dying" is "memorable" because of its "blend of strangeness and a clear-sighted literalness" ("Apocalypse Then" 136) and William H. Rueckert's contention that the poem is "straightforward," "obviously political," and demands neither "analysis" nor "critical mediation" (63), the poem imparts more terrible awe when understood as neither "literal" nor "straightforward"; both views simplify the poem and disempower Merwin's eerie images. Nearly every image occupies a liminal space fraught with decay and death. The poet's eschatological voice depicts a natural life-cycle reversed by "possessors" who have "no past / And fire their only future." Merwin's approach to the horrors of Vietnam is to describe them as a strange retreat into nonexistence. He does not directly harangue U.S. policy. Instead, he follows the advice of the speaker of Dickinson's "1129," which begins: "Tell all the Truth but tell it slant— / Success in Circuit lies."

Merwin's poem reveals truth through slant, indirection, and the images of "possessors" leaving nothing but "ash" in their wake. Unlike the speaker of "Counting Small-Boned Bodies," who mimics official government propaganda, the voice of Merwin's poem is *utterly* different than public discourses and than other political poetry of this era. Even so, he pulls no punches in his descriptions; despite the enigma[13] at the core of Merwin's poetic voice, the language he uses to illuminate the devastation is absolute, unyielding. There is no space for negotiation or compromise when "The ash the great walker follows the possessors / *Forever*" and "*Nothing* they will come to is real" (my emphasis here and below). Thus, the possessors' reign is unbroken by time or space, and nothing they touch will be spared. Further, natural processes such as the cycles of day and night and the body's healing mechanisms are no longer restorative: "The nights disappear like bruises but *nothing* is healed" and "the seasons rock" but they are "calling to *nothing* living." The possessors' power, moreover, is absolute, but derivative: they "move *everywhere* under Death their star." Here, the possessors are drawn in military terms—they "advance" in "columns of smoke." The possessors *themselves* are possessed by Death. They are Death's agents on earth, doing its bidding without discrimination or remorse. They are Death's army, commanded by its ultimate rule over *everything* living.

Edward J. Brunner has noted that death for the possessors is different than death for the Vietnamese. He writes, "The two versions of death radically distinguish Asians from Americans, a distinction underscored with irony: the death the Asians experience leaves them with their eyes open; the death star under which the possessors march leaves them as blind as ever" (148). Brunner's point has merit, but the poem leaves unclear the identities of "the open eyes of the dead"; though Brunner declares unequivocally that these dead are Vietnamese, the poem suggests otherwise: "when the moon finds them they are the color of *everything*." "The color of everything" may suggest brown soil and thus brown Vietnamese skin, but such an interpretation is essentialist and would ignore the African American, Native American, and other nonwhite U.S. soldiers who died in Vietnam. Moreover, the term "Asians" is itself imprecise, equivocal. It is thus important not to consider "The Asians Dying" using Brunner's binary in which Vietnamese die enlightened and Americans die "blind"; the movement of the possessors "everywhere" implies that Merwin is primarily concerned with an American imperial policy that ignores the past and relies on "fire (power)" as the "only future" that will increase its power.[14]

The Vietnam poems of Bly, Merwin, Denise Levertov, David Ignatow, and Robert Duncan are categorically different than the poems of Komunyakaa's *Dien Cai Dau* (1988), Weigl's volume of Vietnam War poetry *Song of Napalm* (1988), and the G.I. resistance poems Bibby discusses in *Hearts and Minds: Bodies, Poetry, and Resistance in the Vietnam Era* (1996). Komunyakaa's, Weigl's, and G.I. resistance poetry are based on first-person experiences of war. Bibby points out that the Vietnam era was "a period in which 'being there' [was] paramount" (ix). Bly's and Merwin's poems are counterpoints to this notion and to poems of experiential agency in which "being there" is of great importance. Rather than depict combat experience, Bly's and Merwin's poems document the effects of an imperial war on the American psyche. Merwin's poem also preemptively circumvents Palmer's implied criticisms of Forché's "soothing" images, grammar, and syntax, while also being more accessible politically than Palmer's poem.

Like the two previous poems, Levine's "They Feed They Lion" (*They Feed They Lion* 1972) does not represent and transform first-person experience. Levine did not participate in or directly observe the 1967 Detroit riots, nor is he an African American subject to racism's injustices. Even so, Levine has pointed out that the poem "comes out of the riots" ("Staying Power" 23) in the city where he was born and raised. Levine thus has both an outsider's and an insider's perspective on the 1967 riots, much as Kinnell's poem has on 9/11. This dichotomy could be a primary reason that he chose to use a different figure of voice for "They Feed They Lion" than he used for most of his other poems of the period. The political poem of equivocal agency is an anomaly for Levine; his poems are mostly in the experiential, first-person narrative vein. They often feature readily identifiable first-person speakers meditating on their experiences of nature, love, poverty, work, and foreign cultures, or third-person speakers meditating on the experience, for example, of a Republican in the Spanish Civil War or an auto worker in Detroit.[15] David St. John claims that Levine's "primary impulse" is narrative, especially one of the "struggle of individuals ignored and unheard by their societies." He points out that Levine's work "gives voice to these 'voiceless' men and women whom he feels have been recognized and honored rarely in our literature" (277). Thus, "They Feed They Lion" has a theme similar to Levine's best poems, but its techniques— lack of narrative, unidentifiable first-person speaker, and the use of AAVE—diverge from his other poems.

"They Feed They Lion" has much to distinguish it from the majority of Levine's work, but also from most contemporary political poems. These differences begin with the title, which immediately brings up several issues that trouble both the poem and this reader. First, the repetition of "They" foreshadows the poem's incantatory use of syntactical parallelism and repetition. Next, the second "They" shows Levine's heavy usage of AAVE—substituting the personal pronoun for the possessive pronoun, dropping the initial article as in "Earth is eating trees," and departing from the standard subject–verb agreement as in "They Lion grow." Third, the prominent repetition of the third-person plural "They" indicates that the poem will be about community and collective agency, what Edward Hirsch has called a "hymn to communal rage, to acting in unison" ("Naming" 348).

The title also indicates that Levine boldly stages a rhetorical voice foreign to him. In doing so, he risks appropriating the voice of an oppressed other in order to stage his own guilt. Levine's comments about the poem nearly twenty-five years later bear out in part such a notion. He says that he saw himself "as a witness to a great American crime" of racism; however, he suggests that the poem seeks to deal with his own place in the struggles against racism. On his visit to Detroit sometime after the riots, he was struck in "realizing that in Eldridge Cleaver's term" he was "part of the problem, not part of the solution" because he is white, middle class, and middle-aged.

He continues that "he had identified at a great distance with the black rage that was exploding" but then saw who he really was: "a guy who'd made his peace with America." He has said, moreover, that "They Feed They Lion" is "an effort to come to terms with [the emotion of] being that guy" ("Staying Power" 23).

This impulsive guilt and confused identity make the AAVE powerful and self-incriminating rather than exploitative, but the reading problematically requires comments outside the poem. The compromised first-person speaker does not appear explicitly until the fifth and final stanza as a collective representative of white guilt and sadness, but also of privilege. The lion, which is fed on the injustices perpetrated against African Americans, literally grows from the white speaker: "*From my* five arms and all my hands, / *From* all *my* white sins forgiven" and "*From my* car passing under the stars" and "*from my* children" the lion grows (34; my emphasis). What Fred Marchant has called the "disconcerting, ambiguous nature of the persona" (306), though accurate and emblematic of equivocal agency, is *less* ambiguous given the prominence of "my white sins" and Levine's comments about his status as "that guy." The poem shows that he himself is the cause of African American rage. Levine's speaker would likely agree with the speaker of Rich's "For the Record" for he has certainly answered its question: "ask yourself where you were."

Levine's inclusive vision of urban poverty (via the specifics of Detroit) is a gumbo of industrial materials, foods, waste products, deceased people, body parts, and rage being cooked "on the oil-stained earth." Detroit is in effect a huge skillet greased with "bearing butter," "tar," "creosote," "gasoline," "rain," and the "sweet glues of the trotters"; "out of" this volatile, highly flammable surface "They Lion" is continually fed. The raw materials of the city go into the skillet; they are the materials of urban squalor that contribute to and are symptomatic of poverty, oppression, and despair. The first stanza reads like a recipe for riot. With its repetition, syntactical parallelism, and de facto ingredients, "They Lion grow(s)" as yeast rises in an oven:

> Out of burlap sacks, out of bearing butter,
> Out of black bean and wet slate bread,
> Out of the acids of rage, the candor or tar,
> Out of creosote, gasoline, drive shafts, wooden dollies,
> They Lion grow.

The materials are earthy, rugged, elemental, and mostly physically tangible objects. In the second stanza, though, they become more emotionally resonant and familial but also more abstract. So while the lion grows "out of buried aunties" and "Mothers hardening like pounded stumps," it also grows "out of the bones' need to sharpen and the muscles' to stretch." The use of "aunties" is particularly resonant as it suggest centuries of African American domestic servitude and oppression. The latter two lines are images of being taxed to physical extremity and the corresponding need to respond to that extremity with focused physical strength.

At the same time though, the symbols of poverty are still present. "Industrial barns," "bus ride," and "gutted cars" mix with disconcerting, abstract images such as "the sweet kinks of the fist" and "the thorax of caves." The result is a ghostly lion, rising both out of mysterious, visionary images resonant with emotional turmoil and the very real materials of the inner-city. In a review of *They Feed They Lion*, Alan Helms claims that the title poem "ignores the 'edges' of syntax, logical relation, propositional sense." For Helms, moreover, much of the poem's imagery does not "make 'sense,' " but "that's one of the points of the poem" (153). Though much of the poem may not make sense from a purely realistic, representational viewpoint, the collection of images make "sense" on a gut emotional, adrenaline-fueled level. Furthermore, from a mainstream media standpoint, riots do not make "sense" either—in their view, riots are self-destructive and pathological. Levine's poem powerfully suggests that riots come "out of" the everyday, mundane realities of bus rides, burlap sacks, and black beans *and* "out of" some abstract, dynamic repository of rage—"From they sack and they belly opened." Therein lies the brilliance of "They Feed They Lion." There is no way to get at the raw emotion Levine is interested in without mixing the inexplicable genesis of pure anger with the raw materials that both embody and create that anger. In this way, the rage is similar to the anger in some hip-hop music with its emphasis on metaphor, hyperbole, and the raw materials of poverty.

Along with its sense of communal rage, the most instrumental aspect of "They Feed They Lion" is its portrayal of collective agency. The lion is the communal agent—it embodies all of the power and anger of Detroit's African American community, and all of the community's energies coalesce in the single figure of the lion. "They Lion" is thus the agent that enables this community to move "from 'Bow Down' " to " 'Rise Up.' " Even though the speaker—outsider and (symbolic) oppressor—"has imaginatively embraced 'They,' and done it in defiant black English grammatical constructions" (Marchant 305), he is still an outsider. He is the symbolic character that the lion acts against. This outside speaker is consumed as "they feed" on him. As Marchant points out, the lion has a connection to Africa as well as to Yeats's "rough beast slouching toward Bethlehem" in "The Second Coming" (305). And, lest we forget, the lion is popularly known as the king of the jungle, and since Bob Marley's "Concrete Jungle" (1970) urban ghettoes have often been referred to popularly as "jungles." Levine's "Lion," then, is an imaginary construct embodying the rage of Detroit's African American community and the guilt of a middle-class white man. The voice of the poem reflects these divided concerns.

Like "They Feed They Lion," a collective experience of oppression is the central tenet of Sherman Alexie's "Evolution" (*The Business of Fancydancing* 1991). However, unlike Levine, Alexie, a Spokane/Coeur d'Alene Indian, uses a narrative voice infused with parody and satire in order to cast the contemporary Indian reservation as a space controlled by the malicious forces of colonialism. In "Evolution," Alexie's rhetorical strategy departs from Native American oral traditions, while foregrounding elements of magic realism. He has said that his work "has nothing to do with the oral tradition" because he "typed it" ("Sherman Alexie" 14), a claim that strikes me as protesting too much and as a dismissal of the historical and cultural forces that shape all writers. In contrast, John Newton writes that Alexie "stresses instead his own easy affiliation" with popular culture and the culture of the contemporary reservation (414), spaces that are hybrid, dynamic, and multicultural, and that are impacted by a variety of traditions, both oral and written, from which Alexie liberally borrows.

Alexie sketches the contemporary reservation in "Evolution" as a surreal combination of popular culture, supernatural occurrences, and what Jennifer Gillan has called "the structural elements of the representation of Indianness—the Indian as savage or child" (103) or, in "Evolution," as savage, childlike alcoholic. These representations of what it means to be an Indian from a stereotypically conservative white perspective, moreover, "are central to the narrative of the United States as a nation" (Gillan 103–104) in that the purity, thriftiness, and Protestant work ethic of white America had a foil in the supposed laziness, savagery, and chemical dependence of the Indian. In "Evolution," moreover, the union of a supernatural world and a rational one in the techniques of magic realism offers an alternative vision to the sterile, stagnant, and oppressive white, Western ethos, and it complicates the relationship between popular and Indian cultures. In doing so, it mocks the supposedly evolutionary superiority of whites to Indians, and shows that oppression is not a historical condition, but a present fact of life. The poem thus foregrounds William Faulkner's famous quote: "the past isn't dead; it isn't even past."[16]

Alexie's satiric narrative of the American Indian's mock
"evolution" begins with a popular culture icon. Buffalo Bill is physically present on the contemporary reservation in present tense verbs
and in the actions they portray. First, he "*opens* a pawn shop on the
reservation / right across the border from the liquor store"
(*The Business* 48; my emphasis here and below). His shop is inside
reservation borders, whereas the liquor store is noticeably on U.S.
land. Like a 7-Eleven, Buffalo Bill's pawn shop "*stays* open 24 hours a
day, 7 days a week," but unlike a 7-Eleven, this shop buys rather than
sells, takes rather than provides. At Buffalo Bill's shop, "the Indians
come running in" to sell first the material possessions prized by white,
mainstream America ("jewelry / television sets, a VCR"), next their
cultural heritage ("a full-length beaded buckskin outfit / it took Inez
Muse 12 years to finish"), and finally their very bodies. This process is
the mock, reverse evolution of North American Indians.

Before Buffalo Bill takes the Indians' bodies, he acts as a bureaucratic
government agency—the Bureau of Indian Affairs or the Department
of the Interior—that keeps meticulous but skewed records of contact
between whites and Indians. Everything he takes he "keeps it / all cat-
alogued and filed in a storage room," where the historical records of
these contacts are controlled, stored, and organized by an Indian
oppressor. When the Indians begin pawning their bodies, the first thing
to go is "their hands," "saving" the final vestiges of humanity (their
thumbs) "for last." After they have pawned "their skeletons"—typical
museum pieces in natural history museums—Buffalo Bill "takes" the
"last" Indian's "heart." At this juncture at the end of the poem, Indians
reach the apex of their (d)evolution as museum items to be gawked at,
laughed at, and cataloged as stereotypes for perpetuity.

When Buffalo Bill has nothing left to take from the Indians, he
"closes up the pawn shop" and "paints a new sign over the old" one.
The new sign reads "THE MUSEUM OF NATIVE AMERICAN
CULTURES." This shift in purpose—from killing Indians as part of
the U.S. "evolution" to mock-celebrating them and exploiting their
cultures for entertainment—continues with further economic exploitation. In the final line of this "Evolution," Buffalo Bill "charges the
Indians five bucks a head to enter" their own museum. Not only are
they exploited in these ways, they are also consumers of their own
history of oppression, their own stereotypes, and their own deaths.
Whereas Stephen F. Evans rightly claims that the implied border
crossing from pawn shop to liquor store is a "powerful metaphor of
recurring Indian defeat by white civilization and the white-conditioned
habit of Indian self-defeat" (56), the more ubiquitous metaphor is the

one that sees pop cultural mythology's (in the guise of Buffalo Bill's) vision of evolution as the death of the Indian as savage and the advent of his proper place—in the museum where other extinct, once wild creatures now reside. Alexie's parody of this vision of (d)evolution ends in that beacon of high culture—the museum—where cultures are supposedly preserved. However, this museum actually represents the deaths and exploitation of indigenous cultures.

In Alexie's usage of magic realism, Buffalo Bill does not miraculously enter the reservation in the late twentieth century; instead, he never left. He has always been there to keep Indians in their proper place in American culture. Buffalo Bill is still the celebrated hero, Indians the primitive savages prone to alcoholism and self-destruction; both are popular images that mask the realities of colonization. Therefore, in "Evolution," the Indians strangely give back to whites the trappings of popular culture (TVs and VCRs) even as they struggle with the alcohol introduced to them by whites. Alexie's Indians are thus trapped in a colonized space wherein they have compromised identities and little self-determination.

"Evolution" is a satirical narrative with a dystopian, parodic voice. Unlike the two Simic poems that employ strange narratives and ironic voices, "Evolution" is more accessible and entertaining and thus more deceptive. John Newton points out that "poetry-shy undergraduates respond to Alexie's work" with "instant recognition" due to its "reader-friendly textures and ambivalent good humor" (414), features that would no doubt disappoint Palmer and the Language poets. But as Newton suggests, something more nebulous is at work in "Evolution," which is nonetheless subtle and indirect. Newton calls Alexie's collection of parodic strategies vis-à-vis white American culture "autoethnographic parody"; in this strategy Alexie works to reclaim the Indian's stereotyped, white-constructed image. Newton points out that Alexie "cannot set the terms of this narrative exchange" because it necessarily takes place in the images, terms, and significations of the dominant white culture (427). Indeed, "Evolution" works as a type of gallows humor, but not an empty one. It takes on the "most vicious and demeaning" (Newton 416) stereotypes held by the dominant culture and attempts to re-imagine them as part of genocide styled as "evolution." But the question remains: does this poetic voice exploit those negative images for poetic gain? I believe, finally, that Alexie's poem documents exploitation and appropriation, but does not traffic in them itself.

If Alexie reconsiders the "evolution" of Indians and white North Americans in the previous poem, in "A Reconsideration of the Blackbird" (*Pyramid of Bone* 1989) Thylias Moss re-imagines the pernicious effects of racism by "reconsidering" the object of one of the most famous twentieth-century American poems, Wallace Stevens's "Thirteen Ways of Looking at a Blackbird" (*Harmonium* 1923).[17] Like Simic's especially, Moss's modus operandi falls squarely within the rhetorical strategy of equivocal agency. And unlike most of Stevens's, Moss's poetry engages pressing social issues, such as racism, violence, and misogyny. Jahan Ramazani writes that Moss's "approach to this weighty material is oblique, riddling, and gnomic." As Ramazani points out, her poems are "digressive, elliptical, allusive" pieces that "ramble associatively," but "tend to return to their central themes" (999). In "A Reconsideration of the Blackbird," the elements Ramazani describes are all in play; the poem is so fragmented and elliptical that the political import is mostly felt rather than rationalized, as is often true of poems of equivocal agency.

Stevens's "Thirteen Ways of Looking at a Blackbird" is well-known for its multiple perspectives, cubist influences, and its celebration of movement. In Stevens's poem the blackbird "whirled in the autumn winds, / It was a small part of the pantomime." Whereas Moss's reconsiderations are often prosaic and flat, Stevens's are often haiku-like and cubist-influenced: "I was of three minds, / Like a tree / In which there are three blackbirds" (*The Collected Poems* 92–94). In Moss's poem, though, there is little motion or faith in language to remake the world for the better. Stevens's poem enacts in part the modernist impetus to create a world out of the individual's imagination and consciousness, and he was primarily concerned with a world that is in constant motion. However, for Stevens and for some of his readers, the negative counterbalance to this continual movement is instability and uncertainty, two notions that Moss explores in her "reconsideration."

Stevens's propensity for linguistic play is the primary element that Moss takes on in her poem. But unlike Stevens's poem, which is methodical and ordered, Moss's is explosive, snarled, and difficult to sort out. It is immediately obvious from the visual texture of "A Reconsideration of the Blackbird" that it is even more fragmented than Stevens's thirteen well-marked sections; Moss's poem proliferates with italicized terms and phrases, questions answered elliptically if at all, and three pairs of "Problem" and "Solution" lines.[18] On this surface, the poem's main linguistic play and conceit emerge—that a crow is a blackbird and a blackbird is a symbol for a black person. Accordingly, the first line is a declarative statement with just such an implication: "Let's call him *Jim Crow*" (10–11; original emphasis here and below). The following couplet takes the next step from thinly disguised racism directed at the blackbird—Reconstruction-era Jim Crow laws—to a declaration of direct racism: "Let's call him *Nigger* and see if he rises / faster than when we say *abracadabra.*" These first three lines make obvious Moss's Stevensesque consideration of the blackbird from multiple perspectives; indeed, the first three lines look at racism from two perspectives. However, the next three fragments/stanzas turn surreal and elusive as if to disrupt any systematic attempt to understand racism and how it affects the identity of the blackbird. Each fragment begins with a perplexing, ungrounded question. They are, in order: "*Guess who's coming to dinner?*"; "What do you find *from here to eternity?*"; and "*Who never sang for my father?*" The first response is comical in the speaker's address to the reader as if she were at the gaming table: "Score ten points if you said blackbird. / Score twenty points if you were more specific, as in the first line." The second "answer" is simple: "Blackbirds."

The third response is lengthy, complex, and violent. The syntax is confusing, but its import is not. Here the blackbirds are not the oppressed but the oppressors. They "landed on the roof / and pressed it down, burying us alive." Are the definitions of *blackness* imposed on African Americans oppressive? Do they bury black people under an array of negative images? The speaker implies these questions and that African Americans neither have the power nor the time to escape negative definitions: "Why didn't we jump out the windows? Didn't we have enough / time?" Here the crushing weight of historical racism is destructive, but a few lines later some of its consequences are styled as positive and unifying. Presumably in the house being "pressed" upon by the blackbirds, the inhabitants unite in common cause for survival: "We were holding hands and hugging like never before. / You could say the blackbirds did us a favor." But—this is a major rebuttal—the speaker immediately denounces this statement with a declarative "Let's not say that however." The speaker seems to think and speak simultaneous to the poem's moment of becoming, rapidly reconsidering each and every thought she has on the blackbird and its blackness.

This refashioning leaves space for negotiation and self-definition and for evading imposed definitions. Immediately after the speaker's rebuttal, she offers an alternative and an ultimatum. The alternative is to "let the crows speak." This ultimatum is formulated simply—"Let them use their tongues or forfeit them"—but difficult in its import, especially as it is unclear how it would be best for crows to use their tongues. More critically, what is the significance of crows speaking? Why crows here and not blackbirds? It is difficult to uncover differences between crows and blackbirds in the poem; they appear to be one in the same, perhaps just "different ways of looking" at or referring to a blackbird.

The final third of the poem takes the image of tongues and submits it to a surreal series of "Problem"/"Solution" statements. The "solutions" are more terse and piercing than the previous "answers." The speaker's short, clipped sentences are disturbing and dismissive. These mock dialogues are structured in the manner of logical, philosophical proofs, but the solution statements are never logical. Here is the first systematic interchange:

> Problem: What would we do with 13 little black tongues?
> Solution: Give them away. Hold them for ransom. Make belts.
> Little nooses for little necks.

In this first "problem," Moss alludes specifically to Stevens, but now the blackbirds are tongues. The "solution," moreover, includes four options, all of which imply that black tongues have no autonomy; the four solutions portend slavery, subjugation, physical exploitation, and murder. No further explanation is needed to elucidate the role of these "solutions" in the historical treatment of African Americans.

The final "Problem"/"Solution" lines appropriately end the poem with the most forthright perspective on the blackbird. The "Problem" is disheartening in that it summarizes the lack of human compassion that characterizes racism: "Problem: No one's in love with the black-birds." Despite the riddling nature of Moss's poem, the sentiment here is understandable. Moreover, it has a crushing pathos absent in the rest of the poem, except perhaps in the line about "holding hands and hugging." The enormity and emotion of this problem is made even more so by the speaker's jarring "Solution." The commas that separate the parts of the solution suggest a logical, step-by-step connection between the parts, unlike in the previous, disconnected, four-part solution: "Paint them white, call them visions, everyone will want / one." This "solution" is ugly, but it is the culmination of a "reconsideration" that starts with *Jim Crow*, moves on to *Nigger*, then to self-destructive tendencies, then to murder and oppression, and finally to a self-effacing erasure of blackness altogether in favor of whiteness.

Moss's elliptical approach aptly ends with this solution. Because the "blackbird" and black identity in general have been historically defined by white, Western, political-religious, imperial powers as evil, primitive, inferior, and/or subhuman, the "rational" culmination is a mandate or "solution" to make all black people white, and therefore desirable.[19] Moreover, in Moss's final "solution," the imperative to "call them visions" subtly denounces poetic tradition, especially its romantic, visionary strains, of which Stevens could be considered a descendant. It further suggests that "vision" has wrongly been considered the province of whites, but not blacks. The message could be construed as: *if you are a black artist, make sure your vision is a white one.* If so, "everyone will want" to read it. Otherwise, your tongue will become a "little noose."

In his review of Moss's *Small Congregations: New and Selected Poems* (1995), Rafael Campo hints at a series of questions that affect politically engaged poetry. For Campo, Moss's poems often "fail to sound beautiful," which betrays "her distrust of poetry." He continues with the claim that "at times, her methods are not equal to her message." He conjectures that her poems are sometimes not beautiful "because it hurts the eye so much to read them, to see the awful truths they reveal." However, he also claims that his is not a "convincing excuse" because poets such as Marilyn Hacker, June Jordan, Thom Gunn, and Adrienne Rich have written beautiful poems about difficult sociopolitical subjects ("Sturdy Boxcars" 348). A comparison, for example, of Rich's rhetorical strategies with Moss's is a byproduct of this book; the more pressing questions, though, are not ones of comparison. Why do poems, especially political ones, have to be "beautiful"? Certainly many hip-hop songs are not "beautiful," but still powerful. Are pain and oppression unacceptable subjects for poetry? Or do these subjects have to be made beautiful as well? What problems result from making beautiful the horrific?[20] Campo's comments get at the heart of the complications and problems with much political poetry. For a poem of equivocal agency, traditional concepts of beauty ought not apply. "A Reconsideration of the Blackbird," moreover, is beautiful primarily in its haunting qualities, ones that make the reader quail and think, rather than appreciate gracefulness and charm. Finally, poems of equivocal agency, such as Moss's, do not betray a "distrust" of poetry; rather, they portray an abiding trust in the ways that poems can be imaginative interventions in the often frightening world.

Summary and Conclusions

The political poems of equivocal agency discussed in chapter 2 are not so much about specific political messages or positions or about the experiences that help create and are created by these positions or worldviews. Instead, these poems' strategies and voices evince greater concern for imaginative visions that do not fit neatly into succinct messages or political positions. They do not order us to act; they move by insinuation, intuition, and in the re-creation of the world rather than in its representation. *The Writing of the Disaster* (1980), Maurice Blanchot's fragmented meditations on disaster, language, and an ethics of responsibility, suggests that literature arrests and impedes the containability of its message, in the process defusing and complicating whatever messages inhere therein. So it is in many of the poems in this chapter, many of which are complex and multifaceted. These poems often display more sweeping, challenging, and surreal visions of the world we live in, the ones we might live in, and the ones that are likely only dreams; they depict not what *is*, but what *might* be or what *might* have been. A few lines from A.R. Ammons's book-length poem *Tape for the Turn of the Year* (1965) sum up the strategy: "in art, we do not run / to keep up with random / moments, we select / & create / the moment occurring forever" (37). So, though the moment—events and experiences in the world—have a place in poetry, in poems of equivocal agency the poet creates and recreates a type of magical, transformative world that is "occurring forever" and is not bound to a limited time and space, even for those poems with particular contexts.

There are many other poems I could have chosen for this chapter, including those in the oeuvre of Yusef Komunyakaa, many of which combine the rhetorical strategies and voices of experiential and equivocal agency. Poems such as "1984," "Landscape for the Disappeared," "The Music that Hurts," "Fever," "Camouflaging the Chimera," and " 'You and I Are Disappearing,' " all of which appear in his Pulitzer Prize-winning *Neon Vernacular: New and Selected Poems* (1993), are some of his most haunting and surreal. Jorie Graham's "Fission" (1991) is another well-known example that combines elements of both experiential and equivocal agency. Amiri Baraka's frequently anthologized "An Agony. As Now" (1964) is also a political poem of equivocal agency, one which stands in stark contrast to his poems of authoritative agency. I refer readers specifically to two excellent examples I did not choose—Robert Hass's "Politics of a Pornographer" (*Field Guide* 1973) and Charles Wright's "Against the American Grain" (*Harper's Magazine* August 2004)—for further ways that contemporary poets, and ones not often considered "political," use the voices of equivocal agency. When reading any political poem of equivocal agency, finally, it is necessary for the reader to be willing to make broad imaginative leaps. As Bruce Weigl writes of

Simic's poetry, the reader "must be willing to enter a wildly imaginative world, willing to jump into the fray surrounded by strangely human and magnificently cosmic forces that radiate within the expansive vistas of his imagination" (2–3). The poems of *migratory agency* in chapter 3 include subtle elements of the strategies outlined in chapters 1 and 2, but they have unique poetic agency, figures of voice, and sensibilities all their own.

CHAPTER 3

Migratory Agency

INTRODUCTION

As in the previous chapters, the goal of chapter 3 is to elucidate one of the primary rhetorical strategies of American political poetry. However, unlike the previous chapters on embodied and equivocal agencies, this one on *migratory agency* makes more significant departures from current poetry criticism and theory. These departures are byproducts of three imperatives: to be inclusive, to embrace multilingualism, and to articulate my belief that poems of migratory agency bring to life a key variation on one of the most important rhetorical strategies of poetry, broadly defined, in the twentieth century. With a few brief illustrative exceptions, the poems analyzed in chapter 3 are by Latina/o poets. However, it is *not* my intention to write a chapter *about* Latina/o poetry; nor is my *primary* goal to argue that these poets deserve inclusion in the much-disputed canon. Because most Latina/o poetry is studied from within the framework of a specific tradition or type of poetry and rarely as part of a larger framework, I hope that one of the byproducts of chapter 3 is a movement of these poems and their languages into the multiethnic mainstream of contemporary American poetry.

In this chapter, then, I discuss the dominant figures of voice and rhetorical strategies in migratory agency, and how these poems depart from and are similar to other prominent literary and cultural movements in the twentieth century. My understanding of migratory agency thus begins relatively broadly and then narrows into what I perceive is its primary domain in contemporary American poetry. In this introduction, I look backward to Modernists Ezra Pound and T.S. Eliot, who strived to create a sophisticated, multilingual poetry that migrates between languages, cultures, and historical traditions; I also turn back briefly to a Neruda poem that illustrates indirectly some key principles of migratory agency. Throughout the chapter,

I keep in mind (and the reader should as well) that the subject of chapter 4—hip-hop music—also actuates a type of migratory agency in its conscious borrowing and mixing (and consequent reshaping) of a variety of languages, discourses, and musical traditions. Though both Modernism and hip-hop migrate between cultural codes, neither of them embody the speaking voice of the migrant. The main figure of voice in poems of migratory agency emphasizes the agency of the linguistic and cultural migrant, who moves between Spanish and English and between the worlds and cultural sensibilities from which these two languages emerge (and merge). These poems foreground the poetic agency of the border-crosser and the voices that are possible only in a bilingual poet.

First, I want to work through my initial two imperatives for chapter 3. Despite two decades of discussing multiculturalism with regard to pedagogy, the canon, and American literature, most critical work in American poetry studies is organized by or dedicated to a specific ethnicity, gender, topic, or to what I consider an elite survey of American poetry and culture. Book-length studies of American poetry generally focus on, for example, African American, Asian American, Native American, Latina/o, Chicana/o, or female writers, or on a topic such as environmental, war, feminist, postmodern, prophetic, Language, or resistance poetry. These thematic works generally exclude Latina/o writers, writers from alternative traditions, spoken word and hip-hop artists, and American poets who write in more than one language. "Comprehensive" American poetry surveys usually consider only canonical (primarily white male) writers with a (white) woman or an African American included for comparative (or P.C.) purposes. More encompassing volumes, such as books of essays edited by Charles Bernstein and Marjorie Perloff, are better, but they do little with bilingual poetry or hip-hop.

Latina/o poets are generally left out of even "comprehensive" critical studies of American poetry. Yet they are not simply marginalized because even marginalization implies an existence at the edges of a critic's scope. For instance, in the seminal *American Poetry and Culture 1945–1980* (1985), Robert von Hallberg focuses on Robert Creeley, John Ashbery, James Merrill, Robert Lowell, Edward Dorn, Mona Van Duyn, and Robert Pinsky, all of whom have "shown marked curiosity about the dominant American culture" (8).[1] To be fair, von Hallberg is interested in poets who "have looked more searchingly and fairly at the national culture"; he claims that the enduring popular perception "that American poets have made themselves cultural outlaws" (244) is inaccurate. Though I agree in part with his claim, it is easily pointed out that middle- to upper-class white males are much more likely to look at the dominant culture more fairly than women, the poor, and minorities; they are, in fact, *part* of the dominant culture rather than *apart* from it. Though von Hallberg would argue that some white poets—Levertov and Bly, for instance—have not looked fairly at the dominant culture, he does not consider that what might be "fair" for African Americans or Latinas/os may be different than what is fair for whites.

The major problem, then, with even a smart book such as von Hallberg's is the title. For him, as for many others, "American poetry and culture" represents an extremely narrow range of poets. Although his book was published in 1985, before hip-hop gained a measure of respect with academics, before spoken-word poetry became popular, and before much of the emphasis on multiculturalism in the academy, the same fundamental dynamics of his study persist today. Any relatively comprehensive study of contemporary American poetry and culture that does not take African American and Latina/o poets into account is very limited, just as any contemporary study that does not take on hip-hop omits the most vibrant poetry scene in the United States. Writing about American poetry with limited breadth is important for understanding specific poets, but a readjustment of scope is necessary if a critic chooses not to write about poets concerned with race, ethnicity, and civil rights.

In many cases, however, critics include one or two poets other than canonical white ones in their books. Kevin Stein's *Private Poets, Worldly Acts: Public and Private History in Contemporary American Poetry* (1996) is a typical example. Stein features chapters on Lowell, Rich, Frank O'Hara, James Wright, Levine, Komunyakaa, Dove, David Wojahn, and Forché. As has become relatively standard of books on American poetry, Stein includes a selection of the frequently discussed (Lowell, Rich, O'Hara, and Wright) alongside several African Americans, here choosing the canonical Dove, and one that fits into his specific framework (Komunyakaa). Stein's book, more impressive in breadth than many, is emblematic of the white–black dichotomy inherent in studies of American poetry. To an extent, African Americans have gained entry into the canon whereas other groups remain outside, even though Joy Harjo is sometimes included in monographs. But rarely is a Latina/o poet, *especially* one who writes in Spanish *and* English, included as one of these additions, despite the potential benefits of the juxtaposition.

The inverse of these dynamics is apparent in the weight borne by scholars of Latina/o and Chicana/o poetry.[2] In their authors' efforts to be comprehensive and illuminating, book-length works often bog down in description and background. Four of the seminal, self-described comprehensive texts—Bruce-Novoa's *Chicano Poetry: A Response to Chaos* (1982); Cordelia Candelaria's *Chicano Poetry: A Critical Introduction* (1986); José E. Limón's *Mexican Ballads, Chicano Poems: History and Influence in Mexican-American Social Poetry* (1992); and Teresa McKenna's *Migrant Song: Politics and Process in Contemporary Chicano Literature* (1997)—have significantly overlapping summaries and descriptive information. When Candelaria briefly outlines a historical context for Chicana/o poetry vis-à-vis the dominant Anglo-American tradition, it is an expeditious, indistinct backdrop to her "exhaustive analysis" (xii). Even Candelaria acknowledges that her self-proclaimed comprehensive study will "fall short" of her goals and reader expectations (xi–xii).

Although books on Latina/o poetry and on other minority poetries are indispensable to scholarly work and essential for illuminating the poetry, they also tend to marginalize further the poetry in American letters. Candelaria's 1986 important claim about Chicana/o literature in relation to the American tradition is still largely unheeded in the academy and by critics: "That Chicano literature is fundamentally 'American' is clearly established, for its origins and influences are all part of the very basis of the macro context that constitutes the U.S. American literary tradition. In this sense, therefore, it, like other ethnic minority literatures of the United States, lies within the *mainstream* of American literature." This mainstream, she points out, is "pluralistic, iconoclastic, democratic, and multi-ethnic," rather than "solely Anglo-American" (15; original emphasis). The rhetorical strategies of migratory agency exist *within* the mainstream of American letters; whereas the poetic agency of the migrant is largely the province of bilingual Latina/o poems, these migrants too are part of the multiethnic, pluralistic American mainstream. They embody the dynamism, multiethnic, and multilingual nature of America and its literature; these poems are thus the most charismatic repositories of the shifting space that meets at the junction of two signifiers—"America" and "poetry"—both of which are fluid terms currently undergoing relatively dramatic changes in meaning.

As I alluded to in this book's introduction, the term "America" has a range of different historical significations. The prevailing English speaker's (and consequently, hegemonic) understanding of "America" is fundamentally different from its denotation and connotation in Spanish. As Debra A. Castillo notes, in English the word "typically refers to a country" and in Spanish to a continent (5). I want to retain the essences of both connotations. The poems discussed in chapter 3 were produced in the place that English speakers understand as America, but they exhibit the values and influences of the broad range of peoples, cultures, and languages of the Spanish speaker's continental understanding of America. This bifurcated understanding of America points up the bilingual, divided voices of migratory agency, in which various registers of two languages vector into and out of each other and into and out of the cultures from which they originate. Further, as Castillo points out in *Redreaming America: Toward a Bilingual American Culture*, the "discourse of plurality" in the American academy is discordant—not to mention disturbing—"in the [university] context of monolingualism" (190) in which English predominates and other languages barely register. Given this language-power imbalance, bilingual political poems, and more specifically poems of migratory agency, serve to redress and correct for academic, critical, and cultural biases.

The use of multiple languages, as I mentioned previously, is not exclusive to Latina/o poets. In their most famous long poems—*The Waste Land* (1922), "Hugh Selwyn Mauberley (Life and Contacts)" (1920), and *The Cantos* (published intermittently from 1917 to 1969)—Eliot and Pound used multiple languages. Eliot used German, French, Italian, and Sanskrit in *The Waste Land* in order to create a polyglot texture of voices, perspectives, and speakers as if mimicking the turning of a global radio dial. He was interested in the fragmentation and uncertainty of the modern world; the use of multiple languages was part of his attempt to find some objective way of seeing this world through a cacophony of voices.

Pound's engagement with languages, on the other hand, was longer and more sustained. Imagism, founded and practiced by Pound, H.D., and Amy Lowell, was influenced greatly by Chinese and Japanese poetry. He translated regularly from Chinese, Japanese, Italian, and Greek, and his translation of T'ang poet Li Po's "The River-Merchant's Wife: A Letter" (1915) is one of the best twentieth-century English translations of any poem from any language. In his own poetry, Pound habitually made allusions in five to six languages. Herein lies a key difference between the strategies of migratory agency, which I fully delineate shortly, and those of Modernism. Pound and Eliot wrote English poems textured with lines and allusions in other languages in part to display the difficulty, authority, and unique individualism inherent in their rigid, authoritarian, and patriarchal version of Modernism. Eliot's and Pound's often arcane allusions in multiple languages were implicitly political in their didactic intentions and in their juxtaposition of languages. They were trying to show that Americans are not provincial and unlearned. Theirs was an attempt to display the agency of the intellectual migrant, who is not only comfortable, but superior, in nimbly moving between languages and historical and poetic traditions.

In Pound's case, for example, *The Cantos* were his attempt at a modern epic encompassing world history, literatures, languages, arts, myths, and economics. He wanted to write a poem with allusions that only classically educated readers would understand; these readers would then work to create an uber-civilization "ruled by right-thinking men of action" (Ramazani Head Notes 367). Eliot's and Pound's use of multiple languages, therefore, was a political strategy for demonstrating authority, learnedness, and superior education. Moreover, they were not directly challenging the primacy or authority of English or its place in the dominant culture, as do the poems discussed in chapter 3. Additionally, their multilingual poems are the product of elite, classical educations, not the life experiences of a migrant moving between languages, which suggests that experience is key to migratory agency in addition to embodied agency, the latter a point supported by Rafael Pérez-Torres when he claims that many Latina/o poems "attempt to represent accurately the culture and economics of specific communities" (*Movements* 17). Finally, then, these Modernists and hip-hop artists generally *borrow* from other languages and cultural codes, whereas the figures of voice in migratory agency are organic, indigenous to the languages and cultures they inhabit. In all three cases, however, the voices remain *poetic*—staged and rhetorical.

Because poems of migratory agency code switch between English and Spanish, I want to review briefly some theoretical parameters outlined in literary and sociolinguistic studies on code switching in poetry and in U.S. bilingual communities. Anthropologist Keith H. Basso argues that code switching—in his study between Western Apache and English—"may be strategically employed as an instrument of meta-communication" and as an "indirect form of social commentary" (8–9). Jeraldine R. Kraver writes that code switching in Latina poetry is a "means of resisting the forces of monoculturalism and monolingualism that threaten bicultural and bilingual writers"; she shows that it also "upset(s)" "the binary oppositions—especially English/Spanish—upon which Anglo society depends" (193, 196). Further, she rightly claims that "introducing" Spanish in a text "disrupts [the] authoritarian discourse" of English (196–197). Poems of migratory agency, which have various amounts of English and Spanish, do all of the above: they challenge the dominant discourse, they reflect the multicultural experiences of poets and their communities, and they interrupt the Anglo-American literary tradition.

In poems of migratory agency, the speaker-poet—to use the words of sociolinguists Eva Mendieta-Lombardo and Zaida A. Cintron—is "the creative actor who uses CS [code switching] as a linguistic/literary device to accomplish an end, for instance, to engage the reader/audience in a culturally significant or culturally intimate way" (567). Code switching not only reflects the speaker's experiences and serves as a means to establishing and recognizing group identity, it is also a strategic, creative device for activating a specific type of poetic agency. The primary and most powerful agency these poets have in the wider culture is their ability to move fluidly between languages and their variant systems of signification. However, the use of multiple languages and cultural codes is just one tool at the disposal of bilingual poets. They employ numerous rhetorical strategies that often dovetail with experiential and authoritative agencies. Furthermore, many Latina/o poems are exclusively in English *or* Spanish, but they are still informed by the rhythms, nuances, and cultural currents of both languages. Four critically acclaimed Latina/o poets—Alberto Ríos, Sandra Cisneros, Gary Soto, and Martín Espada—write almost exclusively in English, but their poems embody the voices and strategies used by other bilingual poets. Also, some bilingual poets—notably Lorna Dee Cervantes and Victor Hernández Cruz—no longer write bilingual poems; Cervantes now writes in English and Cruz writes poems in Spanish and English but not in combination. Cervantes, for example, "decided early in her career that she could not write bilingually, that it was a 'false' and 'clumsy' voice" (Kraver 197). Though I disagree with Cervantes and believe some of her strongest poems are bilingual, readers must decide this question themselves. (Her claim also dovetails in an interesting way with Vendler's presumptive desire for a purity of language discussed shortly.) Ultimately, though, it is unnecessary that a poem be transparently bilingual in order to display the sensibilities, voices, and strategies of the migrant speaker, as I explain later.

Cervantes's and Vendler's concerns are also reflected in the wider literary culture, where there is a palpable resistance to Spanish among many poets, readers, and critics. In a recent essay, Marcos McPeek Villatoro retells the story of Joseph Brodsky's confrontation with Latino writer Benjamin Sáenz. Brodsky, according to the story, "admonished" Sáenz for turning in a bilingual poem in Brodsky's workshop (176). For Villatoro, this anecdote suggests the difficulties and pressures bilingual poets face from a literary culture that often determines a poem's acceptability on the basis of its relationship to an illusory English-only tradition. In his account of the incident, Sáenz writes that Brodsky told him to "keep foreign languages out of [his] poems, since [he] was working in an 'English tradition.' " According to Sáenz, shortly thereafter Brodsky "recite[d] a poem with a Latin phrase in it." Sáenz concludes that Latin, Greek, and French have "an esteemed place in American letters"—and we see evidence of this in Eliot's and Pound's work—and that Brodsky's real problem was with Spanish. "Clearly," Sáenz writes, "some languages are more foreign than others" (524).

Brodsky's apparent disdain for Spanish as well as his upholding of an "English tradition" ignore some fundamental realities. There is no unbroken U.S. "English tradition" handed down from poet to poet. There are *many* English traditions in the United States. A critic could ostensibly trace various strands of poetic tradition: Whitman–Williams–Olson–Ginsberg–Creeley–Baraka; Dickinson–Pound–Snyder–Charles Wright; Stevens–Ashbery–Merwin–Strand–Graham; Longfellow–Frost–Roethke–Kumin; McKay–Hughes–Brooks–Clifton–Dove; Bishop–Lowell–Plath–Berryman–Olds; and Tillie Olsen– Edwin Rolfe–Rukeyser–Levertov–Rich–Forché. Even these are incomplete, contentious, and tenuous. Do you trace "tradition" on the basis of aesthetics, style, theme, subject matter, commitment, or some combination thereof? How do you account for influences on U.S. poets from England, Ireland, France, Spain, Russia, Perú, Cuba, Chile, and Mexico?

There are also many Spanish (and indigenous language) traditions in America and, more specifically, in the land now called the United States. To give just one, José E. Limón thoroughly discusses the *corrido*, which is an oral folk poetry that has been prominent both in Mexico and in the United States, in his aforementioned book. He shows its influence on Chicano Movement poetry in the 1960s and 1970s. Bilingual poetry, moreover, can no longer be ignored by the dominant literary culture as tens of millions of Americans are bilingual, and there are well over 40 million Latinas/os in the United States (many of whom speak two languages). Spanish language poems are also a key component of political poetry in the United States; critics of American poetry should no longer ignore them. Finally, the discourses of "authenticity," as many cultural and postcolonial theorists have shown, often serve "traditions" that seek to maintain linguistic and power inequalities.

The conscious mixing of traditions and languages can create exciting and discordant juxtapositions. The presence of Spanish in an

"English" poem disrupts "tradition" and makes strange not only its sensual textures, but also the import of its messages. A canonical example in Latin American poetry illustrates these tensions, but from the opposite perspective. In Neruda's "La United Fruit Co." (*Canto general* 1950), the presence of English is menacing, disjunctive, and harsh. The title immediately suggests a tension between cultures and languages—the conjunction of the Spanish "La" with the untranslated name of an American company is discordant, especially as United Fruit Company is considered a symbolic representative of U.S. economic imperialism.[3] In the fourth and fifth lines, "Coca-Cola Inc." and "Ford Motors" stand out as harsh linguistic intrusions, aural metonyms for intrusive economic imperialism by multinational corporations. The names sound especially sinister when the poem is read aloud, as they create a break in the mellifluous Spanish:

> Cuando sonó la trompeta, estuvo
> todo preparado en la tierra,
> y Jehová repartió el mundo
> a Coca-Cola Inc., Anaconda,
> Ford Motors, y otras entidades[4] (206–207)

The company names are clunky; the monosyllabics "Ford" and "Inc." especially stand out amid the polysyllabics of a romance language. However, the two North American corporations in the previous line (Coca Cola and Anaconda) sound like Spanish names, but they are made stranger, *more* foreign by the English abbreviation "Inc."

The bicultural, bilingual texture at the beginning of "La United Fruit Co." provides an apt transition into the rhetorical elements of migratory agency. The migration between languages and cultures is central to them; these poems exist within the contact zone between North American and Latin American cultures and between English and Spanish. Their poetic agency works to make multiculturalism (via multilingualism) vital to American literary culture. As Ada Savin notes in her essay on Cervantes, the multilingualism of Latina/o poetry "acts out the living contact between the cultures in contact and their respective languages" (217). This continual migration paradoxically centers these poems in a constantly moving space that does not rest in one culture or language.

The figure of the cultural and linguistic migrant provides the poetic agency in the poems of chapter 3. Teresa McKenna begins chapter 1 of *Migrant Song* by citing a passage from Jimmy Santiago Baca's "In My Land" (1979) to show that the image of the migrant symbolizes

Chicana/o literature. She writes, "the primary metaphor for the experience is the migrant, who is at once the paradigmatic figure of displacement and oppression and the leading force of persistence in the vicissitudes of change. As both, the migrant finally underscores life-generating rebellion against cultural erasure" (9). Arturo Islas also rightly claims that the Mexican in the United States is a migrant, not an immigrant: "Mexicans did not cross an ocean with the intention of starting a brand new life in a 'new' world. They were already very much a part of the landscape even before it changed its name from 'Mexico' to the 'United States' " (5). (This idea informs the title of Baca's first book—*Immigrants in Our Own Land* (1979).) The speakers in poems of migratory agency, then, embody both the *force* of resistance to and the *site* of cultural and linguistic displacement.

In contrast to embodied and equivocal agencies, in which rhetorical strategies are the *means* to political comment/intervention, the rhetorical strategies of migratory agency are in *themselves* political. These poets, in other words, have figured out how to make the *form* of their poetry political over and above its *content*. The multilingual form is itself political in challenging the dominant English discourse. As such, there is a form/content distinction in many of these poems similar to the one I outline in chapter 4 with regard to live hip-hop performance. If a poem's form is political, its explicit content need not be political for it to do political work. However, the poems discussed in chapter 3 are political in form *and* in content; the key figures of migratory agency are both political ends themselves as well as tools for further political comment.

In the readings that follow, I attempt to explain how the movement between languages and cultures creates a unique type of poetic agency. I have chosen poems that occupy varying gradients on the English–Spanish language see-saw—I read poems that are mostly English, equal parts English and Spanish, and one that is entirely Spanish. Taken in combination, I hope that they successfully illuminate the figures, strategies, and voices of migratory agency. Readers will note, however, that many of the poems I read are largely written in English. This fact does not privilege English over Spanish. It merely suggests that the dominant mode for U.S. poetry still occurs on the cultural ground of English, although that ground is rapidly changing. Because Spanish is on this ground, it has even greater significance and power when used in an "English" poem. Some poems have little Spanish, but these few words have powerful rhetorical effects.

Poems of Migratory Agency

In a review of Walcott's *The Fortunate Traveller*, Helen Vendler suggests that using more than one language in a poem is foolhardy. After questioning Walcott's use of patois and his alternations between "high" and "low" diction, she says that multilingual poetry embodies "a macaronic aesthetic" that "has never yet been sustained." She goes on to acknowledge that even though Latina/o poets write in "a mixture" of English and Spanish, "neither language gains mastery." For Vendler, multilingualism "may accurately reflect their linguistic predicament, but the mixed diction has yet to validate itself as a literary resource with aesthetic power" ("Poet of Two Worlds" 31). Vendler's stance on multilingual poetry may be indicative of many critics, but her desire for a "mastery" of one language is undesirable and impossible. The exclusion or erasure of one language via the "mastery" or primacy of another in a poem is an illusion. A language is often haunted by the other languages it seeks to exclude as are cultures and countries haunted by those groups of people they seek to master.[5] Such is the source of rebellion and the eventual erosion of structures of "mastery." Further, I hope to show that the use of two languages is a "literary resource" with dynamic "aesthetic power" and poetic agency.

It is clear that neither language "gains mastery" in Tino Villanueva's "Nuestros abuelos" due to the skewed power relations it depicts. The poem suggests that when one language gains mastery, suffering and oppression come shortly thereafter. Villanueva's first book, *Hay otra voz Poems* (*There Is Another Voice*), appeared in 1972, and his book *Scene from the Movie "Giant,"* which comprises a long poem rethinking the malicious perspective on Chicana/o identity in the 1956 film *Giant* starring James Dean, Rock Hudson, and Elizabeth Taylor, won the 1994 American Book Award.[6] In "Nuestros abuelos" (*Shaking Off the Dark* 1994), Villanueva's systematic language choices create a sophisticated sociopolitical framework. His linguistic choices produce a means for understanding the history of Chicana/o migrant laborers, in this case the struggles borne by current Chicanas/os' *abuelos* (grandparents/grandfathers).

Villanueva's poem shows Chicana/o subjects split not only between languages, but also between their bodies and the actions their bodies perform. Consequently, they are agents fundamentally separated from the objects and results of their actions. They do not, in Marxist terms, have any control over the capital they create for others.[7] Even so,

Villanueva's seamless use of both languages symbolically redeems the "private suffering" (55) they endure in this state of physical, economic, and linguistic limbo. He immediately frames the poem in a state between languages—images of community are in Spanish whereas courtroom legalisms are in English. The first instance of this dualism is an English epigraph from the unjust, predatory courtroom of mid-nineteenth-century California. It appears, as is customary, between the title and the first line of the poem, which is also "Nuestros abuelos," and is attributed to "The Honorable Don Pedro de la Guerra," a California senator, lawyer, and judge of Spanish descent.

The epigraph and its footnote are key to understanding the poem's suggestive framework.[8] According to the footnote below the poem, Guerra's speech was originally delivered in court on April 26, 1856, "in opposition to the 'law to settle land titles in California' " that was "approved by the legislature" that year. The epigraph and footnote suggest to readers that the poem will be directly oppositional as well, but they soon learn otherwise. The italicized epigraph begins with the seemingly rhetorical question, "*Who are the plaintiffs?*," which Guerra answers instantly and unambiguously. The plaintiffs in the case, which gave Chicana/o lands to white settlers, were the "*conquered who are humbled before the conqueror asking for his protection, while enjoying what little their misfortune has left them.*" The plaintiffs, moreover, were unable to comprehend the "*prevalent language*" (English) of "*their native soil,*" which makes them "*strangers in their own land.*" Here Villanueva (and Guerra) portrays the migrant's (*not* immigrant's) lament depicted by Islas, Baca, and McKenna. In choosing this epigraph, Villanueva uses the terms of colonial conquest, terms that highlight the dislocation of Chicanas/os and their inability to resist it due to a lack of speaking skills in the conqueror's language. As such, they have been rendered childlike and obsequious and, most disastrously, silent. They have not been driven off of their own land to other lands, but made inferior on their own lands to "their conquerors," which is colonization at its worst.

The epigraph appears between the repeated "Nuestros abuelos" and is huge and forbidding in relation to them. The epigraph and footnote combine for parts of eleven lines; the poem itself has sixteen lines. Chicanas/os' ancestors are both figuratively and literally made small in the U.S. courts. However, "nuestros abuelos"—represented in Spanish—suggests that identity, family, and heritage are the province of Spanish-speaking roots, not Anglo North American ones. These two words imply that the poem's speaker considers himself a product of a collective heritage of Chicanas/os, not of *our heritage,* but of *nuestra herencia*, in a line of descent from Spanish speakers rather than English speakers, as if to say *the voices of the ancestors remain even in their absence.*

The poem ultimately suggests that silence and anonymity result when languages are made unequal. Bruce-Novoa shows that Villanueva's poetry envisions "oppressive forces" that "threaten to relegate people to a silent, invisible, anonymous state of nonexistence." Villanueva's voice, Bruce-Novoa continues, "is faithful to the silent essences of life's victims with whom the poet identifies." Finally, as Bruce-Novoa is wont to do in his strict structuralism, he suggests that Villanueva's poetry displays a deep structure or essence: "Silence essentially characterizes life's victims, while sound pertains to the oppressors" (131). In "Nuestros abuelos" that silence is pervasive but not total, but that sound is all "conqueror." In the first stanza, in English except for the first two words, the ancestors' "suffering" is "private" and thus silent, anonymous. Moreover, their suffering occurs in an abstract space bounded by "the four winds of heaven / & the fifth sun." This elemental abstraction is interminable precisely because it is bounded only by elements; their suffering, then, appears natural, elemental, and unchangeable, which has potentially devastating implications for the migrant's agency.

In line three, which consists of the single word "toiled," Villanueva begins an axiomatic functional use of English and Spanish. All action verbs are in English: "Nuestros abuelos" "toiled," "carried," and "genuflected." In each of these simple past-tense, preterit verbs, the ancestors act on behalf of their "conquerors." None of their actions work toward their own ends, only to serve the manifest destiny of a growing white North American empire. When the grandparents "carried," they "carried ties / for iron-horse companies." When they "genuflected," they "genuflected / for other similar go-West-young-man / enterprises." Their actions are in English because the beneficiaries of those actions are white North Americans; their work enabled the prosperity and westward expansion of the United States. More hauntingly, their servitude and strength propped up the American Dream and those white Americans who sought it ("go-West-young man / enterprises") on railroads built by Chicanos.

Yet if their actions are symbolically silent because rendered in English and thus lost to them when they enter Anglo culture as completed actions, their worn bodies at least remain their own. In the second stanza, "sus espaldas" carry the railroad cross-ties and "sus coyunturas" bend in obeisance to manifest destiny so that the "go-West-young-man" can achieve the American Dream. The disturbing division goes something like this: the grandparents' Chicano-Spanish backs and joints perform North American-English actions. Such a separation implies *you can have our labor, but you cannot have our voices or our bodies.* This division is crude, especially considering that for indigenous peoples throughout Latin America Spanish is the language of the conqueror. Yet in Villanueva's poem the bifurcation is subtle and clear, as are its implications for the two languages, but nevertheless disturbing.

The final stanza is entirely in Spanish, which might indicate that the English-language actions are completed, silenced, and that there is some hope for a self-determined Spanish-speaking future. Whereas in the first two stanzas the silence and anonymity belonged to "nuestros abuelos," in the final stanza silence and isolation symbolically apply to Anglo Americans who, unable to communicate in Spanish, are now symbolically strangers in *their* new land. Though I do not want to overemphasize technical linguistic terms, the notion of "marked" and "unmarked" choices in code switching are helpful here.[9] Mendieta-Lombardo and Cintron write that code switching "among non-bilingual members of a community has a marked value," whereas "among those who live with two cultures and languages it becomes an unmarked choice" (566). As such, the final stanza has a high markedness value for monolingual English speakers, but for Latinas/os it is unmarked because moving between languages is common for them. The final stanza thus silences monolingual-English readers in much the same way the "conquerors" did to Chicanas/os in mid-nineteenth-century California.

Even as this isolation is enacted in the opposite direction, there is still an abiding silence in "nuestros abuelos." The poem is devoid of interiority; because the ancestors' suffering was "private," it is now somewhat inaccessible to the reader. Everything is action, surface, body. In the final stanza there is no longer any separation between Chicana/o bodies and North American-English actions because only the corporeal remains. The only actions that occur in Spanish appear in the last stanza, but neither are positive. First, "Sus manos se hincharon de años / y de callos." Their hands—here the Spanish is flexible—either *swelled* or *were swollen* as "se hincharon" can be either a simple past tense, reflexive third-person plural verb form or, as is the norm in much Spanish usage, the passive verb form. Accordingly, this action may be imposed upon the Chicana/o ancestors as the passive implies a lack of agency. It forebodes the possibility that even their bodies will be lost to them.

In this final line, the speaker describes his ancestors' deaths in Spanish. Even though Spanish is now the controlling language, they remain silent, wordless, absent. "Sus cuerpos" (their bodies), in Villanueva's final stanza, are "cansadas cicatrices" (tired scars) that have arrived ("han llegado") at a "humilde tumba." Their bodies, then, arrive at a single humble tomb—this communal grave ends the poem on a note of collective experience, community, and heritage. But here humility comes not in the language of the conqueror, as it does in the epigraph, but in the Spanish "humilde," which is a more mellifluous word than its English counterpart, "humble." Small consolation, then, that they die in the beauty of poetry, in "la humilde tumba." For the speaker, this end seems inevitable due to the momentous "por eso" (literally *for this*, but usually translated *therefore*) in the final stanza: "y por eso / sus cuerpos, / cansadas cicactrices, / han llegado / hasta la humilde tumba." Though not as dramatic, this *therefore* hangs on the end of the line and strongly suggests an inevitable outcome much as it does in James Wright's "Autumn Begins in Martins Ferry, Ohio" (1963). In Wright's poem, the destitution, frustration, and latent violence of poor fathers in the steel belt of the Ohio Valley is made manifest in their sons' high school football games:

> Therefore
> Their sons grow suicidially beautiful
> At the beginning of October,
> And gallop terribly against each other's bodies. (636–637)

These lines show how the Spanish "por eso" packs an emotional punch in comparison to "therefore," which sounds cold, distant, and legalistic; "por eso" sounds like a plea, a slow drip into sadness whose three syllables can be painfully drawn out.

Villanueva's poem sets some basic groundwork for my understanding of migratory agency. The poem moves strategically between languages like a migrant worker does between locations. Without this migration, these poems would not be able to exert external influence back on the forces of culture and language that work to dissipate Latina/o communities.[10] Cervantes's "Poema para los Californios Muertos" (*Emplumada* 1981) shares many strategic and rhetorical similarities with "Nuestros abuelos," but Cervantes prominently features the voice of a first-person speaker dramatically present in the poem's actions. This first-person speaker vivifies both the identity of the Chicana agent and her collective cultural memory, thereby bringing greater emotional outrage to the poem than does the third-person narrator of "Nuestros abuelos." Whereas Villanueva's poem enacts a split subject and a cultural/linguistic migrant, "Poema para los Californios Muertos" enacts an embodied first-person subject who is bilingual, bicultural, and fissured between languages as well as between an inaccessible past and a future haunted by a ghostly absence of her cultural heritage.

As in "Nuestros abuelos," Cervantes's poem begins with an epigraph. This one, however, is brief: "Once a refuge for Mexican Californios . . ." It appears on a "plaque outside a restaurant in Los Altos, California, 1974" (42–43). This historical marker, Candelaria suggests, "operates as a mnemonic stimulus" for the speaker's sense of heritage ("Rethinking" 125). The poem thus deals with a local history of small, dying California towns once home to Mexican Californios, and as the first lines make clear, the notion of progress as false promise. An image of violent transformation marks the first lines: "These older towns die / into stretches of freeway. / The high scaffolding cuts a clean cesarean / across belly valleys and fertile dust." Here an image of death exists simultaneously with one of life. As Chicana/o towns die, they morph into that prototypical beacon of prosperity—the freeway—and into the image of an unnatural, invasive parturition. Cervantes suggests that what is progressive is also regressive. The inevitable result of this death and birth is "a bastard child" of a city full of ghosts.

The speaker's sense of dispossession becomes clear in the second stanza when she is physically present in Los Altos. Cervantes writes, "I run my fingers / across this brass plaque. / Its cold stirs in me a memory / of silver buckles and spent bullets." Here the speaker gives us simple information about what she touches, how its surface feels, and what memories it arouses. She narrates in English her actions and the images the cold plaque "stirs" in her memory. These lines betray little emotion or overt opinion. Her actions are measured and composed, and her response is cold, distant. Even "silver buckles and spent bullets" have little affective power despite the reader's suspicion that these objects are symbols of oppression and colonization.

Spanish, on the other hand, plays a role contradictory to the measured English. As Jeraldine R. Kraver explains, Spanish "is the language of anxiety, frustration, and rage" in the poem (202). When the speaker switches languages in the second stanza, she moves from a narrative voice to one of rage, but also one that expresses collective identity, solidarity, and cultural heritage. About the dead Californios ("Californios Muertos") she proclaims: "Yo recuerdo los antepasados muertos. / Los recuerdo en la sangre, / la sangre fértil" that stains the earth. Cervantes's speaker laments and identifies with her "antepasados muertos" (dead ancestors). Her memories of them are literally mediated through "sangre" (blood), both through the blood that courses through her veins and the blood that the dead Californios lost in their violent deaths.[11]

In the third stanza, the speaker's witness to absent presence extends into a pair of questions posed directly to the "ancient Californios." She discovers absence inhabiting the restaurant and its surroundings even though "nothing remains" of their presence but an "old oak and an ill-placed plaque" so that the speaker sees "nothing but strangers." Nihilism ("nothing"), it seems, is key to the speaker's heritage. The second of these rhetorical questions is part existential and part practical. She addresses the absent Californios through apostrophe, which quickens them but makes them present in a landscape that allows their presence only in memorial: "Is it true that you still live here / in the shadows of these white, high-class houses?" The speaker, then, ponders whether or not there are ghosts of the dead Californios in the city as well as whether or not Chicanas/os actually still live there, not in a *refugio tranquilo*, but in the "shadows" of poverty. In either case they are invisible but for the plaque, which the speaker suggests is a fabrication because they likely found no "refuge" there. They are absent both in historical terms and in the "shadows" that hide poverty from the larger white society.

This absent presence ("nothing" that is more than "nothing") is itself a source of identity for the speaker. Eliza Rodriguez y Gibson writes that in Cervantes's work "loss itself becomes a presence that enables" the speaker-poet "to imagine a community" (107). In the third stanza the speaker asserts her identity as a member of this imagined, but lost, community: "Soy la hija pobrecita / pero puedo maldecir estas fantasmas blancas." These lines imply that her cultural inheritance from the Californios is meager, not invested with the agency necessary for social change. She says that she is their poor little daughter; here the Spanish diminutive form (the suffix -cita) suggests smallness, pity, and relative powerlessness. Despite her status as a "pobrecita" (literally, *poor little thing*), language can be a source of power and release. She is able to curse ("puedo maldecir") the white ghosts ("fantasmas blancas") that inhabit this haunted place. Language, then, especially Spanish, is a source of agency for the speaker, a powerful but perhaps unsustainable one. After all, how sustainable is cursing something that is absent?

Lynette Seator claims that "when Cervantes looks to language to connect her to her past, she finds a rupture, a rupture that her words attempt to bridge" (32). In "Poema para los Californios Muertos," the speaker's Spanish declarations of identity and solidarity insinuate that there is a rupture between history (the world of absent presence) and the contemporary North American cityscape (the world of concrete presence). At the end of the third stanza, she says that only the ghosts of the dead Californios should remain ("deben aquí quedarse") in this city, which points to a desire to honor her dead ancestors as well as a fantasy of absolute separation between a white Euroamerican present and a Chicana/o past. Later, it is clear that there has been an erasure of history and that the plaque is but a superficial, dishonest attempt to make that history positively present. All that remains at the restaurant are "bitter antiques, / yanqui remnants," "the pungent odor of crushed / eucalyptus," and "the pure scent / of rage"; none of these presences, it seems, are "de los Californios." Their history is conveniently bracketed in a small plaque—in effect a museum writ small, an image echoed in Alexie's "Evolution" and strangely, in scale, by the finger ring in Bly's "Counting Small-Boned Bodies."

Cervantes's strategies highlight the fissure between history and the living present—even as that history has a palpable presence in each unfolding moment—and between the language of collective ancestral memory (Spanish) and that of her present life (English). Though the migrant agent is able to move between both, her poem shows the difficulty of finding a home in either. Cervantes's speaker fails to carve out a space between the two, for it is here that the most effective poetic and political agency resides. The poem's Spanish, though, refuses to forgo a heritage of absence and loss and to submit fully to the notion of "progress." Moreover, Cervantes's poem denies American cultural progress spoken of in terms of the "melting pot." Some things, she suggests, do not melt easily. They may be largely absent, but they ferment uneasily in "la sangre fértil" and they will eventually manifest themselves in everything planted in the fertile soil. The poem thus seems to say that in making "progress" *you will reap what you sow; if you sow blood* ("sangre") *you will reap it as well.*

The two poems discussed thus far use code switching to foreground the sociopolitical and cultural experiences of the bilingual, Latina/o migrant. But these poems' primary figures of voice do not comment directly on the relations between languages themselves. Many bilingual poems (and a striking number of English poems by bilingual poets) take as their de facto subject the cross-pollination of languages and the cultures they inhabit. Is it any wonder that contemporary poets (*any* poets, for that matter) take language itself as a primary interest? Is it surprising that poems of migratory agency take as a primary figure of voice the self-reflexive voice interrogating language itself? Many of these poems have voices that explore the socioeconomic disparities between Spanish- and English-speaking communities in the United States. Poems such as Victor Hernández Cruz's "Lunequisticos" (*Maraca* 2001) and Martín Espada's "Mariano Explains Yanqui Colonialism to Judge Collings" and "Revolutionary Spanish Lesson" (*Alabanza: New and Selected Poems* 2003) suggest that language itself is a contestatory sphere and an appropriate vehicle for exploring power in a hybrid, constantly mutating culture, much as it is in postmodern literature and theory, especially in the work of Michel Foucault.

Gina Valdez's "English con Salsa" (1993) explores these inequalities and the somewhat superficial language reciprocation within an imaginary "ESL 100" classroom. The poem's speaker, ostensibly an English as a Second Language instructor, sarcastically and enthusiastically welcomes Mexican migrants/immigrants to the class. The poem has three implications. First, the speaker cynically implies that Mexican immigrants learn English only to cook for and to serve food to English speakers. Second, Spanish-speaking immigrants will change, enrich, and enliven English. Third, students will put English on like a mask while retaining the spirit of their native cultures, lands, and languages, as if to say, *we will not be assimilated into your melting pot.*

Unlike the previous poems in chapter 3, Valdez's speaker has biting humor and a sardonic tone. As if spouting off a bizarre confessional first day class introduction, the speaker welcomes her students—"muchachos from Zochicalco," "muchachas from Teocaltiche," and "amigos del sur" (cited in *Touching the Fire* 203). The first word in each of three dense stanzas is "Welcome." The first line, though, begins a general, subversive introduction to the class: "Welcome ESL 100, English Surely Latinized." The syllabus, as it were, starts by dropping the article before ESL, which is common for non-native speakers (further suggesting that this course is taught by an ESL speaker), and by subverting the ESL anagram into "English Surely Latinized." Immediately, then, the speaker undermines a primary purpose of ESL classes—to get students to sound like North American speakers. Instead, English will become "Latinized." As Victor Hernández Cruz claims, Latina/o writers (and, by extension, speakers) are changing English syntax, making it more fluid; he says that Latinas/os "should change the English and give it spice, Hispanic mobility" ("Mountains" 673–674). After decades of the linguistic interchange prominent in a country-wide "ESL 100" classroom, English *will* "surely" be "Latinized."[12]

Mexican (im)migrants do have agency in their ability to transform English, but there is something more invidious at work as well. In the second line, Valdez's speaker begins to suggest that what immigrants will actually learn is service industry English. Although English is "Latinized," it is also "ingles con chile y cilantro" and "English as American / as Benito Juarez," that seedy tourist trap on the Texas border. In a parodic voice the speaker urges her students to learn English so that they can be subservient to white customers. The lines lampoon actual fly-by-night ESL classes that promise future good fortune if the potential student learns English. I recently noticed numerous advertisements on New York City subway trains for ESL classes. The Spanish headlines promised: "Aprenda Inglés. Conoce Amigos" (*Learn English. Make Friends*). In the poem, Valdez's speaker makes unrealistic promises too: "Learn the language of dolares and dolores, of kings / and queens, of Donald Duck and Batman. Holy Toluca! / In four months you'll be speaking like George Washington." Valdez's teacher/advertiser initially mentions that English is the language of money and sorrows ("dolares and dolores") in a remarkably fortuitous combination of Spanish words that sound almost exactly the same—in linguistic terms a "minimal pair." After equating dollars with pain and sadness, the speaker regresses further into the realm of fantasy. No one, except for children, would want to speak like George Washington, cartoon characters, or superheroes. The speaker here sells American culture and fantasies about it, not language skills, just as the subway advertisements prey on immigrants' loneliness, insecurity, and desire for acceptance.

Worse than the comic overtones of learning to speak like Donald Duck, Batman, and George Washington is the likelihood for many Mexican immigrants that they will spend their lives waiting on the wealthy descendants of Washington. For this potentiality, after "four weeks you can ask, More coffee?," and "in two months / you can say, may I take your order?" If the student is persistent or merely seeks to survive in the United States, "in one year you / can ask for a raise, cool as the Tuxpan River." These lines are the most sarcastic of the poem; they condemn the use-value of English when thought of solely as a way for immigrants to earn money. They also implicitly denounce the low glass ceiling for these same immigrants, but they also embody a type of morbid humor, a laughing-at-the-gallows sensibility, and a knowing subversiveness.

Throughout the poem, the speaker connects English with the places, sensibilities, and languages of Mexico. The first metaphor comparing the immigrant's future use of English to parts of the Mexican world appears in the last line of the first stanza: "you / can ask for a raise, cool as the Tuxpan River." Whereas this line clearly has a negative connotation, many that follow do not. The speaker claims that "in this class," they "speak English refrito." This refried English is invigorated and transformed by Mexican places and experiences. They learn to speak English "tuned like a requinto from Uruapan," "lighted by Oaxacan dawns," and "spiked / with mezcal from Juchitan." These juxtapositions exclaim a dissident sensibility: *Students, English is yours, take it, make it your own, and do not lose your language and culture. Speak English like Pancho Villa or Emiliano Zapata, not like George Washington.* She suggests that immigrants must *reimagine* the language of Washington in order to speak it themselves.

The abundance of Mexican place names (Benito Juarez, Zochicalco, Toluca, Tuxpan River, Teocaltiche, Uruapan, Oaxacan, Juchitan, Zapotec, Nahuatl, Lake Patzcuaro, and Jalisco) Mexicanize English and render it accessible to immigrants. More critically, the speaker eventually shifts from what the students will be able to do practically with English to what the students will bring to English and how they will change it—how they will attack it, have fun with it, and stamp new vibrancies on its syntax, its surfaces. These impulses emerge primarily from the notion that these immigrants/students have political agency, as the English they will learn to speak will be "poured from / a clay jug." As such, it will originate with their histories, experiences, poverty, and their sense of the earth; it will not be poured into them by the dominant North American culture (from a Coke bottle, for instance). The students will do the pouring of their cultures into the dominant one, which suggests both a type of power and the potential danger of their culture being swallowed by the dominant one.

Valdez might overestimate the agency immigrants have in their transition between cultures and languages; nevertheless her images of the power of these Spanish speakers to transform English are inspiring and inclusive. When the speaker "welcome(s)" the "amigos del sur," she encourages them to "bring" a variety of things with them, including their "Zapotec tongues" and "Nahuatl tones." In doing so, she opens wide the linguistic and cultural doors of welcome, especially because even in Mexico indigenous speakers of Zapotec and Nahuatl (even if bilingual) are often marginalized from the mainstream. She also encourages them to "bring" their cultural icons with them. If North American "patron saints" are Batman and Washington, their "patron saints" are "Santa Tristeza, Santa Alegria, Santo Todolopuede." Here earlier dualisms prevail—if there is a saint of sadness, there is also one of happiness. For the speaker, all is apparently possible because, she believes, abundant optimism is not only within the purview of North Americans; the saint of you-can-do-anything ("Todolopuede") comes with immigrants rather than it being discovered in the United States.

Such hopefulness is perhaps sardonic, a tongue-in-cheek nod to the unflappable "American Dream" that rejects more dreamers than those who actually live theirs, but there is hopefulness in the speaker's proclamations about immigrants' abilities to change English, and by extension, the United States. The proclamations are playful and witty, but they also suggest an agency capable of enacting transformation: the students "will sprinkle / holy water on pronouns, / make the sign of the cross / on past participles, jump like fish from Lake Patzcuaro / on gerunds, pour tequila from Jalisco on future perfects." Sprinkling holy water, making the sign of the cross, jumping from water to air, and pouring tequila are all emblematic of transformative processes, the passing from one state into another. Each action moves from the quotidian to the transcendent. The students will transform the boredom of grammar to the transcendence of religion, the splendor of flying fish, and the festiveness of revelry. Finally, the students are in power positions. They will act *upon* English pronouns, participles, gerunds, and future perfects.

Like Cervantes's poem, English is the main language of narration in Valdez's "English con Salsa." In the latter, however, the speaker implies that English will be spoken differently by Mexican immigrants, that it will be spoken through a mask. Near the beginning of Ralph Ellison's *Invisible Man*, the narrator speaks of his grandfather's advice to treat white people with the utmost deference and respect when face-to-face with them while silently subverting their authority and power. In other words, his advice is to speak their language but not to believe in it (Ellison 16). Such is the implication in "English con Salsa." In this ESL "course," the immigrant students will have fun with English. They will put it on happily, rejoicing in their new language. They will "say shoes and shit"; they will "grab a cool verb and a pollo loco / and dance on the walls like chapulines." In other words, they will happily do the song-and-dance that some U.S. citizens expect from immigrants: *be happy that you are here, and if you don't like it and don't want to speak English, go back where you came from. Until then, make sure you show gratitude.*[13] As such, the students will act like stereotypical buffoons or children, inanely repeating "shoes and shit," dancing the crazy chicken ("pollo loco"), and bouncing around in ecstasy like grasshoppers ("chapulines"), all the while silently working to change English and "American" culture.

There is great facetiousness in the penultimate line in the speaker's declaration that her students will respond to questions of "Do you speak English?" with "of course. I love English!" This voice and the exclamation mark suggest that the students' "love" of English is an act. The poem's final line is slow and measured after a poem of quick, enjambed rhythms and fast lines. The speaker concludes that speaking English will be undergirded by other more ancient rhythms. She says, "And you'll hum / a Mextec chant that touches la tierra and the heavens." Because the speaker says this line immediately following "I love English!" it is a reminder that the immigrant students will make sense of the world with their native expressive traditions. English will be the language of the everyday business transaction, Spanish and other indigenous languages the media of song, poetry, of "la tierra and the heavens." In this poem, then, the alternating use of English and Spanish enacts the sociolinguistic agency of the migrant even as it foregrounds the glass ceiling that traps and channels them into careers migrating between restaurants and, in light of potential crackdowns on illegal immigrants, safe houses.

Migratory Agency and the *Italics* Question

The previous three poems of migratory agency require competent bilingual readers. They would frustrate monolingual readers, sending them to the dictionary/diccionario too many times to have a fluid reading experience. This disruption is a critical aspect of these poems' figures of voice; each disruption highlights the rift between languages and cultures enacted for bilingual and non-English-speaking Latinas/os on a daily basis. Code switching also interrupts the dominance of English and challenges its "mastery" of lesser "foreign" languages. As such, these poems are intended for competent bilingual readers. If a poet must imagine her audience, the imagined audience for the previous poems of migratory agency is bilingual.

There are, however, poems of migratory agency that are not fully bilingual. These primarily English poems *highlight* or foreground Spanish words, phrases, and titles without excluding monolingual English speakers from comprehending them. Novelist and poet Pat Mora's comments on her use of Spanish in primarily English works is instructive: "I'm writing to a great extent for an English-speaking audience. I am bilingual, though English-dominant. I'm interested in including Spanish because it's part of my world, it's part of my mind . . . There is subversion in the use of Spanish, very consciously."

She goes on to say that she "want(s)" monolingual readers to be able to "stay with" her, but that she also includes "double pleasures"—particularly resonant words and phrases—specifically for bilingual readers (143). I do not want to suggest that Mora's motives are representative of other Latina/o poets, merely that her calculated use of two languages points both to a dualistic voice and a bifurcated audience for this poetry. Her claim also suggests that Spanish lines in primarily English poems are *particularly* resonant and important, and even these few challenge the English "tradition."

The majority of primarily English poems that include Spanish words and phrases literally highlight their Spanish textures in *italicizing* Spanish words, phrases, and sentences. The examples are numerous. Pedro Pietri's "Puerto Rican Obituary" (1973), Baca's "Mi Tío Baca el Poeta de Socorro" (1989), Mora's "Artista Cubano" (1994), Sandra M. Castillo's "En el Sol de Mi Barrio," "Rincón," and "Monday Night at Pedro's" (1997), Judith Ortiz Cofer's "The Changeling" (1993), Virgil Suárez's "Poem for My Father" (2001) and "After Forty Years of Exile, The Poet Arrives" (2002), and Martín Espada's "Searching for La Revolución in the Streets of Tijuana" (2002) are just a few political poems in English that use a proportionately small number of Spanish words and phrases. Their italicized Spanish words foreground these poems' bifurcated worlds—*switching between cultures is analogous to switching between languages.* Many poems of migratory agency do not have an equal number of Spanish and English words; poems migrate between cultures as well as strictly between languages. Even a few Spanish words serve as metonyms for a larger world excluded from mainstream U.S. culture. However, these poems can be politically problematic in that they may exclude a primary audience—bilingual and non-English-speaking Latinas/os. My reading of the next poem implicitly exposes this potential rift.

Baca's "Mi Tío Baca el Poeta de Socorro" includes few Spanish words but nonetheless embodies great departures between English-speaking and Spanish-speaking cultures. These brief italicized phrases are signals or slightly opened doorways to the cultures, languages, and forces that impinge on the dominant culture. This minimal Spanish gives Chicano-Apache Baca's poem its most critical meanings. In the poem, two cultures with unequal power—Chicano campesinos and the U.S. Rangers who repress them—clash. This relationship exposes rifts between languages, generations, methods of activism, and uses of art. "Mi Tío Baca el Poeta de Socorro" is thus primarily English, but its speaking voice laments for Baca's uncle, a deceased poet and labor organizer who in all likelihood wrote in Spanish. The poem thus highlights the chasm between the uncle's politically efficacious Spanish poems and the speaker-poet's self-declared ineptitude.

The migratory agency of Baca's poem is cross-cultural, interlinguistic, and intergenerational. The speaker is self-accusingly cynical and faithless, but the power he summons is politically potent, even if the spirit of that power is eulogized in his murdered uncle. According to the speaker, his uncle's poems were tools used to organize his community's resistance to oppression. As "Poet de Socorro," a title that suggests Uncle Baca was both *a* poet of "socorro" (translated as help, assistance, or aid) and *the* poet of Socorro, the county in which Albuquerque is located, near Baca's childhood home. The title is both honorary and practical. In Tío Antonio Baca's world, poetry was politically effective; his "poems roused *la gente* / to demand their land rights back" (cited in *The Norton Anthology of Postmodern Poetry* 591–593; original emphasis here and below). These are some of the most inspirational lines in contemporary poetry, I argue, because they assert unequivocally poetry's political efficacy. Even though this is one of the poem's few Spanish phrases, it is a repository of hope, power, and solidarity.

As testament to the Uncle's influence in the Chicana/o community and to the force of his poetry, "men wearing remnants of Rinche uniforms" invade his house and assassinate him. "Los Rinches" (the Texas Rangers) are legendary for their history of treachery against Chicanas/os. Rafael Pérez-Torres shows that Baca evokes the historical violence of the Rinches/Rangers as a "disembodied presence," which suggests that "their power lies beyond individuals," a technique that "underscores the impersonality of repressive power" (*Movements* 81). (Baca's poem thus echoes Cervantes's image of "silver buckles and spent bullets" and the claims of absent presence.) Even though this anonymous—their faces are "masked in dusty hankies"—but specific repressive power drags Uncle Baca from his "one-room adobe" and murders him, there are several agents, including poetry itself, that oppose this violence. Uncle Baca's Spanish-language poetry actually organized and energized *la gente* (the people). For the impoverished people of Socorro, then, their power too "lies beyond individuals." The power of the uncle's poetry also resides in part outside poems themselves and with the people who sang and chanted them in opposition to the theft of their lands. His poetry thus lives after his death.

Baca's poem is an elegy not only to his uncle, but to community-based action motivated and organized in part by poems. Though Uncle Baca's "house still stands" and the speaker-poet "drink(s)" in his "spirit," the speaker lacks hope in poetry and in the future.

He claims to "descend / into dangerous abysses of the future" and sounds desperate when he says, "I want to believe / whatever problems we have, time will take / its course, they'll be endured and consumed." Unlike his uncle, the speaker lacks faith. The poem concludes with him imagining following his dead uncle into a church, watching him "kneel before La Virgen De Guadalupe, / bloody lips moving slightly." While the uncle's "great gray head [is] poised in listening," the speaker concludes "considering the words *faith, prayer* and *forgiveness,* / wishing, like you, I could believe them." The speaker thus expresses his lack of faith in poetry, in community-based action (as prayer can be either communal or private), and in human goodness. Whereas Pérez-Torres claims that the poem has an ambiguous ending (*Movements* 83), I see a clear conclusion but an ambiguous future for the speaker. There is, I think, a glimmer of hope left due to his belief in the power of language. In the poem, language is capable of joining generations even as it simultaneously highlights the rift between generations. At the conclusion, the speaker-poet affirms the power of the word—"a prayer on my lips bridges years of disaster between us"—and thus affirms the potential poetic agency of the migrant's language.

If the model for community activism and the roles of poetry have changed from Uncle Baca to J.S. Baca, it may be due partly to a change in what Pérez-Torres calls the "process of affirmation." This process, he writes, occurs on a personal level in Baca's poetry whereas much Chicano Movement poetry was driven by a "desire to organize a community for political action," which is in some ways similar to Black Arts Movement poetry. In contrast, Baca's is not protest poetry or organizing tool; as Pérez-Torres points out, it is more complex, and it "represents a retreat from mass political movement, a reflection of the political situation during the Age of Reagan" (*Movements* 11–12, 47). The poem is thus elegy to the tactics of the Chicano Movement and testimony to a more fragmented political reality; as such, its skeptical, fractured voice reflects this uncertain, but nonetheless palpable, agency.

The gap between Baca's and his uncle's poetics represents a dilemma for poems of migratory agency and it also represents one between notions of the poet's role in Latin and North America. The Latin American testimonio tradition helps elucidate this divide. John Beverley defines the testimonio as a story "told in the first person by a narrator who is also a real protagonist or witness of the event he or she recounts, and whose unit of narration" is "a significant life experience" (24). A testimonio, then, is a "narrative of real historical actors" that "communicate(s) a subject's or subjects' lived experiences" (Rosman 129–130). A testimonio, though, is not memoir or autobiography; it chronicles *una lucha*, a fight on behalf of *la gente* against injustice. As Beverley writes, "The situation of narration in testimonio has to involve an urgency to communicate, a problem of repression, poverty, subalternity, imprisonment, [or] struggle for survival" (26). In Latin America, it has traditionally been expected that poets enter these battles on behalf of *la gente* if they can avoid appropriating and romanticizing their struggles. Testimonio, though, has, if not obviated, then called into question the poet's role as people's representative because the oppressed poor now have a speaking voice.

"Mi Tío Baca el Poeta de Socorro," though not a testimonio, is a variation on it and an implicit commentary on its cultural function. The speaker does not actively attempt to speak for the *la gente* like a poem of authoritative agency does, but in holding up his uncle as an effective poet of the people, he upholds the tradition of representation he denies for himself. Baca's speaker implies that his role is not to speak for the oppressed voiceless nor to found their community. Is this an orthodox North American view of poetry as private, ineffective? Or does the speaker suggest that when you fight for *la gente* and the final poem you write is "scrawled across the page, / '¡Aquí vienen! ¡Aquí vienen! / Here they come!' " as an angry mob comes to " 'Shoot the Mexican!," that in some sense poetry always fails as a political tool? Or does the uncle's murder vindicate poetry's political power?

If Baca is concerned about the poet's role in the community, it relates intimately to what George Yúdice points out about testimonio—that it "has contributed to the demise of the traditional role of the intellectual/artist as spokesperson for the 'voiceless.' " Now, he shows, the "oppressed feel more enabled to speak for themselves in the wake of the new social movements, Liberation Theology, and other consciousness-raising grassroots movements." Consequently, "there is less of a social and cultural imperative for concerned writers to heroically assume the grievances and demands of the oppressed" (42). The issue that concluded chapter 1—the problems of representation when poets assume an embattled first-person "I" in their witness to extremity—is thus even more thorny now that outlets such as the ones Yúdice mentions have empowered the oppressed. Yet this assumes that poets speak *only* for the oppressed, not for themselves as well. Baca's speaker suggests this division—he speaks for himself and no other because he believes himself unworthy of his uncle's public role. Baca's speaker, unlike Baca's uncle, whose poems "roused *la gente*" to fight for their rights, implicitly moves away from the role of representative, in a line extending in the Americas from Whitman to Neruda to numerous rappers. For Baca's speaker, though, the imperative to fight for the oppressed is still urgent, but the means to do so seem inaccessible in an age of cynicism. Yúdice longs for the authenticity of "non-mediated communication that *testimonio* makes possible" (Rosman 128; original emphasis), but the speaker-poet in Baca's poem in fact suggests that the word—prayers, poems, testimonios, stories—always mediates between generations and cultures, and that without the word, any hope for "*faith, prayer,* and *forgiveness*" is lost.

Baca and the testimonio critics are skeptical of the poet's role as representative; however, U.S. Puerto Rican poet Martín Espada's self-proclaimed "poetry of advocacy" speaks "on behalf of those without an opportunity to be heard" (Dick 29). For the former immigrant rights lawyer, creating a global poetics of justice is a primary aesthetic concern. Like Robert Hass, who has claimed—as discussed in chapter 1—that creating images of justice and injustice is the best way for a poet to be political, Espada is primarily concerned with the intersections of poetry and justice. Espada's "Mariano Explains Yanqui Colonialism to Judge Collings" actuates a poetic agency that migrates between three different discourses/languages, while simultaneously searching for a voice that advocates for justice. This brief poem looks like a fragment of a play:

> Judge: Does the prisoner understand his rights?
> Interpreter: ¿Entiende usted sus derechos?
> Prisoner: ¡Pa'l carajo!
> Interpreter: Yes. (45; original emphasis)

The courtroom dialogue features three voices, each of which illuminates a primary space in migratory agency—often oppressive U.S. institutional power structures ("Judge"), U.S. citizens who mediate between presumably extralegal migrants and those structures ("Interpreter"), and migrants who live outside those structures ("Prisoner"). I argue, then, that the Prisoner has not broken a specific law, but the system itself; thus, Espada's title addresses the encompassing context in which the migrant "prisoner" finds himself. Peruvian economist Hernando de Soto explains that extralegal migrants to cities in developing countries—which can be extrapolated here to immigrants from these countries to the United States, where they still live extralegally—do not "so much break the law as the law breaks them," so "they opt out of the system." He continues that "it is very nearly as difficult to *stay* legal as it is to *become* legal" because the existing legal structures do not account for the ways in which they are *capable* of living, given in part their opportunities for *legal* employment (21; original emphasis). Because of these circumstances, migrants have "to compete not only against other people but against the system as well" (84).

De Soto notes that in the nineteenth century, U.S. politicians "expressed the revolutionary idea that legal institutions can survive only if they respond to [the] social needs" of the people, many of whom live, work, and hold property outside of existing legal structures (150). However, they currently have failed to integrate (im)migrants into the legal system. Espada's poem, then, implicitly examines the ramifications of cross-cultural (mis)communication, especially between presumed extralegal migrants and the legal system of the world's imperial power, and how they impact the possibilities for justice.[14] Given the conspicuous title, however, the possibilities for justice are extremely limited. One Spanish-speaking (im)migrant versus U.S. colonialism? An individual charged with a crime versus a judge charged with enforcing colonialism, law, and order? Yet if anyone can "explain" Yankee colonialism, it is a migrant charged with a crime against that colonial power. The title suggests further that Mariano is in the act of speaking truth to that power.

Mariano's confrontational demeanor in front of the Judge and the system of justice he represents belies the fact that the dynamics between prisoner and system are very complicated. These dynamics coalesce in the voice of the "Interpreter," who represents the fluid space between cultures and languages, between ways of understanding the world—not between ideologies, but between the Spanish-speaking extralegal migrant and the English-speaking neocolonizer charged with maintaining the legal structures of U.S. global hegemony. The Interpreter, then, is agent of neither party, but the go-between who mediates the communication between Latin and North American, prisoner and captor, powerless and powerful. If Mariano is charged and Judge Collings is in charge, then the Interpreter is charged with the greatest responsibility. He must facilitate communication and ensure that justice is possible. Without the Interpreter's presence, there can be no cultural or linguistic interchange, especially as Judge and Prisoner never talk to each other directly. In effect, there is no dialogue between cultures or languages or across power differences. Even though the Judge has more power than Mariano, the Interpreter presumably tries to level the playing field. Mariano's power is his subversion of the system and his ability to speak a language (and curse in a language) that Judge Collings does not understand.

Even if upon first reading Mariano does not appear to "understand his rights," after some consideration it is obvious that he does. When the Interpreter translates the Judge's question for the Prisoner— "¿Entiende usted sus derechos?"—the Prisoner replies with an exclamatory expletive: "*¡Pa'l carajo!*" This phrase is an elusive one for non-Spanish speakers. A colloquialism, it can be translated numerous ways, including variations on "prick," "shit," and "damn it!," but the one most appropriate here is a resolute, angry "Go to Hell!" The Prisoner, it appears, understands his rights quite well. He seems to know that he has none, so his response is given in kind. As such, the Interpreter has no choice—"Go to hell!" equals "Yes," or more appropriately, *hell yes.* The implication is that whether the migrant-prisoner responds actively or passively, the result will be the same. Given the title, Mariano's explanation of "Yanqui Colonialism" is just that: "*¡Pa'l carajo!*" Mariano suggests that U.S. imperialism tells the rest of the world, especially Latin America: *go to hell; the only rights you have are the ones we allow you.* Mariano explains this colonialism succinctly and venomously, but unfortunately seems to remain under its boot heel.

To reiterate, it is important that we know nothing about Mariano's alleged crimes. I argue that they consist of his transgression of neo-colonial economic structures; his voice, moreover, is the migrant Spanish-speaker's voice, and it threatens "American" identity. Espada thus opens the door slightly for the *reader as "Interpreter,"* suggesting that bilingual readers are responsible for mediating between cultures in contact, for facilitating real dialogue, and for insuring that the powerless poor can speak in more than expletives. This *potential* voice represents, in part, Espada's notion of advocacy. Santa Arias sums up this imperative in the suggestion that Espada's work "has to be viewed as a bridge between First and Third World culture and politics" (237). Similarly, Gareth Williams "speaks of the need [for scholars] to mediate rather than dominate discourses of cultural exchange between Third World cultural production and First World institutional sites" (qtd. in Gugelberger 16). Espada's poem is just such a mediating intervention, but one that creates a microcosm of the failures of north–south relations in the Americas.

The relationship between constituents in this poem, finally, reflects a variety of non-encounters between the powerful agents of Western free-market capitalism and the migrants traveling from south to north. In his essay on Levine's poem about Hart Crane and Federico García Lorca's 1929 encounter in Brooklyn, "On the Meeting of García Lorca and Hart Crane" (*The Simple Truth* 1994), Carl Good argues that these Modernist poets' failed meeting is one of many telling "non-encounters" in the Americas, one in a long history of missed opportunities for communication between north and south and one that in part symbolizes the "scholarly and literary neglect of the Hispanic dimension in the North American historical and literary imaginary" (234). These non-encounters will become more detrimental in years to come if the voices represented by Espada are not heard and heeded by the legal and economic systems that exclude them and then punish them for their exclusion.

MIGRATORY AGENCY AND SPANISH-LANGUAGE POETRY

While code switching is a vital element of migratory agency, the more complex source of poetic agency in the poems of chapter 3 is the migrant's movement between cultures and sensibilities. The migrant's unique perspective(s) and voice(s) situate these poems in political space. Many Spanish-language U.S. poems also activate this agency. The brief reading that follows represents one of many examples of these poems; it serves here to provide the third critical piece of chapter 3—bilingual, English-language, and Spanish-language poems. As the mostly English poems discussed previously often include a few critically important Spanish words, these mostly Spanish-language poems often have a few critically important English words that serve similar purposes. In Marcos McPeek Villatoro's "La piñata" (2004), for instance, the speaker moves jarringly between real event and frightening vision, between an ahistorical present and a historical memory of the oppression of indigenous people.

The dominant image of "La piñata" is a piñata, full of "dulces atrapados" and "pedazos morenos" (pieces of candy), being beaten by children "con un palo entregado / por las millones de madres a las manos / de los inocentes." This stick ("palo") has been given to the children, whom the speaker calls innocents, by millions of mothers ("millones de madres"). These mothers, the speaker points out, have simultaneously neglected to give to them "la historia" and "la memoria" of—presumably—violence and oppression. Because the piñata resembles "Pocahantas," and because it is not punished for being a tanned Barbie doll made by Disney ("Esta Pocahantas no se sangra / por ser una Barbie curtida y / hecha por Mickey Mouse"), the children are beating the symbolic representative of indigenous culture in North America. Further, because this beating is filtered through the prism of iconic U.S. cultural images, the speaker suggests that violence and oppression are passed down through the oblivion of history and through seemingly innocuous cultural practices. Most importantly, though, the speaker's bicultural vision/perspective—as both Spanish-speaking Latino and English-speaking North American—gives him keen insight into indigenous oppression by both English speakers and Spanish speakers in the history of the western hemisphere. In his vision, therefore, *los palos* become "machetes," and he claims, "Es fácil sacar la sangre dulce / y las tripas azucaradas de los primeros. / Que juguete, cecean, que cosa" (*It's easy to dry the sweet blood / and the sweetened intestines of the first [Indians]. / What a toy, they [the Indians] lisp, what a thing*). This visceral image indicates that the historical memory of oppressed indigenous is easily transformed into a child's game (and reward), even as "El indio patea como conejo" (*the indian kicks like a rabbit*) and "La soga encoge el cuello" (*the rope shrinks its neck*). The poem ends appropriately with the speaker watching the candies scatter in his "yarda del olvido" (*yard of oblivion*).

Villatoro's poem gives insight into how Spanish-language poems can embody migratory agency, but it also signifies how U.S. Spanish poems might have a changing cultural value, and on chapter 1's closing discussion about the embattled, heroic poetic speaker/witness. On the back cover of *On Tuesday, when the homeless disappeared*, in which "La Piñata" appears, in a final section of Spanish-only poems, this section is described as "a statement of ascendance, a strategy for identity preservation, *a gift to the cognoscenti*" (my emphasis). The first two descriptions are detailed in chapter 3; the third strikes me in its claim that Spanish-language poems are elite, intellectual-academic enterprises. Indeed, how things have changed since the Chicano Movement. More strikingly, Villatoro's biography *begins*: "Marcos McPeek Villatoro lived in Guatemala, El Salvador, and Nicaragua during those countries' war years." Thus, before we learn about his writing, we learn that Villatoro has cultural capital as a heroic poet-witness. Michael Palmer, even Carolyn Forché, would cringe.

MIGRATORY AGENCY AND
REGISTER SWITCHING

Victor Hernández Cruz distinguishes between types of bilingual literature, "making a clear differentiation between elite choices and colonial impositions" (cited in Aparicio 164). On one hand there is bilingualism "that is a writer's interest in other languages," and on the other there is "imposed" bilingualism that impacts "an entire group of people, a whole culture" (*Panoramas* 128). This distinction illuminates differences between Eliot's and Pound's Modernist version of migratory agency, hip hop's version of it, and Latina/o poets' more organic version. However, Cruz's differentiation obscures the fact that most poets, and most speakers, borrow from a variety of discourses and codes. Whereas writers such as Eliot and Pound may have used multiple languages to create an "elite" poetry, other Anglo poems emphasize the aural and rhetorical effects of a Romance language such as Spanish—effects that English cannot accomplish. This use of Spanish, for instance, can also contextualize experience. For example, John Balaban's "Agua Fria y Las Chicharras" (*Words for My Daughter* 22–25, which was selected by W.S. Merwin for the 1990 National Poetry Series) has a Spanish title and a few Spanish lines. Yet Balaban, who has translated Bulgarian poets Blaga Dimitrova and Georgi Borisov and Vietnamese poet Ho Xuan Huong,[15] does not speak or read Spanish. In the poem, Spanish authenticates experience and creates key sound effects. Because the poem takes place in three places—the Alhambra; Arroyo Hondo, New Mexico; and Taos, New Mexico—Spanish words authenticate and localize the poem and the experiences therein.

The first part of the poem focuses on sound itself, specifically on how "the voice of the Prophet," the singing of "water-carriers," the "spill of water," and "locusts calling at the edge of wilderness" combine to create elemental motion and tactile and aural beauty. To presage, authenticate, and contextualize these effects, Balaban renders the title, which translates simply as "Cold Water and the Locusts," and the water-carriers' song in Spanish. Balaban's use of Spanish does not indicate "elite" intentions nor "colonial imposition," as a full reading makes clear. But it implies, if not a lesser status, than a supplemental, or ornamental, status for the second language, although certainly not a relationship of "mastery."

Though Balaban's poem actuates a type of migratory agency, I include it here mainly for a different purpose. Code switching between English and Spanish, which is key to many poems in chapter 3 and others like them, is not the only kind of switching that characterize them. Candelaria writes that Chicana/o poetry only appears bilingual "if one is not looking or listening very hard." She rightly claims that much Chicana/o poetry has a "*multi*lingualism" with six distinct dialects—Standard American English, Standard Spanish, English slang/vernacular, Spanish dialects/regional vernaculars, English/Spanish bilingualism, and "an amalgam of pre-American indigenous languages" (*Chicano Poetry* 73; original emphasis). Pérez-Torres also points out that Chicana/o poetry moves not only between languages, but between vernaculars, registers, and colloquialisms. This multilingualism, he writes, is "a verbal strategy for conveying such information as sociopolitical identity and economic position" (*Movements* 17). The use of the vernacular in Chicana/o poetry, he continues, is "an attempt to make present a silenced voice" (233). Candelaria's and Pérez-Torres's comments suggest that most poets, indeed most of society's agents, even monolingual speakers, have many ways of speaking. In this movement between registers and languages there is a powerful agency of representation and re-creation.

Poems of migratory agency, therefore, engage in a special kind of code switching because they involve not only registers of one language, but variations on two or more. To return to Balaban's poem, it shows that code switching works in monolingual poems as well, between registers of the same language. In "Agua Fria y Las Chicharras," Balaban's speaker switches between high poetic diction to a colloquial voice from line to line. The following lines offer a striking example of this juxtaposition: "In the spill of water, the signature of god" to "the few friends he counted / were gone and God knows where." Poets as dissimilar as John Ashbery, who is masterful at switching between jargons and registers, and Yusef Komunyakaa, whose "Changes; or, Reveries at a Window Overlooking a Country Road, with Two Women Talking Blues in the Kitchen" (*Neon Vernacular* 8–10) is a verbal and visual tour-de-force of register switching, utilize different languages in their poems, even if not different standard languages. Chicano Ricardo Sánchez's poems are some of the best examples not only of code switching between Spanish and English, but of switching between multiple registers—beatnik dialect, Caló, regional dialects, and barrio vernacular.[16] It is clear, then, that for as different as poems of migratory agency may seem from the mainstream American English "tradition," they also share a variety of similarities in voice, rhetorical strategy, and the use of diction.

SUMMARY AND CONCLUSIONS

Perhaps nowhere more than for the poems of chapter 3 do Bertolt Brecht's famous lines serve as a better conclusion: "In the dark times, will there also be singing? / Yes, there will be singing. / About the dark times" (27). The poems discussed in this chapter on the figures of voice and rhetorical strategies of migratory agency are dark, often depressing, visions of contemporary America. Though Valdez's "English con Salsa" is hopeful and celebratory, even it is tinged with sadness. I could have chosen, however, to include a poem such as Cruz's "Areyto" (Red Beans 1991), which is a sprawlingly inclusive, utopian vision of a multicultural, continental America joined by music, dance, and song. All of these poems, though, have at their cores a communitarian spirit in search of *shared* space—a nascent desire for a shared, multicultural America acceptable to (im)migrants, indigenous, English- and Spanish-speaking. After all, what these poems *do* is share—languages, cultures, and spaces.

Whereas the poems of this chapter model (and lament for) potential forms of sociopolitical agency, most of their authors already have cultural agency generated by their institutional positions. I have claimed that poetry can be countercultural and counterinstitutional, but—with the exception of Baca—each of the Latina/o poets discussed here teach at U.S. universities. They garner state salaries or ones funded heavily by U.S. corporations and foundations. This fact raises some perplexing questions, not only for the ways that bilingual poetry challenges the English "tradition" taught in most U.S. universities. In writing about the testimonio's introduction to literature classrooms and to critical inquiry, Georg M. Gugelberger asks: "What happens when modes of transgression become sanctioned and canonized?" He suggests that "if you are housed in academia, you will have lost the power" of independence and subversion (2). His question and conclusion are meritable; many transgressive modes, such as bilingual poems and progressive hip-hop music, are in some ways "sanctioned," "canonized," and "housed in academia." But if the goal of much Latina/o activism (and poetry) is full immersion in U.S. culture (while retaining important elements of other cultures), then this institutionalization might begin to look more positive. In this case, bilingual poets at U.S. universities may begin to ensure that Latina/o poetry will reach students who may otherwise be exposed only to Anglo-American and some African-American literature.

With over 40 million Latinas/os in the United States, many of whom are bilingual, and with immigration increasing, the United States may soon become one of the largest *hispanohablante*, or Spanish-speaking, countries in the world. Further, now that NAFTA and other global socioeconomic forces have made for more fluid borders in the Americas, Spanish- and English-speaking cultures are meeting on an unprecedented scale. The poems of chapter 3, then, foreground voices and a type of agency that will become increasingly more common and more important in U.S. culture. They foreshadow coming cultural exchanges and conflicts, protracted linguistic interchanges, and a latent, but powerful, shift to a bilingual country.

In chapter 4 I discuss one of the most popular, powerful, and self-reflexive poetic languages in the world—hip-hop language, which includes a collection of rhetorical strategies that also migrates between cultural codes. Although it is rarely acknowledged, Latinas/os were instrumental in the origins of hip-hop culture in the Bronx and Queens in the mid-1970s. Some of the community-based values and the skepticism about and resistance to the dominant Anglo culture cataloged in chapter 3 also inform much of the hip-hop discussed in chapter 4.

Contestatory Urban Agency

INTRODUCTION

With larger, potentially more diverse audiences and live shows that can create a collective experience of identity, many hip-hop artists have greater political currency than even the best-known U.S. poets. Hip-hop's underlying understanding of agency is best viewed in how it imagines its place in the world through that often hostile, unwelcoming world's eyes. This understanding also gives us some clues to the ways that rappers see geopolitical, economic, and social issues. Their agency and viewpoints are a valuable rejoinder to what the American public hears and reads in the news in most media outlets. After all, how many youthful views are heard? How many African American views? How many views from inside impoverished urban neighborhoods, even from working-class urban neighborhoods? How many views that challenge the economic and political system of the United States itself? How often, on CNN or NPR for example, do pundits, politicians, or artists emphasize community-based values regarding equitable education and health care heard in The Coup's "Heven Tonite": "let's make health care centers on every block / let's give everybody homes and a garden plot / let's give all the schools books / ten kids a class / and given 'em truth for their pencils and pads" (*Party Music*). How many politicians place this much emphasis on health care and class size? How many poets write directly about these issues?

Rappers are like poets who work in print in that they offer listeners/readers alternative visions of the world. They offer visions of possibility and of utopia, but also of witness, outrage, and injustice. In these ways, hip-hop *as* poetry should be considered, in Houston A. Baker, Jr.'s terms, an "alternative space of the conditional" (95). Further, as both Martín Espada and Robert Hass have emphasized, one of the best ways to be political in poetry is to make images of justice; their claim is true for many rappers as well. However, at the same time, some rappers confirm the worst stereotypes about hip-hop culture, and much mainstream hip-hop embodies an individualistic, hyper-materialistic and consumptive agency. Much of it is also violent and misogynistic. The rhetorical strategies of hip-hop's *contestatory urban agency* vary widely, but they consistently challenge hypermaterialism and hedonism.

In chapter 4, I use five songs and parts of a sixth as case studies to explore hip-hop's contestatory urban agency. The first three are about 9/11 and the complexities of post-9/11 America. These songs are especially pertinent given their similarities to and differences from the Kinnell and Baraka poems in chapter 1. They illustrate two distinct, but still overlapping, approaches to political lyrics and contestatory urban agency. In "Are You Satisfied" (*All of the Above* 2002), J-Live, a former New York City public school teacher, destabilizes public officials' unifying post-9/11 rhetoric even as he laments the loss of lives. Mr. Lif's "Home of the Brave" (*Emergency Rations* 2002) directly attacks American imperialism, eschewing J-Live's more even-handed approach. Because I am explicitly concerned with *urban* agency, post-9/11 New York is an apt space for exploration. After those two songs and brief discussions of Mos Def's "What's Beef?" and Jean Grae's "Block Party," I write about the Notorious B.I.G., one of hip-hop's greatest icons. The lyrics of "Respect" and "Things Done Changed" (*Ready to Die* 1994) symbolize the tensions of contestatory urban agency as well as any hip-hop songs.

Hip-hop's contestatory urban agency is bounded by two poles that rappers continually challenge. At each pole, a hip-hop foundation marks the territory—on one side braggadocio, on the other pessimism. The first pole is best expressed in the title of Nas's "The World Is Yours" (*Illmatic* 1994), which implies that urban actors are capable of realizing any goal. "Block Party" echoes this pole when Jean Grae raps, "The world is what you make it." This sentiment has been expressed countless times in what are usually referred to as "uplifting anthems" or some derivation thereof. This pole inadvertently echoes conservative political orthodoxy often used to suggest that poverty is proof of bad character, and that the poor are lazy and the rich simply harder workers. The other pole is best stated by Mos Def's "The Rape Over" (*The New Danger* 2004), a parody of Jay-Z's "The Takeover" in which hip-hop megastar Jay-Z exclaims that he "runs" the rap music industry. In Mos Def's version, "old white men," MTV, Viacom, and "corporate forces" are "running" hip-hop. At this pole young African Americans in hip-hop do not even control their own culture or music, a point echoed by rapper Brother Ali, who claims that hip-hop is "not ours anymore. It used to be anti-establishment, off the radar, counterculture. People in the streets are now being told what hip-hop is and what it looks like by TV" (Kitwana). It is starker in dead prez's "I'm a african" (*let's get free*), which states unequivocally that urban actors are "made" by the social conditions in which they live: "my environment made me the nigga I am." The truth is somewhere between these two poles (as are most hip-hop conceptions of agency), but they are useful in defining the preliminary terms of contestatory urban agency. They provide the outer boundaries for action in urban neighborhoods, but the scene is usually much more complicated than either position asserts.

The tension between acting according to one's purposes and negoti-ating the constraints of racism and socioeconomic inequality frames many conceptions of agency in hip-hop. Rappers often style resistance as fundamentally possible within urban landscapes that work against the goals and aspirations of poor, young, mostly African American agents. In her book on hip-hop culture, Tricia Rose emphasizes the ten-sion between individual agency and the determining social and political counterforces for poor urban actors. It is dangerous, she writes, to "overemphasize the autonomy of black agency in the face of massive structural counterforces." The desire to preserve agency, she points out, must not result in the elision of the "structural forces that constrain agency" such as racism, poverty, and the lack of resources and adequate education. She concludes that the desire for inner-city youth to exercise individual agency/free will "outside of racist and discriminatory con-texts within which such action takes place" is an illusion (141–142). According to Rose's view, any lyrics that stress autonomy and the for-mation of purposes as wholly individual are incomplete and misleading if they do not also acknowledge that all actions are responses to a vari-ety of conditions, some of which constrain possibilities for action. Whereas such a view is accurate from a practical standpoint, it can limit the range of expression for lyrics as political statements (or revolution-ary pronouncements). Foregrounding autonomy and agency is often part of a rhetorical strategy intended to uplift or organize potential actors. In some cases (including in Jean Grae's song), it serves to inspire and to mobilize energy for positive social change. If rappers give too much weight to agency and too little to constraining factors, it may be *strategic* as well as unrealistic.

There is in hip-hop, then, a palpable discursive tension between agency and the determinate factors that limit agency for urban youth. Stuart Hall's distinction between determinism and determination, where the former identifies causes that dictate outcomes, whereas the latter identifies limits and constraints that affect action rather than dictate effects (29, 44–45), suggests a way to understand these factors. Determinism, he shows, is too crude a model because it leaves out the chance for revisability. It gives little space to actors for achieving even realistic goals. Determinate factors, on the other hand, suggest that no outcomes are impossible, but that many are unlikely. The determination approach suggests that moving from poverty in the South Bronx to the ownership of a private yacht is highly improbable, becoming a millionaire small business owner less so, and so on. This approach establishes useful parameters without demarcating absolutes, which the aforementioned poles do. Thus, Hall's framework is more useful in beginning to understand the figures of voice in contestatory urban agency.

Before discussing specific songs, it is useful to consider hip-hop's distinctive linguistic codes, as hip-hop agency is produced by and reflected in a poetics with its own forms of knowledge. First time listeners often attest that understanding hip-hop lyrics is challenging. These difficulties are partly due to the speed of a rapper's delivery, complex rhyme schemes, bass heavy beats that drown out lyrics, or an inability to understand a rapper's denotations. Although these issues affect a novice's capacity for digesting content, another overarching factor is paramount, the ever-mutating hip-hop vernacular. This vast set of terms, phrases, substitutions, metonyms, metaphors, and coded meanings requires active listening and a working knowledge base of hip-hop's discourse conventions. As in Wolfgang Iser's reception theory, there is no work of art without the continuous active participation of the reader/listener. This theory indicates that the reader/listener must understand the conventions and codes that a work uses to create meaning.[1] While Iser's theory has its limitations, such as his implication that only certain readers are capable of a "proper" reading, it suggests the prominence of shared codes of understanding, which are used to disseminate knowledge in a community. Similarly, Russell A. Potter discusses how hip-hop embodies and employs its own forms of knowledge, discursive forms, and traditions (22). Hip-hop's contestatory urban agency, moreover, is expressed in vernacular specific to the hip-hop community. Rappers understand their place in the world, as mentioned earlier, through the lens of their own language(s).

"Throw Your Fists Up": Hip-Hop's Contestatory Urban Agency—Lyrical

J-Live's "Are You Satisfied?" foregrounds several hip-hop tropes in examining post-9/11 America. In doing so, his criticism vacillates between the general and specific: the brutality and inequality of free-market capitalism, President Bush's policies, and what he perceives as the disturbing quietude of the African American and hip-hop communities on these issues. The chorus of "Are You Satisfied?" positions the song as a general critique of American capitalism and imperialism, especially under Bush: "The rich get richer, / the world gets worse, / do you get the picture? / Whoever told you that it was all good lied, / so throw your fists up if you're not satisfied." The chorus decries policies that increase economic inequality, but more importantly it directly questions the hip-hop community and issues a collective call for action with the "fists up" rhetoric of the black power movement and much political-minded hip-hop. Further, "It's all good" is a hip-hop expression—used for more than a decade—usually uttered as a dismissal of problems or as a celebratory declaration. (This phrase is hip-hop's equivalent of Bobby McFerrin's famous song "Don't Worry, Be Happy.") In using this phrase, J-Live not only denounces MCs and listeners who do nothing but say "punchlines and puns" while ignoring urgent sociopolitical problems, especially those stemming from 9/11, he also signifies on and engages the received cultural tradition of hip-hop culture. He frames his reproach in terminology that his audience will respond to with heightened awareness and sensitivity. He also questions the courage of those who have been oppositional critics in the past, when he implies that the president's calls for unity and patriotism have made MCs "scared to debate" with the "same devils" they "used to love to hate." Times such as the present, he suggest, require more courage and persistence in fighting inequality and oppression. Hip-hop's originary voices, he also implies, must be engaged by tackling urgent problems.

When J-Live specifically denounces Bush, he does so via one of hip-hop's primary conceits—time. Potter explains the question "What time is it?" in hip-hop vernacular: "With this question, rappers situate themselves within a black diasporic timezone, outside the 'official' time of calendars" (7–8). Further, Richard Shusterman discusses rap's "frequent time tags" as a "metaphysical position associated with American pragmatism" (626). Both show that hip-hop has its own dynamic conception of time that turns not with Wall Street financial centers, but with the empirical realities of dispossessed African American communities. Rappers project their viewpoints of the world through the lens of this other world. Within this frame-work, one of J-Live's most potent lines asserts that Bush's policies will be so detrimental to these communities and so disorient the country that the hip-hop community will no longer be able to tell time: "By the time Bush is done, you won't know what time it is." For J-Live, Bush's policies dramatically affect not only African Americans, but the ability of those in the hip-hop community to orient themselves, to make sense of their worlds, to *tell time.*

J-Live's approach is most effective not in his denunciation of an administration that "trades books for guns," but in his recontextual-ization of post-9/11 America. Though careful to say there is nowhere else he prefers to live ("the grass ain't greener on the other geno-cide"), he refutes the popular claim that 9/11 changed the world forever: "Now it's all about NYPD caps and Pentagon bumper stickers / But yo, you're still a nigga." He goes on to rap that the attack was "tragic, but it damn sure ain't magic." Here, he takes the most pierc-ing logical step in the song, pointing out that 9/11 has no agency to affect positive change. Events, he implies, may temporarily change conditions, but they may not change beliefs, practices, and attitudes, especially negative ones that impact poor urban communities. Most critically, events do not change the prevailing global economic struc-tures that ensure increased wealth for multinational corporations at the expense of the poor, nor do they eradicate political corruption. He raps in incantatory parallel structure: "It won't make the brutality disappear, / it won't pull equality from behind your ear, / it won't make a difference in a two-party country / if the president cheats to win another four years." Here J-Live juggles the necessary conditions for agency that Rose outlines; he calls for action, vigilance, protest, and a contestatory agency within the constraining contexts of racism, economic and power inequalities, corruption, and the complications of terrorism. He points out that even an event as unifying initially as 9/11 is incapable of changing the fundamental dynamics of racism and inequality. Without oversimplifying, he constructs a protest song that also analyzes the competing variables that affect the exercise of agency.

"Home of the Brave," Boston-based Mr. Lif's commentary on post-9/11 America, is more didactic and aggressive than "Are You Satisfied?" Whereas J-Live ascribes to several tenets of authoritative agency—notably the Whitmanian tradition, here closely allied with the tradition of west African griots—Lif departs from J-Live in his use of an authoritative, confrontational figure of voice. If J-Live is careful to say 9/11 was tragic, Lif—as Amiri Baraka (LeRoi Jones) once wrote in "Black Art"—writes "poems / like fists"[2] that make neither qualification or concession. In the song, Lif works against an artificially constructed consensus that prohibits dissent. Like J-Live, he critiques American capitalism, but more venomously. Lif claims that the role of the current administration is to increase the rich's wealth and to protect American monetary interests—"their only function is to keep the funny money where it's at."[3] After a history lesson on U.S. interests in Afghanistan, Lif questions the U.S. intervention: "Bush disguises bloodlust as patriotism." This base substitution "demonizes Afghanis / so Americans cheer when we kill their innocent families." The brutal, unapologetic imagery reaches a denouement in a recontextualization of 9/11: "You can wave that piece of shit flag if you dare / but they killed us because we've been killing them for years." Here Lif seeks to undermine the flag, represented following 9/11 as a symbol of American unity and freedom. The flag, for him, is not a symbol of innocence. Instead, it shrouds killings and justifies further killings. Unlike J-Live's lamentations for the 9/11 dead, Lif's lyrics contest any declaration of American innocence. He attempts to reveal the duplicity of American imperial identity and to attend to socioeconomic conditions in Muslim countries partially created and sustained by American foreign policy.

In "Home of the Brave," Lif assumes a voice common in hip-hop, especially in the politically conscious late 1980s and early 1990s. First, he references black historical figures and compares himself to them, rapping that he has the "mind of Mandela and the heart of Rosa Parks." After establishing this activist revolutionary link, he moves to an agenda to dispel illusion. When he raps "here's what your history books won't show / you're a dead man for fucking with American dough," he engages an emceeing tradition that flows through Chuck D, KRS-One, Paris, X-Clan, Poor Righteous Teachers, dead prez, Talib Kweli, and others. A substantial part of hip-hop's contestatory urban agency is its truth-teller function. Many rappers feel charged with the role of liberating listeners from lies and illusions perpetrated by the government, corporations, the military–industrial complex, public school curricula, and the police. They redress historical inaccuracies that slight black achievement and educational imbalances that maintain racial inequalities and the "official story." Part of this technique is an occasional indulgence in conspiracy theories, many of which are credible.[4] So, when Lif raps that "it's easy to control the scared / so they keep us in fear / with their favorite Middle Eastern villain named Bin Laden," he engages a historical voice of hip-hop distrust for supposedly beneficial policies that are detrimental to urban African Americans.

Like Lif's song, Mos Def's verse on Black Star's "What's Beef?" criticizes American geopolitics and economics, but unlike Lif, Mos Def speaks directly to the hip-hop community about its misdirected resistance. First performed on Comedy Central's *Chappelle's Show* in 2003, its main conceit is the concept of "beef." In hip-hop, a "beef" is a public feud between rappers in which each stakes a claim as the more skillful MC, often using ferocious insults. A "beef" is more than a "battle"—the latter implies a verbal contest between MCs, whereas the former suggests a more personal conflict. Hip-hop has had many "beefs," most of which have produced records rather than physical confrontations, between Roxanne Shante and the Real Roxanne, KRS-One and MC Shan, LL Cool J and Kool Moe Dee, Dr. Dre and Eazy-E, and famously, between 2Pac and the Notorious B.I.G.

"What's Beef?" is a series of terse statements that redefine "beef." Mos Def addresses his audience via hip-hop terminology, and he speaks for that same audience when he addresses the larger political context. In doing so, he utilizes rap's "dual identity as both head and limb, speaking both to and for its audience" (Costello and Wallace 38). He begins by referring to the recent beef between hip-hop icons Jay-Z and Nas. Mos Def's redefinition of "beef" dramatically shifts contexts away from music and into the communities in which hip-hop was born: "Beef is not what Jay said to Nas / Beef is when the working folks can't find jobs / Beef is when the crack babies can't find moms / Because they're in a pine box or locked behind bars." Beef, according to Mos Def, does not consist of what Jay-Z said to Nas, or what "Ja said to 50" (Ja Rule and 50 Cent); instead, beef is unemployment, crack, jail sentences in lieu of rehabilitation, and an inability to secure home loans. Hip-hop, Mos Def suggests, loses its ethic of resistance when it focuses on internal conflicts; he redirects "beef" in much the same way as Public Enemy and Chuck D, who has said that hip-hop draws power from anger, but this anger is often "directed at other rappers." Instead, Public Enemy directed anger at "the government and people who were responsible for what was happening in society" (Hillburn). Beef, according to Mos Def and Chuck D, should not be directed internally but at the forces that oppress African Americans and the poor, thereby preventing them from exercising agency to improve their communities.

When Mos Def addresses the hip-hop community, he tries to shatter some enduring illusions. The misconception, he reiterates, is that "what y'all call beef is not beef at all." Hip-hop's feuds, he charges, must engage a wider social context. This redefinition of "beef" is an aspect of signifying that Henry Louis Gates, Jr., discusses in *The Signifying Monkey* (1998)—rewriting the received textual tradition, in this case the tradition that defines "beef." In doing so, Mos Def moves from hip-hop "beef" to larger "beef," including the Iraq War and AIDS. Beef, for him, is the tension in the Middle East, not the tension on New York radio station "Hot 9–7." Mos Def unequivocally raps that beef *is* "geopolitics" and the situations in "Iraq, the West Bank, and Gaza Strip." Focusing on beefs between rappers distracts from problems in African American communities—poverty, unemployment, inadequate health care, and greedy foreign wars. Mos Def's voice redirecting anger from internal targets to the perpetrators of oppression has long been an impetus for African American artists. Richard Wright's "A Five Dollar Fight" (*Black Boy* 1945) and Ellison's "battle royal" (*Invisible Man* 1952), for example, depict black men being turned against each other by powerful white men, both for entertainment and to focus their frustration internally instead of on their oppressors.

Because an equal chance to outshine one's opponent verbally is a cornerstone of hip-hop beefs, Mos Def delivers a supreme insult in demanding that hip-hop move away from celebrity squabbles: "Beef is not what these famous niggas do on the mic / Beef is what George Bush would do in fight." According to Mos Def, it is *time* for hip-hop to battle those who oppress African Americans. Yet changing the significations for the term "beef" is insufficient for creating change. Stuart Hall warns that rearticulating values alone will not change sociopolitical realities: "No ideological conception can ever become materially effective . . . until it can be articulated to the field of political and social forces and to the struggles between different forces at stake" (42). The project of addressing African Americans' "beefs," then, is shared by rappers, activists, politicians, and communities.

The previous songs diagnose problems but do little to propose solutions. Jean Grae's "Block Party" (*Attack of the Attacking Things* 2003) criticizes negative aspects of hip-hop culture and sketches a plan for making a more educated and self-aware community. In denouncing "materialistic values," insularity, and violence, she works against two hip-hop tropes—defending one's neighborhood and flaunting material wealth. She raps, "stop acting like your flesh is metal / and your hood's a magnet" because "protecting your turf" is "bullshit." Her condemnation of the hypermasculine "thug" posture of toughness, loyalty, and pride is severe, as is her rebuke of individual wealth. For her, "ownership" is "bullshit"; one reason the African American community lacks "wealth" is that in economic terms "it's every man for himself." Her criticism excoriates when she raps that many—presumably rappers—would rather "be chilling with rich white folks" as a sign of success. She laments that some would let their "kids go hungry" before their "wardrobe is outdated." But as "What's Beef?" condemns, she targets hip-hop values when she could indict instead the dominant American culture they imitate.

Jean Grae's harsh criticisms of hip-hop, and her solutions for them, are admirable but idealistic. In lieu of machismo and material wealth, she emphasizes education and travel. Everyone in the hip-hop community, she raps, should "pick up a book," "read a paper," "take a free class," and "get out your house / get off your block / travel the world." These actions would create more enlightened communities, but they hide pragmatic concerns—traveling requires leisure time and economic resources, two privileges the poor lack. In a desire to nurture hope and possibility for change, Grae attributes too much agency to African American communities. As Rose warns, songs that "overemphasize" African American agency ignore constraints that can prevent them from achieving their goals (141–142). As such, the lines "If the system's corrupt, change it. / Fought for the right to vote, don't even use it" deny how corporate, institutional powers systematically resist progressive change and the empowerment of urban communities. Yet the spirit of these lines descends directly from civil rights leaders, Freedom Marchers, the SCLC (Southern Christian Leadership Conference), and SNCC (Student Nonviolent Coordinating Committee), all of whom worked tirelessly for voting rights and an end to segregation in the 1960s. Jean Grae's song thus shows in part the difficulty of articulating feasible, but also engaging, solutions to problems in hip-hop culture.

Whereas J-Live, Mr. Lif, and Jean Grae are independent artists, and Mos Def is better known as an actor, even those unfamiliar with hip-hop will recognize the name Notorious B.I.G., if only for the circumstances of his murder and Tupac Shakur's. The year 1994, when his debut album was released, is widely considered one of the best in hip-hop history, due in part to the release of B.I.G.'s *Ready to Die* and Nas's *Illmatic*. The lyrics and sensibilities of *Ready to Die* illustrate both poles that bound contestatory urban agency. They show the perplexing binary enabled by the conditions of urban poverty: an obsession with death apparent in the album title and a revelatory celebration of life's possibilities. The urban African American male, for B.I.G., is hemmed in on one side by the likelihood of a violent death and on the other side by a life that is difficult to live free of abject poverty, violence, and crime. *Ready to Die* is thus obsessed by the material conditions of childhood poverty, the trappings of drug dealing, and the financial benefits of hip-hop stardom.

On "Respect," B.I.G. envisions the individual's entrance into the social world, and thus the formation of self, beginning *prior* to birth. Thus, chances for successful actions are shaped by the conditions into which an individual is born. Even in the womb, though, the individual has powerful agency. B.I.G. raps that his "moms is late," so after "ten months" in her womb, he decides to "plan [his] escape" into the world. Is this claim overcompensation as Rose would claim, characteristic rap braggadocio, or a wish for greater African American agency over living conditions from birth to death? Or is it a preemptive attack on the socioeconomic conditions faced by poor urban youth? The last question strikes the deepest chord, especially as the following lines show a desire to seize life actively rather than to enter it as a passive figure: "I wish moms'd hurry up / so I could get buckwild, juvenile, ripping mics." Here, B.I.G.'s persona desires to *begin* life as a rap star, bypassing the poverty into which he will be born. Thus, B.I.G. does not *ignore* Stuart Hall's determinate factors; he *wishes* to *erase* them through hip-hop, which suggests a limited field of possibilities for poor black males.

The lyrics of "Respect" indicate an anxiety about determinants that precede action as well as abiding impatience with the inability to act. B.I.G. raps, "I'm seeing my death / and I ain't even took my first step." Here, he imagines dying in the protective—but ultimately restrictive—womb. However, a potential death in the womb points to the historical oppression of African Americans, as the "umbilical cord" is wrapped "around [his] neck." This disturbing image alludes to hangings and lynchings during Reconstruction and Jim Crow and suggests that African Americans enter the world subject to forces of historical oppression and violence. Before he takes his "first step," the song's persona is thus immersed in a world of violent racism.

Another mediating socioeconomic factor impacts the impending birth. The persona's notably single mother goes alone to the hospital; self-reliance, then, is a necessity in urban communities with high out-of-wedlock birth rates. Given this factor, when rappers ascribe extra credence to autonomous individual agency, it seems reasonable because of self-reliance as a survival tactic for those who have often experienced deep cuts in welfare and other support services. It is notable too that braggadocio does not preclude lyrical complexity. In her article on hip-hop as a tool for political activism, Angela Ards argues that "organizing for social change requires that people tap into their mutual human vulnerability and acknowledge their common oppression." She continues by claiming that hip-hop will have difficulties as part of any political movement because it "builds walls to shield" against vulnerability. Though she is correct that braggadocio in part shields against vulnerability, she also claims that it will be tough for hip-hop to begin "speak[ing] of individual frailty and collective strength" (19–20). I argue, however, that there *is* vulnerability and frailty in many hip-hop lyrics, especially in B.I.G.'s lyrics above. They just *seem* dwarfed by macho posturing. He never makes it to collective strength, but many rappers do, some of whom are discussed in the second half of chapter 4. Collective strength is more a province of independent artists and overtly political ones, than mainstream ones, as community-based marketing, distribution, and performance reflect and encourage collective values, whereas the high-budget, rapper-as-celebrity marketing of mainstream artists does not.

Although difficult conditions await the African American child, the persona in "Respect" imagines a world of pleasure and virtuosic performance. He "bring(s) mad joy," and he is born to be a rap star "ripping mics." After his birth, the doctor says that the baby will be "a bad boy." Naming the speaker "a bad boy" at birth helps produce identity through existing negative definitions of black males as presumptive, latent criminals rather than as college graduates. As Judith Butler might say, selfhood is produced through extant social meanings; the act of naming, moreover, exists within the dominant culture's sanctions and power structures. The way Butler understands public power as literally "writing" one's selfhood is so invidious that it allows little of the agency B.I.G.'s song wants to ascribe to young African Americans.[5] If the persona is "a bad boy" at birth—here the name should be viewed via Butler *and* the allusion to Sean "P-Diddy" Combs's Bad Boy Records, B.I.G.'s record label—his chances of avoiding violence are delimited.

When B.I.G. ponders the narrow field of possibilities for poor urban youth, he calls attention to the competition that permeates global capitalism, which is especially detrimental in areas of limited resources. In doing so, the lyrics suggest that the struggle for symbolic and economic capital can be devastating for urban communities. Pierre Bourdieu writes that "symbolic capital is the product of a struggle in which each agent" is "both a ruthless competitor and supreme judge." This capital is defended "by means of a permanent struggle to keep up with and identify with the group immediately above" and "to distinguish oneself from the group immediately below" (136). Many rappers' lyrics suggest that those in the hip-hop community who flaunt materialistic values—it is tempting to think of iconic figures such as Combs, Jay-Z, and 50 Cent—strive to identify with America's ultra rich and to distinguish themselves from poor African Americans, thereby judging them for perceived inadequacies. In disidentifying with poor urban communities, they inadvertently identify with the richer, disinterested larger American culture. In B.I.G.'s "Things Done Changed," an urban African American male has just three options— hip-hop, drug dealing, or athletics—for gaining either type of capital, which is a common but dangerous perception in much hip-hop. He raps: "if I wasn't in the rap game / I'd probably have a key knee deep in the crack game / because the streets is a short stop / either you're slinging crack rock or you got a wicked jumpshot." Being a drug dealer or star basketball player can provide inner-city youth with symbolic capital—status, distinction, and a command on resources independent of economics—and potential economic capital. For the former "occu-pation" the economic gains can be immediate, but unsustainable, as Boogie Down Productions' "Material Love (Love's Gonna Getcha)" shows (see note 1); for the latter, however, a big payday may never arrive even for an extremely gifted player. Thus, though Cheryl L. Keyes rightly suggests that hip-hop music is a symbol of socioeco-nomic mobility in the inner-city (172), this position glosses over the lack of practical alternatives for poor African American youth. How many, after all, become rap stars or basketball stars?

In "Respect," B.I.G. ultimately exposes the mutable nature of material ambition. He extols material success even as he laments—in hindsight—his bad decisions. While he celebrates money made from selling drugs ("making cream / on the drug scene") and his hopes of becoming the "king of New York," he realizes that these pursuits are fraught with peril. After being incarcerated he realizes that "all the money stacked was all the money for bail." Even though socioeco-nomic conditions limit possible actions, until actions fail, the individ-ual is not likely to modify them. But when they do fail, the individual, in this case B.I.G.'s drug dealer persona,[6] can move from "practical consciousness," which is based on a tacit knowledge of constraints— here a lack of choices and economic resources—to conscious reflec-tion (Giddens 5). B.I.G.'s persona's conscious reflection thus leads to a reassessment of the relative worth of drug dealing. "Respect" indi-cates that this type of feedback loop is built into both the actions of inner-city actors and into hip-hop's contestatory urban agency.

Hip-hop's contestatory urban agency is—if these songs represent how progressive and iconic rappers poeticize agency while challenging dominant culture's frameworks for understanding it—complex, irreducible to a simple formula. Its figures of voice draw from and foreground a mutating vernacular that frames agency in hip-hop terminology. Though unrestrained agency is a utopian dream in some lyrics, artists often acknowledge factors that influence an actor's capacity for achieving her purposes. This fundamental dynamic frames contestatory urban agency and hip-hop's legion of protest songs. So though there is great truth in the claim that "old white men" run hip-hop, there is also some truth—at least through rap music—that for young urbanites "the world is what you make it," if we consider that rappers remake the world each time they grab a microphone. Finally, from a lyrical standpoint, hip-hop embodies a diverse range of poetics; as such, it is reasonable to claim that rappers activate, to some extent, variations of experiential, authoritative, equivocal, and migratory agencies as part of its main form—contestatory urban agency.

"Get Live Y'all": Hip-Hop's Contestatory Urban Agency—Live Performance

In this section I explore the political aspects of live hip-hop at small independent clubs. Unlike the private political exchange possible when an individual reads a poem or listens to a song, a hip-hop show is capable of creating a participatory political space involving upward of 600–700 people. Live hip-hop aesthetics are the primary elements for giving the art form and its performers more political strength than printed poetry. They also illuminate further hip-hop's contestatory urban agency and how it is transformed and magnified in the spaces of live hip-hop.

Given the increasingly oppressive influence of multinational corporations and multimillion dollar campaigns on the American political process, average citizens across the country are largely being precluded from participatory politics. As Michael Parenti writes, "The power of money works ceaselessly to reduce the influence of citizens who have nothing to offer but their votes" (219). Further, an abiding belief in isolated bourgeois individualism forestalls citizens from impacting politics, where only collective, not individual action, is capable of creating social and political change. One of the results of these two conditions is a lack of substantive participation in the public sphere. Richard Sennett notes that citizens' engagements with public life are now a "matter of formal obligation" and "resigned acquiescence," which leads to a fundamental suspicion of strangers and "the bond of a crowd" as opposed to the bonds of intimates (3). Live hip-hop shows, however, are existing sites where rank and file citizens can participate in a coordinated political practice that generates collective agency. Live shows that take place in small, independent clubs are powerful instances of both community outreach and community-building. In these shows, hip-hop artists, in conjunction with a responsive audience, create a collective agency, wherein the audience members are at least momentarily empowered to enact change, to practice subversive action, and to speak out about injustice and current political issues. Michael Eric Dyson has suggested that the rap concert "creates space for cultural resistance and personal agency" (5–6), but the primary focus should not be on individual agency because it is problematic in the political realm. Instead, these shows ultimately create space for collective agency and identity, and audience members partly forgo their personal agency for a willingness to "act in concert."

In this section I draw upon Hannah Arendt's notion of "acting in concert" in order to illustrate the ways that the live hip-hop show can be an interactive space of collective agency and coordinated political practice. In live shows, performers and audience jointly produce a space of interactive engagement in which they can contest dominant cultural values. In the following pages I outline the dynamics of live shows at small clubs, briefly discuss five shows as case studies, and consider some significant problems with audiences at live shows, including the difficulties of translating political action from the clubs into larger public spaces. My face-to-face experience with the live performances of the following artists contributes to my conclusions: Rob Base and DJ E-Z Rock, De La Soul, A Tribe Called Quest, Biz Markie, The Roots, The Coup, Talib Kweli, Eyedea & Abilities, Living Legends, Murs, Little Brother, Dilated Peoples, Prince Paul, Aceyalone, Mr. Lif, Aesop Rock, Brother Ali, Micranots, Atmosphere, Cunninlynguists, Brand Nubian, C-Rayz Walz, Cannibal Ox, J-Live, Sadat X, and Zion I. These shows, and others like them at small, independent clubs across the country, help illuminate the ways that hip-hop artists utilize alternative channels for community-building and participatory political engagement. These shows all took place in small clubs or on college campuses; such venues are crucial to my interpretation of hip-hop shows as examples of Arendtian public spaces and should be differentiated from large arena shows. I return to the problematics of large arena shows later in this section. Finally, all of the shows I discuss as case studies took place at Cat's Cradle (capacity 600–700), located a mile from the campus of the University of North Carolina at Chapel Hill. As such, these examples should be considered local, specific ones, but also ones that provide evidence for the dynamics of live shows at small clubs throughout the United States. The demographics of Cat's Cradle, moreover, bring up some difficult but illuminating questions about the state of hip-hop, which I discuss later in this chapter.[7]

The otherwise lost experience of the political—citizens acting together in a public space with coordinated effort—is a distinctive characteristic of the hip-hop show that points to the inroads many hip-hop artists make against a politically disinterested individualism that encourages us "to get what we can for ourselves and not be too troubled by the problems faced by others" (Sennett 31). The hip-hop artists I discuss here often challenge this brand of individualism; as such, their shows have different social and political value as well as a different niche in the consumer market than contemporary multi-platinum, mainstream hip-hop. Their live shows balance the way that much mainstream hip-hop styles "socially competitive consumption as a viable mode of civic participation and personal fulfillment" (Smith 71). In his article on social mobility and the "hip-hop mogul," Christopher Holmes Smith suggests that for wealthy hip-hop luminaries such as Combs and Master P and the artists who emulate them, a successful rapper's "upwardly mobile ascent is not tethered to a sense of either individual propriety or communal accountability" (80). Under these prevailing mainstream conditions in which individual wealth and a "consumptive ethos" (71) are paramount, the live hip-hop show at a small club is a sorely needed corrective. These shows unveil an aspect of hip-hop culture that is concerned both with collective experience and with collective—rather than individual—identity. As Patrick Neate writes, hip-hop must maintain some independence from the "corporate giants that do neither the form nor its worldwide consumers any favors" (257–258). Live shows at small clubs work to counter unchecked individualism, passive consumerism, and big business.

During these live shows artists and audience create a community-based space. Hannah Arendt's work on the necessity of well-defined public spaces for participatory politics illuminates the hip-hop show as a space that enacts collective agency and identity while giving citizens an experience of a practice that is fundamentally political. Arendt's critique of Western representative democracies focuses on the ways that they exclude citizens from "participating, and having a share in public power" (*On Revolution* 255). She contends that the primary understanding of citizenship in contemporary Western cultures centers on the self-interested, economically inclined, politically detached individual. For Arendt, such an exclusion from the political realm is disastrous. Only in these spaces can citizens discover their identities, since identity is only possible as a product of intersubjective relations.

In these public spaces, power is created when "people gather together and 'act in concert' " (*The Human Condition* 244). Hip-hop artists have figured out how to be political by enacting a sense of collective identity between themselves and their audiences during their performances, by "acting in concert" with their audiences. Thus, despite her inability to take into account economic inequality and her claim that freedom is a luxury item,[8] Arendt's notion of public space frames the hip-hop show as a realm of freedom, a place where action can occur and in which spontaneity is enabled. Tricia Rose's claim that rap is a "contemporary stage for the theater of the powerless" (125), and that rap groups use the show setting to address social and political issues, is further illuminated by Arendt's concept of freedom, in that hip-hop artists have a certain freedom on stage they may not have in the larger sociopolitical world. Moreover, Arendt wants to carve out boundaried public spaces where action is undetermined. These public spaces call forth performances that would not be possible in other spaces; they also dramatically enable performances that question authority and challenge audience members to act for social change, even as they entertain. For Arendt, this space has two dimensions material to hip-hop shows—the individual performance and the intersubjective relations that allow the space to function. Action can occur in this *displayed* space, which constitutes a political realm, only if there are spectators who are not intimates. These characteristics work toward a description of many hip-hop shows with their vibrant and young multicultural audiences full of people who do not know each other, generally affordable ticket prices, and dynamic performances.

Whereas Arendt's work on public space and freedom illuminates some characteristics of live hip-hop, Miriam Hansen's foreword to Oskar Negt and Alexander Kluge's *Public Sphere and Experience* clarifies some key components of "counterpublic" spaces that can be applied to live shows as well. She points out that in "alternative public spheres" (xiv) lived experience is "organized" from " 'below,' by the experiencing subjects themselves, on the basis of their context of living" instead of from "above," "by the exclusionary standards of high culture or in the interest of property" (xxxi). At live hip-hop shows at small clubs, performers and crowd act in concert and in doing so "organize" their experience from below, literally from the underground, which is what independent hip-hop music is often called. This "radical form of democracy" organizes actors and performers and empowers people who are often left out of public debates due to age, race, education, and socioeconomic status (xxxi). However, as Negt and Kluge admit, "no local counterpublic can emerge today outside or independently of" larger, more powerful commercial structures (Hansen xxxv). As such, the small club show exists in an implicit relationship to corporate power and mainstream hip-hop riches. To begin to address this concern, I want to take a brief detour into postmodernism and hip-hop as a radical political "practice."

If live hip-hop shows can organize experience in order to enact coordinated collective identity and agency, it is crucial to understand hip-hop as a political practice. Live hip-hop must be *the* fundamental component of Russell A. Potter's and Richard Shusterman's assertions of hip-hop as a cultural practice. In 1991, pragmatist critic Shusterman tentatively proposed that hip-hop was the "new radical cultural politics" Fredric Jameson claimed was only "hypothetical" in his much-discussed "Postmodernism, or the Cultural Logic of Late Capitalism" (627). Potter claims that hip-hop is "a vernacular practice" that depends on audience and performers collectively producing "a zone of sonic and cultural bricolage." Hip-hop, he says, is a "practice in action" (45–46). Shusterman's and Potter's notions of hip-hop as a practice and as a form of cultural politics is best activated by—and indeed, is dependent upon—live shows, where it is possible to see hip-hop as a political practice in action. Though both understand hip-hop as a fundamentally postmodern art, I want to suggest that even if its production and its musical form are postmodern, the space and form of the small club live show are not. Here, many basic features of postmodernism are trampled: the subject is alive not dead, agency is present not absent, uncertainty and ambiguity are difficult to find (confidence is paramount), and community is active instead of simulated via passively received simulacra. A postmodern musical form need not obviate concerted political action. In live hip-hop shows, finally, it is not futile to dissent, mobilize, and speak truth to power. Active participation works against cynicism and complacency.

Unlike political poetry, where a poem is adjudged to be political based largely on its content, language, or rhetoric, hip-hop's political import is partially a function of the *form of* its performance and the *context for* the performance. The shows I discuss here occupy specific historical moments, moments that are important for those live shows in which performers comment on current issues. However, the political work of a live hip-hop show does not rely exclusively upon the particular historical moment during which it occurs. A performer can abstain from making any definitive political comment during a show and still work to enact in the audience a sense of collective agency. Therefore, a primary difference between the political work of printed poetry and hip-hop is the striking form/content distinction in hip-hop performance. Whereas it would be exceedingly difficult for poets such as Mark Strand, Sharon Olds, Louise Glück, or Dave Smith to politicize a reading of their poetry due to its generally politically disinterested *content*, hip-hop artists have figured out how to make the *form* of their shows political. Even if the overt content of an artist's lyrics is not political, their show can be political due to the ways that shows build collective agency and identity. The functional and intimate interaction between performers and audience foregrounds the form of the show, even if its content is not candidly political. In contrast, poetry readings are often dour affairs with polite applause; even in poetry slams there is often little interaction other than in voting or in encouraging.

The primary methods of interaction in hip-hop shows are long-standing traditions in African American culture. Many of hip-hop's most astute critics have alluded to these techniques, but none have given extended treatment to live hip-hop performance, with the exception of Greg Dimitriadis and Tricia Rose, who ably tackles the "context for its public reception," primarily focusing on large arena shows during the early 1990s. She also alludes to the form/content distinction when she warns against the pitfalls of saying hip-hop artists who do not have explicit political subjects do no political work (124). William Eric Perkins rightly points out the influence of call-and-response on live hip-hop techniques, in lines of descent from western Africa to African American gospel performances to the present. He draws a connection between jazz band leaders and hip-hop's MCs in his discussion of the "reciprocity between the band and the audience," where the performer "shapes the audience's participation, which then spurs the band leader to further improvisation" (2–3). This reciprocity is the crucial interchange that functionally enables the quasi-public space in which agency is created. Annette J. Saddik, in an essay on the performance of black male identity and hip-hop, asserts that hip-hop is a "postmodern form of drama that draws on a long tradition of African-American performance—incorporating, revising, and re-creating as it sees fit to serve more current social needs" (112). Cheryl L. Keyes also briefly discusses the "verbal and physical interplay" between artist and audience (151), and Nelson George points out some essentials of hip-hop performance when he writes that Cowboy of early hip-hop group Grandmaster Flash and the Furious

Five invented phrases such as "Throw your hands in the air and wave them like you just don't care!" (20). Call-and-response staples such as this one help to structure live hip-hop. They provide the working blueprint for the fashioning of collective identity and collective agency; in each of the following case studies call-and-response anchors performer/audience collaboration.

On February 15, 2003, when the San Francisco-based group Living Legends performed on the "Creative Differences" tour at Cat's Cradle, it was just over one month away from President Bush's declaration of war against Iraq, during a time when it was becoming obvious that such a course of action was imminent. Although Living Legends, a collection of eight MCs, was primarily interested in entertaining the audience, there was no shortage of social and political commentary. The prominence of calls for peace and demonstrations of peace signs in call-and-response between stage and audience, often done in explicitly stated reference to the building war effort, was one of the most salient features of the evening. The crowd was buoyant and responsive, thus enabling the features Arendt claims are necessary to constitute this public space of action—courageous individual performance, intersubjective relations between relative strangers, "acting in concert," and collective identity. The participatory *form* of the show created a politics of engagement between audience and performers and within the audience that superseded the actual political content. Each time the audience called for peace in response to Living Legends, it was "acting in concert" and creating a collective identity.

Nearly a year earlier, on April 12, 2002, the Oakland-based rap group The Coup, widely considered one of the most political groups in the hip-hop community, performed at Cat's Cradle. This show, unlike most of Living Legends' performance, united explicit political content with the political form inherent in small club hip-hop shows. On their latest album (*Party Music* 2001), MC Boots Riley uses Marxist rhetoric to attack multinational corporations, the oppression of wage laborers via exorbitant rents and unfair wages, American imperialism, unchecked capitalism, and institutionalized religion's willful ignorance of socioeconomic justice issues, all the while proclaiming pro-union, pro-Zapatista, and pro-revolution stances. The proletarian message is best distilled in one line, rendered in Spanish: "Pro-La Raza sayin' 'Fuck La Migra!' " ("Ride the Fence"). This exclamation is an explicit refusal to accept the immigration authority's likely attempts to send Chicanos out of California from land that was ceded from Mexico in the Treaty of Guadalupe–Hidalgo in 1848. The result of such moves by official power structures and the greedy rich leaves only crumbs to the race ("La Raza" here is read as encompassing African Americans, Latinas/os, and the poor in general). The Coup's song is a call to action for social change and a dramatic redistribution of wealth via the land.

Between politically resonant songs such as these during the April 2002 show, Boots Riley assumed the role of a grassroots political activist. He spoke to the audience about police brutality and inequality in North Carolina, growing poverty in the United States, the war on terrorism, and the war in Afghanistan. He carefully oscillated between stories of police brutality in Durham (ten miles from Cat's Cradle) to global issues, continually imploring the audience to fight against war, inequality, and the conditions that enable terrorism. The show ended with what amounted to a demand for assent from the audience. To paraphrase Riley—"You're not going to go home and forget about this, are you? It's up to you all to act." Crucially, the reception of such a message is contextualized within the public space of freedom, where collective agency empowers the audience to act. Under such auspices, Riley's message is not unsolicited proselytizing or a threatening demand, but an interactive exchange with the audience. Arendt's desire to remove a means/end vocabulary from public spaces and the actions contained therein demonstrates that the audience is not a passive recipient of a performer's message. If the audience is not solely a means to an end for the performer's goals, the interaction can create a collective political engagement.

On November 17, 2003, the Minneapolis-based hip-hop group Atmosphere performed at Cat's Cradle. Though Atmosphere's songs are generally not overtly political, this particular show had an overtly political ambience, immediately visible upon entering the club. In the small booth where artists sell CDs, t-shirts, and other products, there were anti-George Bush t-shirts for sale. During the last section of the show Atmosphere MC Slug derided the policies of the president and implored all audience members to take but one message home— to go to the polls and vote. During the processes of direct address and call-and-response he urged everyone in the audience to look around at the other audience members, saying—and I paraphrase—this is your community, one created through hip-hop music; you all must look out for each other and help each other, so get together, vote, and create change. Miriam Hansen notes that "the language of community provides a powerful matrix of identification and thus may function as a mobilizing force for transformative politics," a possibility I saw at work in this Atmosphere show. However, this language must also "admit difference and differentiation within its own borders" (xxxvi), a task many artists view as difficult, a point I return to later in this section of the chapter.

This message of community, though, is largely untenable in a realm other than the public space of the show, for example, in a poetry reading or public speech when it can become uncomfortable when a poet grows preachy or didactic. For Arendt, the public space of the political is a "realm of freedom and equality precisely because the realm dissolves when it is not the product of an intersubjective 'acting in concert' in which every participant engages willingly" (McGowan 73). At a show such as Atmosphere's, all participants engage in the collective action willingly. This enthusiastic "acting in concert" both enables the space to exist and is enabled by the space. Such willingness makes tenable Slug's attempts to mobilize youth for a cause. This tactic links to Arendt's efforts to think of a public space as a place wherein citizens can interact without the influence of the state, institutions, and corporations, since institutionalization, she believed, kills the spirit of action. This show encouraged audience members to harness the state (through voting and collective action) even as it circumvented the institutional, corporate influence that undermines so many mainstream musical acts. Recording on an independent record label and performing at venues that are not sponsored by large corporations (such as large arenas, amphitheaters, and concert halls) may allow for more piercing social and political commentary and a political space unhindered by overt commercialization.

On September 30, 2004, the night of the first presidential debates, Cunninlynguists opened for Brand Nubian at Cat's Cradle. The show demonstrated the potential for what can be done when people "act in concert." Further, it showed the Arendtian notion of power as a force "that makes it possible to achieve some ends that cannot be reached individually" (McGowan 75–76)—widespread social and political change as well as a collective experience of the political. Cunninlynguists' call-and-response "Fuck George Bush, say fuck George Bush" united a group of citizens in a coordinated political practice that is literally unachievable in an individual forum. The call-and-response created collective motivation in the audience. Creating political change at the highest level is not possible from an individual perspective, but collective identity and agency *are* capable of creating change. This show showed citizens acting at a local site that makes possible "the direct participation" of citizens in "the public affairs of the country" (*On Revolution* 263). Though this type of participation is possible at political rallies, these rallies are often party- or organization-sponsored. The hip-hop show, on the other hand, is an art form that entertains, enables collective agency, and gives its participants an experience of the political.

"The Best Damn Rap Tour," which stopped at Cat's Cradle on June 27, 2005, is the last case study discussed here. The show included C-Rayz Walz (recently featured on an issue of MTV's *Made* as a freestyle rap coach), Vast Aire and Cannibal Ox, and J-Live. The most striking aspect of this show was its myriad subversions of the corporate-dominated music world. First, the show cost just $12 for nearly four and half hours of music by three reputable artists; second, the artists mingled with fans in the audience during the opening acts, talking and listening; third, the artists were at the "merch" (merchandise) table selling (and autographing) their records directly to fans. (It is easy to notice the similarities to poetry readings, which usually include merchandise tables for purchasing poets' books.) This direct relationship between performers and their audience is a much needed intervention in the mythology, distance, and wealth of highly mediated celebrity and corporate cultures. It moves hip-hop away from videos and celebrities and back to its beginnings in the late 1970s and early 1980s when it "was dependent upon face-to-face interaction and small-scale mediation" in which the "event itself was more important than any particular separable discourse" (Dimitriadis 184). For many independent artists, the live show is still the cornerstone of the art, although a skeptic could say that these artists simply do not have access to larger commercial channels and would use them if they did. But as C-Rayz Walz raps on his latest album, "I won't dumb it down to double my dollars" ("First Words Worse" *Year of the Beast* 2005). This *stated* ethic permeates the independent hip-hop music scene, but is difficult to parse for its truth-value.

The centrality of live hip-hop to independent artists and audiences may partially alleviate the concerns of many critics and fans. Central to their concerns is the prominence of costly videos and marketing at the expense of "face-to-face community building practices" (Dimitriadis 191). Regardless of the differences between the two, the *visual* is key to both. Things were not always this way. In Elizabethan England, theatergoers went to "hear" a play. Now, however, U.S. theatergoers, although largely from a different socioeconomic class than most theatergoers in sixteenth- and seventeenth-century London, go to "see" a Broadway play. Twenty-first century audiences go to "see" a hip-hop show, whether that show is in a small club or in a large arena. Even if the audience attends in part for the aural experience, the visual dimension takes precedence in the way that encounters with live musical performances are explained. This modest sociolinguistic change is just one of many wrought by a visually -dominated consumer culture of films, music videos, television, and the Internet. But for hip-hop, it points to an existential crisis. Nelson George, one of hip-hop's most astute mainstream commentators, laments that music videos, though indispensable in disseminating hip-hop culture globally, have transformed the art form's fundamental aesthetic from its very public gestation period in city parks and on street corners in the Bronx and Queens to one that thrives on sophisticated marketing, image construction, and video editing. He claims that hip-hop video "has removed live performance from the center of its aesthetic" (111–113). Of greater consequence is the danger this dynamic presents to the axiomatic exchange between audience and artist key to hip-hop aesthetics.

In contrast to George's claim and Greg Dimitriadis's concern that there is an "increasing lack of space for live production and congregation" (191), hip-hop shows at small clubs work to keep live performance at the center of the aesthetic partly by engaging hip-hop fans in a coordinated political experience. But the question remains: What is it about the small club hip-hop show that brings the hip-hop aesthetic back to live performance as a central aesthetic axiom? What is it more specifically about the hip-hop show in a small club that is different from a hip-hop show in a large arena or stadium? Are the dynamics of a politically engaged public space unique to small clubs? In addition to dramatically cheaper ticket prices and a relative freedom from corporate and institutional influence, the primary factor that differentiates small clubs from large arenas is the sense of immersion possible in a small club.

The full immersion of the audience in a show is due somewhat to the close architectural confines, the usually hot temperatures inside, the high decibel sound levels, and the inability to separate oneself from the energy unless one leaves the club. The close confines and small stage, which usually separates the audience from performers not with floor space but vertically by just a few feet, lead to increased intimacy between performers and their audience. In this atmosphere it is not unusual to see artists walking around the club before or after the show, signing records, and directly engaging audience members during the show by addressing them, talking to them, and giving them handshakes. All of these possibilities are dramatically foreclosed during the large arena show. It is reasonable to conclude that large arena shows may be capable of creating a sense of collective identity, but not coordinated collective agency, since collective agency and political practice, as Arendt shows, depend upon intimate intersubjective relations. The large arena show, with its implicit emphasis on spectacle and the resulting wide-eyed consumption of that spectacle, has a fundamentally different and distant dynamic.

American pragmatism's rejection of Cartesian subject–object dualism is a key to understanding the immersion possible in a live hip-hop show at a small club. As outlined by Cornel West in his book on pragmatism, Charles Sanders Peirce, William James, and John Dewey rejected Cartesian subjectivism and its attendant "fictive" spectator theory of knowledge, which is predicated upon a subject/object dualism in which the self (the "spectator") is a detached observer who comes to know an object from a position fundamentally apart from what she comes to know. Peirce, James, and Dewey reject the subject/object binary and show that the individual is always embedded in relationships with other people, social, political, and economic conditions, and the "furniture of the world" that predate any separation of subject and object and that are continuously subject to change. The individual always finds herself *in medias res*—in the middle of things—so that all experience is prior to a subject/object split (West 44, 56, 89, 91–92).

This is exactly the type of immersion that exists in a small club. If the handful of people lingering at the back of the club are bracketed, there are few "spectators" at a small club hip-hop show. The vast majority are active participants emerged fully in the middle of things. The only way one can really *know* the small club show is not by being a detached observer but by sweating and participating in the calls-and-response, by chanting song choruses when prompted, by joining in the enactment of collective agency, and by "acting in concert." In many of the live shows I have attended, the artists have often ridiculed ("called out" in hip-hop vernacular) or encouraged the few stragglers usually present in the back of the room. These outliers, the artists imply, are antithetical to the art form and to live hip-hop aesthetics. In large arena shows, this level of intimacy and interaction is much more difficult, and passive consumption is closer to the norm, especially if we consider applause and screaming not primarily participatory but congratulatory. A crude maxim largely holds: in a small club the audience participates, in a large arena the audience observes, at a poetry reading the audience politely applauds.

Another way of describing the immersion possible in a small club is in terms of synaesthesia. The experience of collective identity and agency created in the space of the live show to some extent cannot be separated from the multiple sensory experiences that merge into each other and the senses that are elicited by other senses. *A Handbook to Literature* defines synaesthesia as "the concurrent response of two or more of the senses to the stimulation of one." The primary senses directly stimulated during a small club hip-hop show are hearing, sight, and touch, which is not to mention the sense of taste often stimulated by alcohol or the sense of smell created by alcohol, sweat, and smoke. Without one of these elements, the others would have a less palpable effect. For instance, if the sense of touch—largely a product of venue size—were sacrificed, the intimate connection with other audience members so crucial to Arendt's theory would be greatly compromised. One cannot merely "watch" the artists on stage without being assaulted by the sonic power of microphones, recorded bass lines and snare drums, and other people's bodies. But perhaps the most interesting synaesthetic-like experience is the way that the audience experiences the political through intense sensory stimulation. It is rare for citizens to have an intimate *political* experience via their senses, especially an interactive experience that joins them to other people.

A further dynamic illuminated by the form/content distinction in live hip-hop is the role of lyrics in live hip-hop performances. Though lyrical content is to some extent immaterial to the political work of live hip-hop, it is important to hip-hop aesthetics as a whole. Understanding many hip-hop lyrics requires intensive listening and well-trained ears. This task is especially difficult at live shows, where the acoustics and sound levels may not be conducive to understanding all of the performer's lyrics. For example, if the bass levels are tuned too low (where lower means more bass) and the microphones' volumes are not loud enough, it may be difficult to understand an MC's lyrics. So, though it is easy to understand calls-and-response, it may be difficult to understand the lyrics themselves. But as Potter writes, "Hip-hop audiences do not, at any rate, merely *listen*—passive reception is no longer possible" (108; original emphasis). Passive reception is difficult in a live show at a small club as MCs demand that their audiences stay responsive. As such, the live show functionally eliminates the problem outlined in Little Brother's "The Listening" (*The Listening* 2002). The song suggests that passive reception is not only possible but may be the norm for many fans who listen to hip-hop in their home or car.

In "The Listening," Little Brother's two MCs, Phonte and Big Pooh, rap about the current state of hip-hop music, reminiscing about their childhood obsessions with memorizing rap lyrics while lamenting that currently, "don't nobody care what you're saying." During one verse, they dramatize an encounter with a fan who says that "all she listens to is beats," meaning that she cares only about the rhythm, melody, and bass line of the song, not its lyrical content. The quick-witted chorus further elucidates the problem for MCs with carefully written lyrics. It claims that people "ain't listening / they're thinking about their Timberlands / they say the shit we talk about ain't interesting / we got a better chance of blowing up in Switzerland." According to the chorus, active listening has been symbolically replaced by an icon of consumer culture (Timberland boots). Additionally, they self-deprecatingly claim that they have a much greater chance of becoming popular in Switzerland, where English is not even the primary language, than in the United States.[9] The song points to some potentially disturbing questions about the state of hip-hop (and American) culture, and it also suggests that live shows help to eliminate what Little Brother views as a big problem in contemporary hip-hop—disengaged, passive listening. Passive listening, even if one cannot understand all of the lyrics, is exceedingly difficult in a small club hip-hop show due to the emphasis given to active participation that is always a product of paying close attention to the performers' engagements with the audience and responding to them quickly and energetically.

If we consider not participating an untenable option at a small club hip-hop show are there elements of coercion present? In other words, do artists pressure, coerce, and force their audiences to participate as they wish? Some basic assumptions need to be addressed to answer this question. First, artists seemingly must speculate about their audience's viewpoints. Unlike records, live performances call forth immediate feedback and judgment. As Arendt might have said, individual performances in these public spaces require courage. Further, because live hip-hop at small clubs is wholly dependent upon its audience's active participation and consent, performers must work to ensure that their audience is engaged. However, audience members have presumably entered the space of their own volition with relatively full knowledge of what they must bring to the show. They are also free to leave if they do not want to participate in the collective experience.

The most difficult aspect of the previous question concerns potential "groupthink" problems. Slug of Atmosphere evinced a keen understanding of this issue at the November 2003 Cat's Cradle show. After an interlude between songs in which his DJ played the Rage Against the Machine lyrics "Fuck you I won't do what you tell me," he sheepishly mentioned to the crowd the irony of such lyrics in light of his calls-and-response that the audience follows without hesitation or deviation. It seems prudent to attribute Slug's commentary more to egotism than to a submissive, mechanistic audience. Or, as Hansen points out, he understands that his actions function "as rhetoric" and "as a trope of impossible authenticity" (xxxvi). In any case, "acting in concert" involves collectively working to achieve what cannot be done individually. The power of acting together inherently includes the danger of blindly following.

This issue also points to the indispensability for live hip-hop of magnanimous personalities capable of virtuosic performances. Arendt writes that the virtuosity of performance in spontaneously created political space should not be thought of as a consumable product. She writes that "virtuosity" is "an excellence we attribute to the performing arts (as distinguished from the creative arts of making), where the accomplishment lies in the performance itself and not in an end product which outlasts the activity that brought it into existence" (*Between* 153). The virtuosity of a hip-hop performance is categorically different than the albums fans buy. The quasi-public space of the show, its audience participation, and the ability of performers to connect with that audience create a virtual space of interaction, impossible when a private citizen listens to a record in her home, office, or car. One pressing question remains: Can the agency of a live hip-hop show translate from the public space of the show into the larger realms of representative democracy, where urgent social problems and economic inequalities remain, and where money, not virtuosity or audience participation, controls politics?

Many readers may question any premise about the political potency of live hip-hop shows if it is not also possible for the collective agency and political experience created by "acting in concert" to translate into action and change in the larger world. Angela Ards, in discussing the difficulties of moving from hip-hop as entertainment to hip-hop as activism, claims that "what look like mere social events may represent a *prepolitical* phase of consciousness building that's integral to organizing" (14; my emphasis). I believe, though, that it is important to think of live shows not as "prepolitical" but as fully *political* events in that they establish community-based interpersonal relationships and create democratic, political spaces. They *are* organizing. According to Arendt, action in these public spaces "always establishes relationships" (*The Human Condition* 190). Moreover, the "extent of those relationships and their consequences are impossible to know (and hence control) in advance" (McGowan 68). Arendt claims that every action is a "miracle" since it introduces something new into the world; consequently, it is not possible to predict with accuracy an action's future effects or how it will translate outside that space. Arendt wants to preserve public spaces for actions that can be creative, world-disclosing, and unbounded by the limitations of reductive cause and effect calculations. As such, the long-term political and social effects of a performance are unknowable in advance. An artistic performance, we could say, often enters the world as an Arendtian "miracle" whose effects in the wider world are initially unknowable. Finally, it seems fatuous to claim that at any moment in history one can know the lasting sociopolitical effects of a single hip-hop show, poem, novel, or painting. An element of the unknown accompanies all forays into and out of what Arendt calls the public space of freedom and action.

Ultimately, the live hip-hop show depends on the performances of both artist and audience in a way that poetry, most other art forms, and many political performances such as debates do not. For collective agency to be enacted and for assent to be elicited and channeled into creative energy, both artist and audience must "act in concert." The audience's collective identity, then, is created intersubjectively between themselves and between the artists and themselves. If we can view live hip-hop as a way of making inroads against any notion of art as fundamentally separate from its audience, the live hip-hop show at a small club can be seen as a crucial element of localized participatory democracy. In a country where actual participation in politics is becoming increasingly more difficult and expensive, the hip-hop show stands out as a remarkable event not only in the music industry, but in a tradition of local participatory politics in American history.

However, as with any art form or consumer product, the greatest power resides largely with audiences. The space of a live hip-hop show, then, is enabled by the people who buy tickets and travel to shows. Also, it is advantageous (but not necessary) for the audience to know the artists' music before they see them perform as it allows audience members to recite song choruses when they are called to do so. So in another way, the audience is in further control of the show's level of engagement depending on how familiar they are with the performers. For these reasons, when hip-hop luminary Prince Paul told the June 13, 2003, crowd at Cat's Cradle that the future of hip-hop is in their hands because they buy both profound and vapid hip-hop records, he was largely correct.

The power of the audience may help democratize and make more dynamic artistic performance, but even partial audience control over hip-hop music may have serious ramifications when one considers that a large percentage of that audience will likely be white. According to one *estimate* from "fans, promoters, and independent MCs who play live more than half the year," overall small club audiences are 85 to 95 percent white (Kitwana). Many African American rappers have long been perplexed by the lack of African Americans in their audiences at shows. In The Roots's "Act Too (The Love of My Life)" (*Things Fall Apart* 1999), guest MC Common evinces a keen awareness of the issue, but without pontificating or editorializing: "When we perform it's just coffee-shop chicks and white dudes." Common points out an unavoidable reality for many artists—the large percentage of whites at hip-hop shows—but his lack of further comment implies that MCs do not know yet how to interpret this dynamic.

A large white presence in audiences is presumably a more pressing problem for artists who care about the cultural and political impact of their music than for artists who care solely about making money. Nelson George implies that white suburban audiences are a problem within the historical context of hip-hop music's development. When he writes about his perceptions of a 1995 Run D.M.C. show that had a "99.9%" white audience as a "sweet memory of childhood fun" in which "a frenzy of rhymed words, familiar beats, and chanted hooks" allowed the suburban crowd to drink and laugh, he laments that this scene "may not be what many folks want hip-hop to mean, but it is a true aspect of what hip-hop has become" (75). Scenes like this are common, and though they are striking for their lack of an edge and their lack of resistance to the inequalities against which hip-hop has long fought, they should not be overly alarming if they are considered "snapshots of a movement" (Potter 148). And though this scene is not surprising at a Run D.M.C. show—perhaps the first hip-hop (along with the Beastie Boys) that suburban white kids listened to in the 1980s—it is perplexing when Run D.M.C. is one of the most important acts in hip-hop history and is widely respected in African American communities. Why didn't African Americans (other than George) attend this show?

This question is especially pertinent for groups such as dead prez, Immortal Technique, and The Coup, who make some of hip-hop's most politically committed music. If their live shows are any indication, much of their audience is white. The Coup's Boots Riley believes that marketing decisions are partly responsible for the predicament. When asked about the lack of African Americans at hip-hop shows in general and at The Coup's shows in particular, "he blames such scarceness on the manner in which promoters advertise his concerts, targeting them specifically for and to white middle-class or suburban youth venues" (Keyes 3). Riley points to marketing as a primary reason that crowds are white, an assertion I find difficult to disagree with, but his claim does beg a question: if The Coup were to play a city venue marketed to African Americans, would an African American audience attend in full?

While Riley's claim about marketing and promotion is largely correct, many hip-hop shows at Cat's Cradle reveal limitations with any view that does not also consider other factors. Despite doing primarily street-based marketing in the area and the presence of a large African American population in the areas immediately surrounding the club, Cat's Cradle hip-hop audiences are often largely white, even for iconic, Afrocentric groups such as Brand Nubian. In general, the hip-hop acts that perform at Cat's Cradle do not get a lot of mainstream airtime on radio or cable television. As such, it is reasonable to assume that urban radio stations influence not only the purchasing decisions of African Americans, but to some extent they also determine the artists with whom their listeners are familiar. This situation is problematic for groups such as The Coup and dead prez in light of Dyson's accurate claim that radio executives usually opt for "pop rap as more acceptable than its realistic, politically conscious counterpart" (8). For those urban hip-hop fans who do not have ready access to the Internet or college radio, this situation could prevent them from not only hearing a group like The Coup, but from hearing *of* them. So if white kids are attending hip-hop shows and listening to music intended primarily for African American audiences, it is partly due to choices made by urban radio stations, television executives, and corporate media near-monopolies such as Clear Channel. Consequently, The Coup often "acts in concert" with an audience different than the one their music is made to reach.

The blame, though, does not rest solely with promoters, clubs, radio executives, and television producers. The political *content* of an act such as dead prez may turn off some African American (and white and Latina/o) listeners. The cover of their debut album *let's get free* (2000) shows young sub-Saharan Africans raising automatic weapons in a revolutionary stance; a sticker that covers the guns claims: "this artwork has been censored by the powers that be, due to its political content." Thus, dead prez preemptively claims that their music enters the market under prohibition; they are keenly aware that their message may marginalize them. When dead prez engages an audience with the call-and-response question "Where are all my vegetarians at?" before they perform their vegetarian anthem "Be Healthy," it is likely that they are not trying to reach a mainstream audience, black or white. They could be said to marginalize themselves in much the same why that the Language poets do (although with entirely different motivations and aesthetics). Finally, revolutionary content may not appeal to listeners who believe in social mobility via striving for individual wealth. Or more simply, some fans now want no more than to be entertained by easily accessible music.

Shows at small clubs such as Cat's Cradle do not attract multimillion selling stars, but artists such as The Coup whose record sales may range from several thousand to hundreds of thousands of records. So, though many of these artists will not sell millions of albums, their shows will continue to create interactive political spaces that enact collective agency and identity. Their shows will give 25–700 young people at a time what has largely become a lost participatory experience in America—"acting in concert" as a coordinated political practice. In part because audiences may include many white people, shows will also continue to "invite identification across forbidden lines" (Potter 10) of race and socioeconomics even if that message is not reaching much of its intended audience. Without live shows, hip-hop's political potency would be palpable, but live shows are fundamental to its status as an evolving cultural practice that challenges various power structures and the meanings of participatory democracy and American individualism.

To sum up, then, the small club hip-hop show is just one "snapshot of a movement" (Potter 148). This segment of hip-hop culture is a necessary corrective to a largely insipid, corporate-controlled mainstream hip-hop obsessed with wealth and individualism. It is also a return to principles that nurtured the culture in its early years—community-building, direct participation, and live performance. When we understand the live hip-hop show as Arendtian "acting in concert" in order to build collective agency and vibrant public spaces and to organize experience from "below," it transforms hip-hop from primarily entertainment to powerful political practice. For these very reasons, a small club hip-hop show—assuming the audience is sufficiently energized by the artists and vice versa—does not need explicit political content in order to be a functioning political space. In the final analysis, independent hip-hop acts need live shows to disseminate their music and messages (and to make a living), whereas independent-minded hip-hop fans seem to crave the energy, creativity, participation, and community that is not possible through mainstream channels. Thus, despite significant problems with live shows at small clubs, not the least of which are audience demographics and occasional less-than-capacity crowds, these spaces actively create a motivated hip-hop community. If these shows were able to reach more African Americans, the small club live hip-hop show would be without peer in the intersection of politics and literature.

SUMMARY AND CONCLUSIONS:
A GLOBAL HIP-HOP FUTURE?

Hip-hop is now an entrenched part of the dominant cultural landscape rather than a threat to that landscape. Chuck D's claim that hip-hop is the Black CNN, cited in the introduction to this book, is no longer accurate; it is currently more appropriate to see mainstream hip-hop as an African American *Lifestyles of the Rich and Famous*, a claim that MTV's *Cribs* supports. Now that there are few self-conscious, progressive political voices—*perhaps* with the exception of Kanye West—alongside the merely entertaining ones on MTV and BET, as there were in the late 1980s and early 1990s, the critical, introspective, and innovative voices of contestatory urban agency, like those discussed here, carry hip-hop's torch as a force of resistance to social injustice.

To watch videos on MTV and BET for an afternoon is to see hip-hop as a shallow, image-driven culture of exaggerated masculinity, misogyny, gratuitous sex, audacious wealth, and unabashed consumerism. In this visible segment of hip-hop, individual consumption and wealth are primary values and means to social advancement. Much of commercial hip-hop's ethos of hyperconsumerism, which includes the ostentatious flaunting of luxury items such as jewelry and cars, serves in part to encourage listeners and viewers to " 'buy in' to the emerging paradigm of accessible luxury" (Smith 71)—an American Dream in which anyone can have a mansion. In this way, hip-hop becomes a symbol of upward mobility via material gain that drives an economy based on consumption. Christopher Holmes Smith suggests that this paradigm departs from civil rights "communal development blueprints" (71). Mainstream hip-hop thus arguably reinforces some negative values that the civil rights movement fought.

Yet what is most interesting about this *mainstream* dynamic is initially suggested by Patrick Neate. He claims, "It is white, corporate America that bestrides the globe economically," but "it is black America in general and hip-hop in particular that bestrides the world's popular culture" (13–14). If this is true, and I believe it is, then these two previously disparate forces have joined together in a strange partnership in the ultimate service of wealth creation. Given hip-hop's changing roles in U.S. culture, Rose's claims about rap's marginality in 1994 now seem tenuous. She wrote then that hip-hop was "part of the dominant text, and yet always on the margins of this text; relying on and commenting on the text's center and always aware of its proximity to the border" (19). Now, though, rap is so imbricated in the dominant text that the margins *within* hip-hop comment on the center, both in hip-hop and in the greater culture. This dynamic makes small club live shows and the voices of contestatory urban agency critical because they often interrogate the consumerism that marks commercial rap. Potter's analysis of this commodification aptly sums up this situation: "since bourgeois culture craves difference, appropriating subcultural forms and turning them into commodities solves two problems in one blow" (120). As such, dispossessed black youth are transformed from threat to commodity, and now, more dangerously, into tools for promoting capitalism and consumerism. Strangely enough, though, what threatens hip-hop culture also invigorates it. There is both a creative and market equilibrium that keep the diverse culture in balance, at least for those participants capable of and willing to search beyond the mainstream. If there is hedonism, there will also be a community-based ethos, and so on. However, that balance has tilted negatively since the late 1980s and early 1990s, which suggests that hip-hop values may be cyclical; that corporate-run record companies and radio and television stations have greater control than they did then; or that there is more money to be made and the temptation to make it too great.

The paradoxes of hip-hop are too complicated to sort out in a single chapter, however, as a scholar and fan of, and a participant in, hip-hop culture, I can draw one certain conclusion. In the twenty-first century, responses to urban crises of racism, oppression, poverty, and inadequate water supplies and health care will be more important than ever. Here's why: In 1950, there were 86 cities of one million-plus inhabitants. In 2004, there were 386 cities with these demographics. By 2015, at least 550 cities will have populations exceeding one million. Further, the current global urban population of 3 billion is greater than the *world's* 1960 population, and, in 2004, the world's urban population surpassed the number of rural inhabitants for the first time in recorded history (Davis "Planet" 17). How are these demographics relevant to hip-hop? With the growth of urban populations and of "megacities" (over 8 million) and "hypercities" (over 20 million), poor urban residents will struggle to survive and to be heard, and because much of this population will be minorities and indigenous, they will face institutionalized racism. Hip-hop artists have struggled with these forces in similar contexts for nearly three decades. The voices of contestatory agency, then, will echo, whether consciously or not, millions of pleas from Bogotá, Mexico City, Lagos, Dakar, Rio, and Jakarta. Governments in the developed and developing worlds will not be able to ignore the issues that affect these populations. Hip-hop, the poetry of disaffected urban American youth,[10] will make its way into and out of these crowded urban spaces, in voices of hope, revolution, resistance, anger, and, for the foreseeable future, darkness and decay. Most voices will remain young and black, others will be white, and yet others Latina/o and mestiza/o. They will join the expanding range of hip-hop, changing and refashioning the worlds it engages.

Conclusion

PART ONE

In this book I have tried to chart what I perceive are the major rhetorical strategies of political poems in the United States from the mid-1960s to the present. In order to explain the general distinguishing features as well as the subtleties of each strategy, especially their attendant figures of voice, I chose poems that best represent that strategy's overall qualities. However, many of these poems push, challenge, and sometimes overrun the boundaries I established. I fully believe that the strategies are distinct, but they can overlap in interesting ways. I leave it to the reader to make the overlapping connections between strategies within individual poems. I tried to strike a balance between having firm, well-delineated categories and flexible ones that are critic-, reader-, poem-, and poet-friendly. In other words, I did not want to isolate strategies in a mutually exclusive way. Levine's "They Feed They Lion" exemplifies a poem that shades into another type of poetic agency. Though its primary strategy is *particular equivocal agency*, Levine draws heavily on his own *experiential agency*. Yet he abstracts, disguises, and redirects that personal experience so as to conceal its connection to him in a transparent way. Further, this connection is understandable mostly due to his comments in interviews about the poem. "They Feed They Lion" thus shows *primarily* equivocal agency; only an extensive investigation reveals how experience shapes the poem.

Poems that evade strict categorization reveal the limitations of my (or any) theoretical framework, but they also reveal much about poets' nuanced approaches to political poetry. In this same vein, the poetry left out of this "comprehensive" book reveal much about *my* strategies, proclivities, and commitments. The political party "big tent" platform inevitably excludes capable participants and constituencies (or takes them for granted and thus ignores them). My big tent approach similarly leaves out some forms of political poetry. I did not include spoken word, performance, or slam poetry; I have thus omitted poems performed at vibrant, multicultural, political spaces such as El Puerto Rican Embassy, Nuyorican Poets' Café, Tía Chu Cha Café Cultural,

Def Poetry Jam, and local sites across the country.[1] A simple explanation for their exclusion is my knowledge of and passion for printed poetry and hip-hop rather than spoken word, but another is more convincing. Spoken-word poetry embodies voices and strategies that draw on the types of poetic agency detailed in this book. Performance pieces could conceivably fit into any of the agencies described here. Much slam poetry, moreover, utilizes the language/vernacular and contestatory urban agency of hip-hop music; hip-hop *also* draws on spoken-word traditions *and* grew out of them—Last Poets, Black Arts poets, signifying, and playing the dozens inform the fundamental aesthetics of hip-hop as well as spoken word.

Some readers may take issue with the poems I have chosen to discuss here. It is possible to find countless other poems that fit into the strategies I outline. I view this not as a problem but as a positive generative quality of my categories. That generation, after all, is part of the purpose of this project. To reiterate, I also chose to discuss poems by living, working poets. Thus, I did not include political poems by deceased poets (with the exception of the Notorious B.I.G.) such as June Jordan, Gwendolyn Brooks, Robert Lowell, Allen Ginsberg, Etheridge Knight, Audre Lorde, James Wright, Denise Levertov, and Ricardo Sánchez. Others may see an oversight in my decision to exclude Language Poetry (while yet other readers may cheer).[2] I believe, as many other critics and readers do, that though Language Poetry is certainly political in its conscious subversion of poetic tradition(s), commodified corporate language(s), and MFA workshop poetry, it fails as *a language of politics.* Another reason is the lack of human agency in most Language Poetry, which is one of my primary concerns in this book. Alicia Ostriker claims that Language Poetry is politically vacuous, despite its practitioners' insistences to the contrary, because it denies that "the morally responsible human subject is even theoretically possible" ("Beyond Confession" 35), a claim also advanced in part by Charles Altieri in "Without Consequences is No Politics." As I discussed in relation to Michael Palmer's "Sun," if the political content of a poem is obscured or inaccessible, it will likely fail as a political figure of voice.

In summary, then, this book explores the ways that poets engage pressing social and political realities and the ways they figure human agency. In chapter 1 I selected and analyzed poems of *embodied agency,* which include *experiential* and *authoritative agencies.* They support Adrienne Rich's claim that a poem is "not a philosophical or psychological blueprint; it's an instrument for embodied experience" (*What Is Found* 13). Poems of experiential agency, moreover, draw from what Muriel Rukeyser called poetry of "documentary fact" (cited in *What Is Found* 21) in commenting on historical events, but they also often foreground voices of experience with regard to historical conditions and trends rather than to specific events. These poems are sometimes criticized as mere documentary or polemic, especially when written by women or minorities, but they reimagine experience in ways that transform as they document. Poems of authoritative agency embody experience, but they extrapolate from that experience the authority to speak for entire communities in the traditions of Whitman and the griot. They are uncompromising, and their grave, urgent voices tackle directly pressing injustices. They do not, as poet David Mura writes, "surrender vast realms of experience" to the "objectivity" of disciplines such as journalism, economics, and political science as "the sole voice[s] which speak on events and topics of relevance to us all" (cited in *What Is Found* 121).

In chapter 2 I discussed two types of *equivocal agency, comprehensive* and *particular*. These strategies are often more difficult to describe than those of chapter 1. By nature, these poems are often indirect, mysterious, haunting, enchanting, duplicitous, or some combination thereof. They generally depart from simple linear narratives and from identifiable first-person speakers. They often have parodic, distant, satirical voices. For example, Simic uses first-person speakers, but they are ghostly, more present in their absence than in any physical body. His speakers and characters "vanish / With a touch of the hand" ("Cameo Appearance"). Poems of equivocal agency are primarily political through the imagination, which is itself the uncompromising force that refuses capitulation to repressive sociopolitical paradigms or the limitations of a poetry of experience.

In chapter 3 I discussed poems of *migratory agency*, which are not simply "hybrid." They do not foreground multiple languages in service of a hybrid, modern (or postmodern) art. Their figures of voice migrate between languages, cultures, worldviews, and geographies, and in doing so begin to challenge how we speak of America. The *skin* of these poems holds a multiplicity of living, breathing communities moving between languages and cultures. These poems—whether mostly in English or in Spanish—actively create a multicultural, multilingual poetry of the Americas and of the United States. They are, moreover, at the forefront of a burgeoning Latina/o century in U.S. literature and culture.

In chapter 4 I argued that hip-hop has a unique form of poetic agency activated by its progressive voices, live performances, and community-based values. The chapter captures only a small, but vibrant, part of the culture, nevertheless I believe that this part is critical to the culture's place as a dynamic political art, capable not only of poetic agency, but political agency in the public sphere. I hope that those readers familiar with hip-hop will find the chapter illuminating, innovative, and an impetus for further inquiry. For those readers familiar with hip-hop only through its dominant cultural images, I hope that chapter 4 offers an alternative perspective into the culture, and an entrance point into those aspects of it that elude mainstream publicity.

Now that I have summed up the four chapters, I want to consider a poem that has multiple poetic agencies. Then, following my reading of this poem, I discuss a poem that uses humor as its primary form of agency, before making some general conclusions about politics and poetry in the United States. In "The House Slave" former Poet Laureate (1993–1995) Rita Dove creates a figure of voice that imagines the first-person speaking "I" of a slave. The speaker narrates the poem contemporaneously as if she were present on a nineteenth-century plantation. She speaks in present-tense, active first-person verbs in order to describe the horrors of witnessing her family's mistreatment: "I watch them driven," "I cannot fall asleep again," "I lie on my cot," and "I weep" (29). The reader knows that Dove was not a slave herself, but the poem works because we are willing to go along with her experience of being an African American woman. Yet what is more important is the poet's and reader's temporal distance from slavery. Just as the house slave in the poem is insulated from the greatest suffering—she is inside and not subject to the horrors of the fields—and witnesses it from the window, the poet is both insulated by over one hundred years but still witnesses it through the window of the poem, the history that informs it, and the racism that still pervades American society. After all, do not hundreds of thousands of African American women keep house, so to speak, in large corporations and universities—"houses" run by rich white men? The poem enacts the isolation of the house slave, the isolation of the poet, and the suffering they both witness.

"The House Slave" has two overlapping types of poetic agency. It is a poem of experiential agency, but with a difference. There is the first-person speaking "I" witnessing and narrating. There is the reimagining of collective experience. There is the force of her status as an African American woman. But there is also a palpable discursive tension with equivocal agency. The scene she describes certainly happened, but it never happened to the poet or to anyone she has known. This poem thus illustrates how and why poems are not subject to evidentiary justification. Dove stages a voice of historical imagination and collective oppression. The voice is both hers and not hers. But the phrase *this did not happen* never enters my mind. The poem is convincing precisely because its speaker becomes not the poet's voice but the slave's.[3]

If poems such as Dove's span the agencies discussed here, others' voices do not fit into any of my categories. I want to reflect momentarily on just one—humor—and its possibilities in contemporary culture. One could make the claim that humor is one of the best political tools in twenty-first century U.S. society. *Chappelle's Show* and *South Park* are incisive political art, and Jon Stewart's "fake news" show *The Daily Show* has not only brilliantly subversive political commentary, it is also the most insightful *news* program on cable or network television. Parody and satire are tools in trade for comedians and for poets. Some contemporary American poems have striking humorous voices: Gregory Corso's "Marriage," Sylvia Plath's "Daddy," Martín Espada's "Revolutionary Spanish Lesson," Victor Hernández Cruz's "It's Miller Time," Gina Valdez's "English con Salsa" (discussed in chapter 3), Campbell McGrath's "Capitalist Poem #5," among countless others, including many by Alexie.[4] Since the Beats, the combination of subversive politics and humor has been a cornerstone of poetry as countercultural art.

Gary Soto's "Mexicans Begin Jogging" is an accomplished example of a contemporary poem that uses humor in a political, but subtle, way. In the poem, the speaker-poet narrates a worker's experience of fleeing a factory on a border patrol raid. Thinking he is an illegal immigrant, the boss yells at him, " 'Over the fence, Soto' " (cited in Suárez *Red, White, and Blues* 173). The speaker-poet protests that he is an American, but the boss insists and "press[es] / A dollar into [his] palm." So, he follows the running illegals "through the back door" saying to himself "I was on his [the boss's] time." The second stanza begins with the speaker-poet running with the others. The dominant image of this run is fascinating, absurd, and darkly comic; Soto styles it as a surreal road race—a marathon or charity race—that the Mexican factory workers join accidentally. They run "past the amazed crowds that lined / The street and blurred like photographs, in rain" and past "sociologists" who "clock" the speaker-poet as he goes past on a "jog into the next century / On the power of a great, silly grin." Because Soto's name appears in the poem, and because this technique is poetry faux pas, it likely points to an actual experience that was funny for just one participant—the poet. Thus, the image's comic absurdity for the speaker-poet opens the poem up to undertones of fear, ethnocentricity, xenophobia, repression, dangerous working conditions, and heartache for illegals. Soto's voice is humorous and political, even if it gains part of its edge from a position of privilege—legal U.S. citizen versus illegal Mexican immigrants. Humor, then, can be a viable, if occasionally risky, figure of voice in U.S. poetry, especially when it is used to comment on difficult political issues such as immigration.

PART TWO

I conclude here by returning to the overarching debates that frame this project in the preface and introduction. In 1949, when Muriel Rukeyser wrote that "anyone dealing with poetry and the love of poetry must deal, then, with the hatred of poetry, and perhaps even more with the indifference" (6), she was engaging a long tradition of poets who have felt compelled to view poetry through the lens of its detractors. In eighth-century China, for instance, Tu Fu "brood[ed] on the uselessness of letters," lamenting that "Poetry and letters / Persist in silence and solitude." What good is poetry, he asked, when his country is "Overrun with war" and citizens view poets with "contempt"? (cited in Rexroth *One Hundred* 6, 29, 8, 15). Rukeyser's suggestion that the "economy of the nation" and the "empire of business" within it "both include in their basic premise the concept of perpetual warfare" (61) still rings true—if the United States exists in a state of "perpetual warfare," poetry will always face contempt and indifference.

Tu Fu articulated better than most the strained relationship between poetry and a society at perpetual war. His poems were valued in the T'ang Dynasty for their *Yi*, or Confucian moral instruction, as well as for their rigorously rule-bound verse. During the second half of his life Tu Fu became increasingly concerned with the ravages of war, and for good reason. In AD 742, the Chinese census numbered nearly fifty million; in AD 764—just twenty-two years later—there were approximately seventeen million citizens. The capital city of Chang-an, where Buddhists, Taoists, Christians, Jews, and Manicheans held counsel together, was destroyed in a bloody rebellion. Tu Fu—a descendent of thirteen generations of Confucian literati and an exile from Chang-an—and his poetry show an obsession with poetry's place in war.[5] The twenty-first century, then, is more similar to Tu Fu's than not. Though the wide-scale devastation now happens in places other than the United States, those who make war and those who make poetry are still at odds.[6]

The debate about the usefulness of poetry began in earnest in the United States in 1991 with the appearance of poet-critic Dana Gioia's "Can Poetry Matter?" in *The Atlantic*. Nothing, however, has been resolved or calcified in this debate but the debate itself. As mentioned in the preface, the debate pits—centuries after Tu Fu—those who want to make poetry "obviously important" and those disparate factions who want to disparage poetry as useless at best, an obstruction to might and power at worst.[7] My goal here is not to stake my own claim in this debate; I mention it simply as a checkpoint on the way to a more critical question. In lamenting the *place* of poetry in U.S. culture, many critics miss most of its *places*. Tu Fu wrote, in the poem that laments poetry's solitude, "Everywhere the workers sing wild songs" (29). These songs, the poem suggests, thrive and inspire even as we lament for "poetry." Poetry, then, is song—Bob Dylan's, Bright Eyes's, and Jill Scott's; slave spirituals and working-class chants in stands of soccer stadiums in Quito and Lima; and Rita Dove's, June Jordan's, Anthony Hecht's, Simon Ortiz's, Li-Young Lee's, and Def Poetry Jam. But it is also the force that inspires, enchants, and mobilizes poor city youth the world over in the many forms of hip-hop music, in Tokyo, New York, Cape Town, Mexico City, Vancouver, and Los Angeles. What is needed in the debate about poetry, and what I have tried to create in this book, is a wider frame of reference for poetry and for the criticism that should nurture, challenge, and promote it.

The terms of the debate, in other words, have not kept up with the object of the debate. Poetry reinvents itself, much as hip-hop does, as it goes, and our critical understanding of it lags behind. David Haven Blake's recent article "Reading Whitman, Growing up Rock 'n' Roll" claims that if Whitman were alive in the 1960s and 1970s instead of one hundred years previously, he would have been a rock star or folk singer-songwriter.[8] Bob Dylan has mentioned in passing that if he were born in the 1970s or 1980s he would be a rapper rather than a singer. These two anecdotes suggest that poetry—both performed and printed—reifies itself in unpredictable ways over time. Critics, unfortunately, have a difficult time keeping up with the changes and the ways that poetry lives and reinvents itself in the margins.

Both anecdotes also indicate that poetry is reifying as a musical rather than literary form. Poets such as Joy Harjo, Miguel Algarín, Sherman Alexie, and others perform their poetry with bands. Robert Hass's comments about the political nature of rhythm point directly to the power of poetry and music together: "Because rhythm has direct access to the unconscious, because it can hypnotize us, enter our bodies and make us move, it is power. And power is political." He claims that the relationship between rhythm and power makes rhythm a perpetual "revolutionary ground." Rhythm, he continues, "announces the abolition of tradition" (*Twentieth Century* 108). Hip-hop and performed poetry, then, foreground this relationship in creating revolutionary ground that announces the abolition of printed poetic traditions. These poetries enter listeners' bodies and make them move.

Despite the possibility that much mainstream rap music implicitly promotes conservative values—a claim made by performance poet, MC, and actor Saul Williams—it can unleash the political powers of rhythm in ways that printed poetry often cannot.[9] When I began thinking about, researching, and writing this book, I was asked if I had an image in mind of the "perfect political poem." My answer then was silence, now it is more certain: a hip-hop song, precisely because it *moves* me in a way that the printed page often cannot. I get chills when I read a striking poem, but when I hear a remarkable hip-hop song, I get chills and nod my head to the rhythm. Additionally, the physical experience of live hip-hop gives songs more experiential resonance and memorial power than printed poems. Public Enemy's "Black Steel in the Hour of Chaos" (1988)—which I listened to for the first time at twelve years old, not yet capable of understanding its subtleties and extended metaphors—is a potential choice.[10] It engages a long tradition of African American art's eloquent, angry depiction of the quest for freedom from oppression, from Claude McKay's "If We Must Die" to Robert Hayden's *Middle Passage* to *Invisible Man* to Toni Morrison's *Beloved*.

To my twenty-first century sensibilities, Public Enemy's song sounds more powerful, and immediate, than these predecessors. The booming amplification, directness, urgency, and conviction of Chuck D's voice resonate more than the sound of my own voice when I read even the most moving political poem. Whereas hip-hop has more sound bites suitable for political pronouncement than does printed poetry, partly because songs are often more immediately accessible than poems, the political power of hip-hop is attributable not only to live performance, lyrical content, and rhythm—it is in the *voice* of the performer. In finishing up the final draft of chapter 4 I discovered a difference in how I write about voice in that chapter compared to the first three, where I use "speaker," "narrator," or occasionally "speaker-poet" in describing a poem's figures of voice. In chapter 4, I never use "speaker" or "narrator." I use, albeit awkwardly, "persona" when discussing a Notorious B.I.G. song, but I mostly use the artist's name.

For example, I write "J-Live raps" or "Mr. Lif claims." I have come to believe that this difference is not merely one of convention or personal preference. Even though rappers rhetorically stage a variety of voices and personas in their songs, their voices are more direct than the voices in printed poems. The *sound* of the human voice in all its inflections, intonations, rhythms, and emotions makes hip-hop more immediate and personal. When Rich wrote about how "the art of the griot, performed in alliance with music and dance" can be used "to evoke and catalyze a community or communities against passivity and victimization," I think she had in mind this immediacy and urgency. This use of voice, appropriately, is "at the heart of the renascence of poetry as an oral art" (*What Is Found* 86).

Hip-hop voices, too, show us that we live in a country at "perpetual war," in which poetry and institutional powers are at odds. Many rappers suggest that there is no reprieve in urban ghettoes from the conditions of war. Mobb Deep's "Survival of the Fittest" (1995) expresses this notion best—"there's a war going on outside no man is safe from"—and KRS-One, in the epigraph in the introduction to this book, raps that *poetry* must "conquer it [war] and its law." If the United States as global hegemonic power is in a state of perpetual warfare, then questions about authority and usefulness will always hound poetry. Poets will always face varying pressures—to tackle geopolitical realities, to evade them, to feign indifference, to defend poetry, to lament poetry's place in the world, to create images of justice, possibility, and community. As such, the various articles and books that appear every so often about "the writer in wartime" or some deviation thereof are slightly off the mark. If poets take for their imaginative realm the entire world, then there is never a time when the debates about "the writer in wartime" do not apply, especially because the United States is at least minimally implicated in most conflicts. If there's not a war on directly involving the United States, there is one brewing, or one in a country from which many have immigrated to the United States. Or, there is one on that cultivates the disgust, sympathy, or fear of U.S. citizens, some of whom are poets. As Galway Kinnell writes in "When the Towers Fell," the searchlight that look for bodies "always goes on / somewhere, now in New York and Kabul," soon Baghdad, Darfur, Uzbekistan, London. And, as Martin Luther King, Jr., said in his famous Riverside Church speech of April 4, 1967: "A nation that continues year after year to spend more on military defense than on programs of social uplift is approaching spiritual death" (King). This "spiritual death" is exactly what poets and poetry fights against and exactly why poetry remains at odds with a society at "perpetual war."

This context, in other words, is inescapable. In a column in *The American Book Review* (2005) appropriately titled "The Writer in Wartime," Harold Jaffe debunks the illusory binary between "committed or engaged writing" and "so-called autonomous writing," which he says is a "quintessential" American notion. In other countries, he points out, committed writing does not face "condescension." Jaffe debunks as nonsense the argument that writers need independence from events in the world to maintain artistic integrity. He says that the "restrictive imaginative repertory" (no political themes) of MFA programs and many journals and presses does not make a writer independent, but the opposite. Jaffe cites South African Nobel Laureate J.M. Coetzee's claims that all writers should *promote* works of literature "as instruments of action" and social change because "it is not in the interest of those who actually wield power to disabuse anyone" of the idea that literature is ineffective, just idle people playing with words while the powerful make decisions about real issues (3, 6).

It is always wartime and the writer is never autonomous. Poetry is thus always "a reflection of and a response to contemporary culture" (Jaffe 3). But a question persists: What *authority* do poets have to write about war, genocide, poverty, capitalism, globalization, and other issues? Jaffe's suggestions, to me, are incomplete. He says that writers have authority from three primary conditions: they have freedom from a 9 to 5 job and thus more time to think, they are not "beholden" to "benefactors," and they can publish and thus distribute their ideas to readers (3). I believe, however, that writers have no more *authority* than other citizens to speak about injustice. They are simply better at the speaking than other citizens, so they have a type of authority from their creative talents. Yet discussing a writer's authority misses the point. The issue is not authority but *power*. Who has the *power* to speak? This is why it is crucial that at least some poets and rappers stay engaged with geopolitical and sociopolitical realities. They have powers that most citizens do not. They do not have the power of CEOs, bankers, politicians, filmmakers, and the wealthy, but poets and rappers have the power of their voices and visions, and if they can make it through the interferences of the corporate world, the potential ability to disrupt the hegemony of that world.

When we speak of *authority* in debates about poetry's usefulness, we mean *power*. And I think that there is an underlying fear of poets, rappers, and artists gaining traction against elite corporate and governmental forces that control the flow of ideas. I end then with Charles Molesworth's rhetorical questions about Gary Snyder's "authority" as a citizen-poet because it suggests that power, not authority, is the issue at hand. He asks, "Can Snyder claim for his (or can his readers claim on his behalf) any authority other than that of the aesthetic realm?" Molesworth then goes on to ask if it is possible to understand Snyder's "notion that trees and animals should be represented in Congress" as "anything but an amusing [literary] conceit." We have to *believe*, as Coetzee suggests, that it is much more than a simple conceit. Molesworth allows that Snyder's claim might be a "serious critique of representational government" because "banks and corporations command a share of representative power in our legislatures, and they are no more capable of speaking for themselves, without human mediation, than are trees and animals." He concludes, asking "If humans can find a way to define the rights of a corporation, why can they not do the same for the forest?" (154–155). What *representative power* do poems and rap songs have? The power readers, listeners, critics, poets, rappers, and citizens ascribe to them. And, unfortunately, what power corporate moguls, politicians, and moneyed interests cede to them. As both a critic and a poet, I am ready to give American poets who work in print and in song the power to start the widespread shift in consciousness needed to make this country and world a more just and equitable place. That, after all, is *faith* in poetry, in the human voice itself.

Notes

Introduction: Political Poetry in the United States

1. I use "rap" and "hip-hop" interchangeably in this book. I usually prefer the term "hip-hop" because I see it as more inclusive and encompassing. Most critics use the terms interchangeably, as do most in the culture. Some artists, though, see rap as a style of music, hip-hop as the larger culture of which rap is a part. KRS-One, for instance, draws a distinction between rap "as something you do" and hip-hop as "something you live," in other words a culture. Hip-hop culture includes four basic elements—rapping, dj'ing, graffiti writing, and breakdancing. See the liner notes to *KRS-One: A Retrospective.* I also use the terms "rapper," "MC," and "hip-hop artist" interchangeably.

2. It should be noted that Walt Whitman's understanding of the poet's public role as people's representative influenced many of these Latin American poets, even if indirectly. In "Song of Myself," he writes, "It is you talking just as much myself . . . I act as the tongue of you, / It was tied in your mouth . . . in mine it begins to be loosened" (lines 1244–1245). For an analysis of Whitman's debatable influence on Latin American poets, see Enrico Mario Santí's "The Accidental Tourist: Walt Whitman in Latin America" in *Do the Americas Have a Common Literature?*, ed. Gustavo Pérez Firmat (Durham, NC: Duke UP, 1990), 156–176.

3. See Stephen Burt's "Portability; or, The Traveling Uses of a Poetic Idea" in *Modern Philology* 100.1 (2002): 24–49, for an in-depth discussion about this issue. He asks, "How far can we take a poem—and a person—before they cease to be what they were?" (28).

4. See Terry Eagleton's overview of Gadamer's Hermeneutics in *Literary Theory* (New York: Oxford UP, 1984).

5. See Don L. Lee, "From a Black Perspective," *Don't Cry, Scream* (Detroit: Broadside P, 1969).

6. Zinn cites these particularly powerful lines from the poem: "Rise like lions after slumber / In unvanquishable number! / Shake your chains to earth, like dew / Which in sleep had fallen on you— / Ye are many, they are few!"

7. However, as contemporary U.S. politics show, political discourse may appear to be clear, but much is smoke and mirrors and deception. Giddens, for example, believes ideology is primarily rhetorical. It is the form argument takes in the public sphere. In other words, the speeches given to the public usually appeal to universal needs or welfare. There is

thus a striking contrast between the "front" and the "back" where the "front" is the appeal to general welfare (for instance, "what's good for General Motors is good for the country") and the "back" is the underlying, unspoken intent (to siphon off wealth to the rich at the expense of local communities and workers).

8. Adrienne Rich's now famous proclamation appeared in its inchoate form in 1971 in "When We Dead Awaken: Writing as Re-Vision," cited here in the Norton Critical Edition of *Adrienne Rich's Poetry and Prose* (New York: W.W. Norton, 1993), 166–177: "I think I began at this point to feel that politics was not something 'out there' but something 'in here' and of the essence of my condition."

9. See McGann's *The Romantic Ideology: A Critical Investigation* (Chicago: U of Chicago P, 1985).

10. Dove's "Parsley," which explores the brutal actions of Rafael Trujillo, former dictator of the Dominican Republic, has two sections. The first is a nonrhyming villanelle, the second a sestina. See *Selected Poems* (133–135).

11. See Helen Vendler's *The Breaking of Style: Hopkins, Heaney, Graham* (Boston: Harvard UP, 1995) for a discussion of why and how these three poets changed their style from poem to poem as well as over their careers.

12. See Levertov "On the Edge of Darkness: What is Political Poetry?," von Hallberg's Introduction to *Politics and Poetic Value*, and Ostriker's "Dancing at the Devil's Party: Some Notes on Politics and Poetry," in von Hallberg's *Politics and Poetic Value*.

13. See Gibbons's discussion of Burke (280–281).

14. See Barthes's *Roland Barthes by Roland Barthes* (Berkeley: U of California P, 1994). Also see Paul de Man's "Autobiography as defacement" in *Deconstruction: A Reader*, ed. Martin McQuillan (New York: Routledge, 2001), 171–174. The controversy in Winter 2006 about the veracity of James Frey's memoir *A Million Little Pieces* popularized debates about truth, experience, memoir, and autobiography.

15. In the last decade there has been a shift in mainstream hip-hop into rural places, especially in the South. Groups such as Nappy Roots show that hip-hop can be thoroughly rural. In fact, traditions such as playing the dozens and signifying, which have contributed greatly to core hip-hop values, have rural roots.

16. Clear Channel owns over 1,200 radio stations and controls 70% of major live music venues in the United States. See Damien Cave's "Clear Channel: Inside Music's Superpower" in *Rolling Stone*, September 2, 2004, 53–56, for background on the corporate influence on recorded and live music.

CHAPTER I   EMBODIED AGENCY

1. Poetry and testimonio are very different traditions. See Silvia N. Rosman's essay on Neruda for an example of how they have been studied together.

For background on testimonio, see Beverley's *Against Literature* (Minneapolis: U of Minnesota P, 1989); the Gugelberger edited *The Real Thing*; and two special issues of *Latin American Perspectives* titled *Voices of the Voiceless in Testimonial Literature* (18.3 (Summer 1991): 1–120 and 18.4 (Autumn 1991): 1–120) edited by Gugelberger and Michael Kearney. The premier example of testimonio is *Me llamo Rigoberta Menchú y así me nació la conciencia* as told to Elisabeth Burgos by Guatemalan Indian activist and Nobel Peace Prize–winner Rigoberta Menchú (Barcelona: Editorial Argos Vergara, S.A., 1983).

2. See Jonathan Levin's *The Poetics of Transition: Emerson, Pragmatism, & American Literary Modernism* (New Americanists Series. Ed. Donald E. Pease. Durham, NC: Duke UP, 1999), which draws on Emerson, Dewey, James, and Santayana, for further discussion of Wallace Stevens's understanding of the dynamic between resistance and evasion, especially in relationship to imagination. See pages 87–89. Levin writes, "Imagination responds to material conditions—natural, social, and cultural—and has no possible existence apart from them" (88).

3. Was Komunyakaa familiar with Forché's poem when he wrote "We Never Know"? Given that Forché's book is well known, I assume that Komunyakaa was aware of "The Colonel." Whether or not he consciously imitated her line is uncertain. This argument on Komunyakaa draws on my article "Working in the Space of Disaster: Yusef Komunyakaa's Dialogues with America," *Callaloo: A Journal of African Diaspora Arts & Letters* 28.3 (2005): 812–823.

4. Tim O'Brien's "The Man I Killed" (*The Things They Carried*) deals with how collective guilt overwhelms even soldiers who did not kill a Vietnamese soldier personally, only *saw* one killed.

5. In this book I use the term "stanza" for simplicity and convenience. Though some critics would insist that a "stanza" is part of a formal, metered poem, and that a "stanza" in a free verse poem should be called a "verse paragraph," I find the semantic difference unnecessary. If it looks like a stanza, I call it a stanza. For instance, I would call the first six free verse lines of Merwin's "For a Coming Extinction" (*The Lice* 1967) a "stanza" because it is a self-contained unit of lines separated from the next "stanza" by a blank line:

> Gray whale
> Now that we are sending you to The End
> That great god
> Tell him
> That we who follow you invented forgiveness

6. This object position is important in that it reflects the African American male's historical position as an object to be used and ultimately rejected by the dominant culture; it also suggests the African American *subject*'s historically compromised agency in American society.

7. The best creative work on the "official story" occurs in O'Brien's *The Things They Carried* (1990). See "How to Tell a True War Story" for perspective on objectivity in the context of war.

8. Gibbons explains that exteriorism was developed by Cardenal in response to the abstractions, romanticism, and symbolism of Latin American poetry in the 1960s and 1970s. Cardenal's poetics have "a diction that is concrete and detailed with proper names and the names of things in preference to the accepted poetic language, which was more abstract, general, and vaguely symbolic" ("Political" 278).

9. Altieri's conception of this visionary leap in 1980s poetry is strikingly similar to von Hallberg's understanding of much Vietnam-era poetry.

10. Collins's poem (76–77) has eerie reverberations with Uruguayan Cristina Peri Rossi's story "El prócer," which is about the life, geopolitical ramifications, and malleability of a war memorial statue in an unnamed Latin American plaza.

11. See "The Ethics of Living Jim Crow: An Autobiographical Sketch" for the humiliations of giving concessions to white people and "staying in your place." See also "Fire and Cloud" for the tension between active resistance and protest and the need to "wait" and be patient, both in *Uncle Tom's Children* (1938; New York: Perennial, 1993). See also *The Best of Nina Simone* (New York: Polygram Records, Inc. 1969).

12. In "The Black Arts Movement and Its Critics" David L. Smith suggests that "Black Arts writing directly addressed a black audience." As such, it "demands of its reader (or listener) a sympathy and familiarity with black culture and black idioms" (102). In contrast, Phillip Brian Harper's essay "Nationalism and Social Division in Black Arts Poetry of the 1960s" claims that "The True Import" has its "maximum impact" when "understood as being *heard* directly by whites and *over*heard by blacks" (247; original emphasis).

13. See U.S. congressman and former SNCC leader John Lewis's memoir of the civil rights movement for an excellent interpretation of the tension between working within existing political structures and an unyielding and uncompromising dedication to social change. See Lewis with Michael D'Orso, *Walking with the Wind: A Memoir of the Movement* (New York: Simon & Schuster, 1998).

14. Rich's strategic use of apostrophe is both clever and perhaps self-defeating. It certainly challenges readers to understand the import of their inactions; however, Rich's audience is likely already acutely aware of social justice issues. This poem might be an example of "preaching to the choir."

15. Many readers remotely familiar with hip-hop may instantly object that hip-hop is no longer a "fugitive means of expression" because it is so commercially successful, ubiquitous in many different media, and supported heavily by suburban white kids. These readers have a legitimate point, one that I explore in chapter four.

16. See Ben Lee's " *'Howl' and Other Poems:* Is There Old Left in These New Beats?" in *American Literature* 76.2 (June 2004): 367–389, for a discussion of Allen Ginsberg's use of anaphora and "who" in *Howl.* Ginsberg's use of "who" to begin lines is a precursor and likely influence on Baraka's "who" lines in "Somebody Blew up America." Lee writes about *Howl:* "The form of the poem leads us to wonder when exactly—and with whom—these actions and attitudes originate. Through force of repetition, one might say, the relative pronoun 'who' becomes interrogative, and the form of Ginsberg's poem subtly undermines the notion that generations break away cleanly" (383).

17. It is crucial not to mistake AAVE or other vernaculars as improper or inferior. They are systematic, dynamic, rule-based variations on SAE rather than lesser versions of English.

18. See Michael J. Sidnell's essay "Yeats's 'Written Speech': Writing, Hearing, and Performance" in *Yeats Annual* 11 (1995): 3–11, for an analysis of how Yeats's "Adam's Curse" stages spoken voices. Yeats's rhetorical staging and Sidnell's discussion of it influenced my understanding of the two spoken voices in Forché's "Return."

19. Joan Didion's *Salvador* (Washington Square P, 1983) is a short, captivating, impressionistic sketch of El Salvador during this time period. One passage particularly resonates with Forché's poem. Didion writes, "Whenever I hear someone speak now of one or another *solución* for El Salvador I think of particular Americans who have spent time there, each in his or her own way inextricably altered by the fact of having been in a certain place at a certain time. Some of these Americans have since moved on and others remain in Salvador, but like survivors of a common natural disaster, they are equally marked by the place" (98; original emphasis).

20. César Vallejo's "Un hombre pasa con un pan . . ." ("A Man Walks by with a Stick of Bread . . .") offers an alternative justification. It suggests that poetry (especially intellectual poetry) is difficult, if not impossible, to write in the face of human poverty and suffering. See *César Vallejo: The Complete Posthumous Poetry,* trans. Clayton Eshleman and José Rubia Barcia (Berkeley: U of California P, 1979), 176–177.

Chapter 2   Equivocal Agency

1. As noted in chapter one, this discussion is not to imply that all poems in chapter two are about war. War simply provides an accessible and easily illustrated context with which to frame the ways that poems of equivocal agency depart from poems of experiential agency.

2. For present purposes, I do not make a stark distinction between magic realism and the fantastic real, as originally advanced by Cuban writer Alejo Carpentier. For background, consult Alberto Ríos's website on

magic realism: <http://www.public.asu.edu/~aarios/resourcebank/definitions/>.

3. In *The Afro-American Novel and Its Tradition* (1987), Bernard W. Bell briefly discusses the dynamic between truth of sensation and truth of fact in relation to Morrison. See the chapter on Poetic Realism.

4. For further reading on trauma theory, see Cathy Caruth's *Unclaimed Experience*; Shoshana Felman and Dori Laub's *Testimony: Crises of Witnessing in Literature, Psychoanalysis, and History* (New York: Routledge, 1992); Cassie Premo Steele's *We Heal from Memory*; Kai T. Erikson's *Everything in Its Path: Destruction of Community in the Buffalo Creek Flood* (New York: Simon and Schuster, 1976); Richard J. McNally's *Remembering Trauma* (Boston: Belknap/Harvard UP, 2003); and Frederick Crews's "The Trauma Trap."

5. See Albee's *The American Dream* (New York: Coward-McCann, 1961), Baraka's *Dutchman* (New York: Morrow Quill Paperbacks, 1964), and Dragún's *Historia del hombre que se convirtió en perro (History of the Man Who Was Converted into a Dog*; 1957. *Aproximaciones al estudio de la literatura hispánica.* 5th ed. New York: McGraw Hill, 2004: 282–288). Also see Leslie Catherine Sanders's chapter on Jones/Baraka and her discussion of the Theater of Cruelty in *The Development of Black Theater in America*.

6. Hurricane Katrina and its aftermath in New Orleans and along the Gulf Coast brought these faces and ministrations to the shores of the United States in late summer 2005. See Spike Lee's *When the Levees Broke: A Requiem in Four Acts* (A Spike Lee Film, HBO, 2006) for a captivating look at the lives behind these disconnected media images.

7. In the novel *Reservation Blues* (New York: Grove P, 1995), Sherman Alexie expresses a similar sentiment, in this case in relationship to music: "Big Mom played a new flute song every morning to remind everybody that music created and recreated the world daily" (10).

8. In *Beloved* (New York: Vintage International, 1987), Morrison writes, with regard to the relationship between schoolteacher (the brutal slaveholder) and Sixo, his slave: "schoolteacher beat him anyway to show him that definitions belonged to the definers—not the defined" (225). As in the Thylias Moss poem discussed in chapter two, Morrison and Harjo suggest the importance of *redefinition* to freedom and autonomy.

9. There are thirteen years between *The Country Between Us* and *The Angel of History*. Editing the voluminous *Against Forgetting* by many accounts took a remarkable amount of Forché's time. In a 1988 interview, Forché hints that work on *The Angel of History* had already been underway for years. See her interview with Montenegro.

10. Palmer's reference to Benjamin in one of the series of title poems suggests interesting connections. The line "This is how one pictures the angel of history" (227) directly quotes Benjamin. The title of Forché's book and the inclusion of the entire passage from Benjamin's work as

an epigraph indicate that whatever their differences, Palmer and Forché share theoretical influences.

11. These examples are from Richard Wilbur's "Grace" (1947) and Adrienne Rich's "The Uncle Speaks in the Drawing Room" (1951). See von Hallberg's *American Poetry* (129–130).

12. In the essay at the conclusion of *Selected Poems*, Bly writes that he used this line in *The Teeth Mother Naked at Last* (1970), but I argue that it applies especially well to "Counting Small-Boned Bodies."

13. In their introduction to *W.S. Merwin: Essays on the Poetry* (1987), Folsom and Nelson point out that the word "enigma" became a prominent "part of the vocabulary" in writings about Merwin's poetry beginning in the mid-1960s (9).

14. Much the opposite may actually be true. See John Perkins's *Confessions of an Economic Hit Man* (San Francisco: Berrett-Koehler Publishers, 2004), a memoir about the American "corporatocracy" that keeps developing nations under its economic and political control through, among other things, massive World Bank loans, IMF structural adjustment programs, and incentives to liberalize their economies.

15. Poems such as "Saturday Sweeping" (*They Feed They'Lion*) and "On the Birth of Good & Evil during the Long Winter of '28" and "For the Poets of Chile" (*The Names of the Lost* 1976) are more indicative of Levine's narrative voice and use of experience than is "They Feed."

16. These lines appear in *Requiem for a Nun* (1951; New York: Vintage, 1975).

17. Robert Kroetsch's "Sketches of a Lemon" (1981) is one of the best poems to sound off on Stevens's poem. Unlike Moss's poem, Kroetsch's is playful, irreverent, and unconcerned with sociopolitical issues. See Kroetsch, "Sketches of a Lemon" in *The Contemporary Canadian Poem Anthology*, Vol. 3, ed. George Bowering (Toronto: Coach House, 1983), 162–176.

18. This "Problem" and "Solution" section is reminiscent of Merwin's "Some Last Questions" (*The Lice* 1967), except that Moss's eerie solutions are often more literal (even if absurd) than Merwin's surreal, disconnected images.

19. In Chapter 42 of Melville's *Moby Dick*, "The Whiteness of the Whale," Ishmael describes how disconcerting Moby Dick's whiteness is for sailors. He goes into a lengthy treatise about how whiteness "typifies the majesty of Justice" (192) as well as the way it "exaggerates" the "terror of objects otherwise terrible" (197). See *Moby Dick; or The Whale*, ed. and intro. Tony Tanner (New York: Oxford UP, 1988).

20. Brazilian photographer Sebastião Salgado's *Migrations: Humanity in Transition* (New York: Aperture P, 2000) has been acclaimed as well as scorned for its photographs of refugees and displaced people (from war, environmental disaster, and migration to cities) in the hypercities of Asia, the Americas, and Africa. They suggest that it is possible to make beautiful the horrific despite questions of appropriation and

exploitation. Susan Sontag's criticism of Salgado is especially fierce in "Looking at War: Photography's View of Devastation and Death" (*The New Yorker* December 9, 2002). For an alternative view, see Ian Parker's "A Cold Light: Sebastião Salgado sails to Antarctica" (*The New Yorker* April 18, 2005).

CHAPTER 3 MIGRATORY AGENCY

1. Among numerous books that generally fit this paradigm are: Altieri's *Self and Sensibility in Contemporary American Poetry* (1984), which includes Creeley, Rich, Ashbery, Merrill, Hass, and others; Nick Halpern's *Domestic and Prophetic: The Poetry of Lowell, Ammons, Merrill, and Rich* (2003); Jerome Mazzaro's *Postmodern American Poetry* (Chicago: U of Illinois P, 1980), which includes Auden, Jarrell, Roethke, Ignatow, Berryman, Plath, and Bishop; and James E.B. Breslin's *From Modern to Contemporary: American Poetry, 1945–1965* (Chicago: U of Chicago P, 1984), which includes Ginsberg, Lowell, Levertov, Wright, and O'Hara.

2. Chicana/o refers to those of Mexican descent born in the United States. Latina/o is a more encompassing term used to refer to all people in the United States of Latin American descent. I use them accordingly. See Suzanne Oboler's *Ethnic Labels, Latino Lives: Identity and the Politics of (Re)Presentation in the United States* (Minneapolis: U of Minnesota P, 1995) for a thorough exploration of how these markers develop and how they affect the lives of whom they are attached.

3. For a concise history of the United Fruit Company, Guatemala, and the 1954 CIA-orchestrated coup, see Richard H. Immerman, *The CIA in Guatemala: The Foreign Policy of Intervention* (Austin: The U of Texas P, 1982), 68–82.

4. Bly's translation of Neruda's "La United Fruit Co.": "When the trumpet sounded, it was / all prepared on the earth, / and Jehovah parceled out the earth / to Coca-Cola, Inc., Anaconda, / Ford Motors, and other entities." See *Neruda and Vallejo: Selected Poems*, ed. Bly, trans. Bly, John Knoepfle, and James Wright (Boston: Beacon P, 1971), 84–87.

5. In *The Writing of the Disaster*, Maurice Blanchot suggests that language and writing are incapable of mastery: "To want to write: what an absurdity. Writing is the decay of the will, just as it is the loss of power, and the fall of the regular fall of the beat, disaster again" (11). For a short story about the dangers of "mastery," see Angela Carter's "Master" in *Fireworks: Nine Profane Pieces* (New York: Penguin Books, 1974), 78–87.

6. See *Scene from the Movie "Giant"* (Willimantic, CT: Curbstone P, 1993). For an analysis of Chicana/o identity in *Giant*, see Pérez-Torres's "Chicano Ethnicity, Cultural Hybridity, and the Mestizo Voice," *American Literature* 70.1 (1998): 153–176.

7. See Anne Shea's " 'Don't Let Them Make You Feel You Did a Crime': Immigration Law, Labor Rights, and Farmworker Testimony" in *MELUS* 28.1 (Spring 2003): 123–144, for an in-depth discussion of this issue.

8. There seem to be substantially more epigraphs in bilingual than in monolingual poems. See, for example, Villanueva's "I Too Have Walked My Barrio Streets" (*Shaking Off the Dark* 51–54), where the Spanish epigraph is from Neruda, the opposite of the case in "Nuestros abuelos." Another example is Maurice Kilwein Guevara's "The Easter Revolt Painted on a Tablespoon," in *Poems of the River Spirit* (Pittsburgh, PA: U of Pittsburgh P, 1996), 55.

9. Although the concept of markedness was developed by Roman Jakobson and the Prague School of Linguistics and later conceived as a Markedness model by Carol Myers-Scotton to account for code switching in speech, for current purposes it is most simply elucidated by Mendieta-Lombardo and Cintron.

10. See José Montoya's "Pacheco Pass," in *In Formation: 20 Years of Joda* (Aztlán: Chusma House Publications, 1992), 81–82; See also Sandra M. Castillo's "Rincón," in *Paper Dance: 55 Latino Poets*, eds. Leroy V. Quintana Cruz and Virgil Suárez (New York: Persea Books, 1995), 16, for examples of migratory agency similar to "Nuestros abuelos."

11. The image, language, and voice in the lines "Los recuerdo en la sangre, / la sangre fértil" echoes Montoya's lines "la sangre de / La Raza" in "Pacheco Pass" (see the previous footnote).

12. This change is already happening. The prominence of Spanish place-names in the United States and the popularity of Latin music are two prominent examples.

13. While walking past a T-shirt kiosk at a recent street fair in Manhattan's Little Italy, I noticed a T-shirt screen printed with these words: "Welcome to the U.S. Now Speak English!" This couplet captures perfectly the sentiment I discuss here regarding "English con Salsa."

14. See Mexican Victor Hugo Rascón Banda's play "La mujer que cayó del cielo" (*The Woman Who Fell from the Sky*) (Mexico City: Escenología, A.C., 2000) for a trilingual (Spanish, English, and Tarahumara) commentary on cultural and linguistic miscommunication. It is based on the true story of Rita Quintero, an indigenous woman from Mexico who appeared in a small Kansas town in the early 1980s without a clue as to how she arrived there.

15. Balaban's translation of Borisov's "Let Him Be," *New Orleans Review* 11.1 (1984): 82 is one of my favorite contemporary translations. Balaban's *Spring Essence: The Poetry of Ho Xuan Huong* (Port Townsend, WA: Copper Canyon P, 2000) has garnered critical acclaim, commercial success, and controversy. Ho Xuan Huong was an eighteenth-century Vietnamese poet, and some Vietnamese believe she never existed and that hers was a pen name for a male government official. For other Vietnamese, she is a national hero.

16. Some of the finest examples appear in *Canto y Grito Mi Liberación* (1971; Washington State UP, Pullman, 1995). See especially: "and it . . ."; "migrant lament . . ."; and "smile out the revolú." For a critical study, see Miguel R. López's *Chicano Timespace: The Poetry and Politics of Ricardo Sánchez* (College Station: Texas A&M UP, 2001).

CHAPTER 4   CONTESTATORY URBAN AGENCY

1. See Eagleton's discussion of Iser in *Literary Theory* and Iser's *The Implied Reader: Patterns in Communication in Prose Fiction from Bunyan to Beckett* (Baltimore: Johns Hopkins UP, 1974).

2. LeRoi Jones's "Black Art" first appeared in the *Liberator* (1966). It established many of the commitments and aesthetics of the Black Arts Movement.

3. This claim has been borne out by Bill Moyers. See "Bill Moyers's Keynote Address: Call to Renewal," in *Sojourners Magazine* (August 2004), on-line at <www.sojo.net>.

4. One of hip-hop's most portable conspiracy theories is the CIA's orchestration of the late 1980s crack cocaine epidemic and the agency's connections with Latin American drug cartels. For ample evidence and sources for these claims, see Parenti's *Democracy for the Few* (156).

5. See Butler's *Bodies that Matter: On the Discursive Limits of "Sex"* (New York: Routledge, 1993). See the introduction for a discussion of citationality, interpolation, and naming in the construction of gender.

6. Though I know that B.I.G. (as Christopher Wallace) was once a drug dealer, I implicitly argue here that all rappers stage or perform personas that depart from their lived experiences. Arguments about "authenticity" have long been central to hip-hop culture, and though these questions bear on the argument advanced in this book, they are not central to them.

7. Smaller clubs such as S.O.B.'s in Manhattan, North Six in Brooklyn, the 9:30 Club in D.C., and Five Spot in Philadelphia feature cutting-edge hip-hop on a regular basis.

8. See Kenneth W. Warren's "Ralph Ellison and the Problem of Cultural Authority," *boundary* 2.30.2 (2003): 157–174, for a discussion of Arendt's controversial comments on the 1957 integration crisis in Little Rock and on her relationship with Ellison, especially with regard to notions of authority and freedom.

9. In this regard, hip-hop is following the trajectory of jazz, which is currently more popular in Europe than in the United States. My good friend Peter Agoston, a journalist, DJ, and owner/operator of an independent hip-hop label, has embarked with his artists on successful tours of Europe, where he reports that the reception is much more

enthusiastic for, and knowledgeable about, independent artists than it is in the United States. His latest European tour featured Sadat X (of Brand Nubian), Greg Nice (of Nice and Smooth), and Ge-ology.

10. U.S. hip-hop is becoming increasingly rural, southern, and Midwestern, and many of its loyal followers suburban. Even so, hip-hop is a thoroughly urban art form, especially abroad.

CONCLUSION

1. Poems lose some magic in the transcription from performance to page, as often happens with hip-hop lyrics. Please see the following sources for an introduction to spoken-word poetry: *Nuyorican Poetry: An Anthology of Puerto Rican Words and Feelings*, eds. Miguel Algarín and Miguel Piñero (New York: Morrow, 1975); *Listen Up!: Spoken Word Poetry*, ed. Zoë Anglesey (New York: One World, 1999); *Aloud: Voices from the Nuyorican Poets' Café*, eds. Miguel Algarín, Bob Holman, and Nicole Blackman (New York: Owl Books, 1994); and *Bum Rush the Page: A Def Poetry Jam*, eds. Tony Medina and Louis Reyes Rivera (New York: Three Rivers Press, 2001). See also *Slam*, dir. Marc Levin (Vidmark/Trimark, 1998) and *Def Poetry—Season 1* (2002).

2. Over the last half decade hip-hop has developed its own language poetry. Experimental, often frustrating, but usually entertaining, challenging, and thought-provoking, it is overtly political in small snapshots and in its overall approach. Some MCs who make what I call an exploratory language-based hip-hop—but remain grounded in its basic values, principles, and aesthetics—are underground icons MF Doom, Aesop Rock, Del the Funky Homosapien, El-P, Busdriver, and to some extent, Ghostface Killah.

3. Dove uses this dual approach often. In *Selected Poems*, see "Belinda's Petition," "The Abduction," "The Slave's Critique of Practical Reason," and "Kentucky, 1833." James Wright's "Saint Judas" has a similar historical imagination and is just as moving and haunting as Dove's.

4. McGrath's poem appears in *Capitalism* (Hanover, HH: Wesleyan UP, 1990). I initially found it in *Poems for America: 125 Poems that Celebrate the American Experience* (New York: Scribner, 2002), 216.

5. Balaban's "Reading the News and Thinking of the T'ang Poets," *Locusts at the Edge of Summer: New & Selected Poems* (Port Townsend, WA: Copper Canyon P, 1997), 135, deals with these very issues. Much of my information on T'ang poetry comes from Balaban's lectures in a Spring 2001 graduate course on East Asian Literature at North Carolina State University.

6. It is prudent to note that epic poems such as *The Iliad* and *The Odyssey* celebrate warfare, and in a different way so does *Paradise Lost*.

7. Victor Hernández Cruz argues that consumer society does not value poetry because it lacks extrinsic sale-value: "In the United States, people see poets as just playing word games, unimportant to the real operation of a materialistic society. In capitalism, there isn't a place for poetry. 'The books don't sell,' they would say. This doesn't change the function of the wordsmith in society. The poet makes awareness available to the masses" (Dick 62).

8. See *The Virginia Quarterly Review* (Spring 2005): 34–47. This issue celebrates Whitman and the one hundred and fiftieth anniversary of the publication of *Leaves of Grass*.

9. "Commercial rap is Republican" is a contentious but legitimate claim. The dominant tropes of commercial hip-hop include: individual wealth as key to happiness, upward social mobility, and power; you can achieve your (material) dreams if you work and hustle hard enough (that is, *nothing can stop you from getting rich if you want it enough*); there are clearly delineated traditional gender relations with men having more power than women; negotiation and compromise are for the weak; and militant action can solve problems. These are caricatures, but they hold as generalizations. For example, 50 Cent's multi-platinum debut album is titled *Get Rich or Die Tryin*. On another note, *Slam*, starring Saul Williams as a poet/drug dealer living in the Washington, D.C. housing projects, won the 1998 Sundance Film Festival grand prize. It is an apt introduction to the energy, creativity, and multiculturalism of spoken-word poetry.

10. "Black Steel in the Hour of Chaos" appears on *It Takes a Nation of Millions to Hold Us Back* (New York: Columbia Records, 1988). "Fight the Power," *Fear of a Black Planet* (New York: Columbia Records, 1989), which originally appeared in Spike Lee's *Do the Right Thing*, is another of Public Enemy's powerful anthems.

References

Primary Sources: Printed Poetry

Alexie, Sherman. *The Business of Fancydancing.* New York: Hanging Loose P, 1991.

Ammons, A.R. *Tape for the Turn of the Year.* Ithaca, NY: Cornell UP, 1965.

Auden, W.H. *Collected Poems.* 1976. Ed. Edward Mendelson. New York: Vintage International, 1991.

Baca, Jimmy Santiago. *Immigrants in Our Own Land.* Baton Rouge: Louisiana State UP, 1979.

———. "Mi Tío Baca el Poeta de Socorro." *Postmodern American Poetry: A Norton Anthology.* Ed. Paul Hoover. New York: Norton, 1994. 591–593.

Balaban, John. *Words for My Daughter.* The National Poetry Series. Port Townsend, WA: Copper Canyon P, 1991.

Baraka, Amiri. "Somebody Blew Up America." *African American Review* 37.2/3 (2003): 198–203.

Bly, Robert. *Selected Poems.* New York: Harper & Row, 1986.

Brecht, Bertolt. "Motto." *Against Forgetting: Twentieth-Century Poetry of Witness.* Ed. Forché. New York: Norton, 1993. 27.

Cervantes, Lorna Dee. *Emplumada.* Pittsburgh, PA: U of Pittsburgh P, 1981.

Cruz, Victor Hernández. *Maraca: New and Selected Poems, 1966–2000.* Minneapolis, MN: Coffee House P, 2001.

———. *Red Beans: Poems.* Minneapolis, MN: Coffee House P, 1991.

Dove, Rita. *Selected Poems.* New York: Vintage, 1993.

Eliot, T.S. "The Waste Land." 1922. *Selected Poems.* New York: Harcourt Brace & Co., 1988. 49–74.

Espada, Martín. *Alabanza: New and Selected Poems 1982–2002.* New York: Norton, 2003.

Forché, Carolyn. *The Country Between Us.* New York: Harper & Row, 1981.

———. *The Angel of History.* New York: Harper Perennial, 1994.

Frost, Robert. *The Poetry of Robert Frost: The Collected Poems.* Ed. Edward Connery Lathem. New York: Henry Holt & Co., 1987.

Giovanni, Nikki. *The Collected Poetry of Nikki Giovanni: 1968–1998.* New York: Morrow, 2003.

Harjo, Joy. *How We Became Human: New and Selected Poems 1975–2001.* New York: Norton, 2002.

Hamill, Sam and Sally Anderson, eds. *Poets against the War.* New York: Nation Books, 2003.

Harper, Michael S. *Dear John, Dear Coltrane.* Pittsburgh, PA: U of Pittsburgh P, 1970.

Kinnell, Galway. "When the Towers Fell." *The New Yorker.* September 16, 2002.

Komunyakaa, Yusef. *Dien Cai Dau.* Middletown, CT: Wesleyan UP, 1988.

———. *Neon Vernacular: New and Selected Poems.* Hanover, NH: Wesleyan UP, 1993.

Lee, Don. L. *Don't Cry, Scream.* Detroit: Broadside P, 1969.

Levine, Philip. *They Feed They Lion & The Names of the Lost.* New York: Alfred A. Knopf, 1999.

Merwin, W.S. *The Second Four Books of Poems: The Moving Target, The Lice, The Carriers of Ladders, Writings to an Unfinished Accompaniment.* Port Townsend, WA: Copper Canyon P, 1993.

Montoya, José. *In Formation: 20 Years of Joda.* Aztlán: Chusma House Publications, 1992.

Moss, Thylias. *Pyramid of Bone.* The Callaloo Poetry Series. Vol. 8. Charlottesville: UP of Virginia, 1989.

Neruda, Pablo. *Canto general.* 1950. 2nd ed. Ed. Hernán Loyola. Barcelona: Random House Mondadori, S.A., 2005.

Palmer, Michael. *Codes Appearing: Poems 1979–1988.* New York: New Directions, 2001.

Pound, Ezra. "In a Station of the Metro." 1916. *The Norton Anthology of Modern and Contemporary Poetry.* 3rd ed. Ed. Jahan Ramazani, Richard Ellman, and Robert O'Clair. New York: Norton, 2003. 351.

Rexroth, Kenneth, trans. *One Hundred Poems from the Chinese.* New York: New Directions, 1971.

Rich, Adrienne. *Your Native Land, Your Life.* New York: Norton, 1986.

Rodríguez, Luis J. "Then Comes a Day." 1989. *Poetry Like Bread: Poets of the Political Imagination from Curbstone Press.* 3rd ed. Ed. Espada. Willimantic, CT: Curbstone P, 2000. 183–184.

Simic, Charles. *The Voice at 3:00 AM: Selected Late & New Poems.* New York: Harcourt, 2003.

Snyder, Gary. *Turtle Island.* New York: New Directions, 1974.

Soto, Gary. "Mexicans Begin Jogging." *Red, White, and Blues: Poets on the Promise of America.* Ed. Virgil Suárez and Ryan G. Van Cleave. Iowa City: U of Iowa P, 2004. 173.

Stevens, Wallace. *The Collected Poems of Wallace Stevens.* 1954. 2nd ed. New York: Vintage, 1990.

Troupe, Quincy. "Boomerang: A Blatantly Political Poem." *Against Forgetting: Twentieth-Century Poetry of Witness.* Ed. Forché. New York: Norton, 1993. 665–666.

Valdez, Gina. "English con Salsa." *Touching the Fire: Fifteen Poets of Today's Latino Renaissance.* Ed. Ray González. New York: Doubleday, 1998. 203–204.

Villanueva, Tino. *Shaking Off the Dark.* 1984. Tempe, AZ: Bilingual P/Editorial Bilingüe, 1998.

Villatoro, Marcos McPeek. *On Tuesday, when the homeless disappeared.* Tucson: U of Arizona P, 2004.

Walcott, Derek. *Collected Poems 1948–1984.* New York: Farrar, Straus & Giroux, 1986.

Wright, James. "Autumn Begins in Martins Ferry, Ohio." 1963. *Contemporary American Poetry.* 6th ed. Ed. A. Poulin, Jr. Boston: Houghton Mifflin, 1996. 636–637.

SECONDARY SOURCES: PRINTED POETRY

Alexie, Sherman. "Sherman Alexie, Literary Rebel." Interview with John and Carl Bellante. *Bloomsbury Review* 14 (1994).

Altieri, Charles. *Self and Sensibility in Contemporary American Poetry.* New York: Cambridge UP, 1984.

———. "Without Consequences Is No Politics." *Politics & Poetic Value.* Ed. Robert von Hallberg. Chicago: U of Chicago P, 1987.

Antonucci, Michael. "The Map and the Territory: An Interview with Michael S. Harper." *African American Review* 34.3 (2000): 501–509.

Aparicio, Frances R. "Writing Migrations: The Place(s) of U.S. Puerto Rican Literature." *Beyond the Borders: American Literature and Post-Colonial Theory.* Ed. Deborah L. Madsen. London: Pluto P, 2003. 151–166.

Arias, Santa. "Inside the Worlds of Latino Traveling Cultures: Martín Espada's Poetry of Rebellion." *Bilingual Review* 21.3 (1996): 231–240.

Baer, William. "Still Negotiating with the Images: An Interview with Yusef Komunyakaa." *Kenyon Review* 20.3–4 (1998): 5–20.

Bernstein, Charles. "Poetics of the Americas." *Modernism/Modernity* 3.3 (1996): 1–23.

Bibby, Michael. *Hearts and Minds: Bodies, Poetry, and Resistance in the Vietnam Era.* New Brunswick, NJ: Rutgers UP, 1996.

Blake, David Haven. "Reading Whitman, Growing Up Rock 'n' Roll." *The Virginia Quarterly Review* 81.2 (2005): 34–47.

Blasing, Mutlu Konuk. *Politics and Form in Postmodern Poetry.* Cambridge Studies in American Literature and Culture. Vol. 94. New York: Cambridge UP, 1995.

Bloom, Harold. Introduction. *Bloom's Modern Critical Views: Derek Walcott.* Ed. Bloom. Broomall, PA: Chelsea House Publishers, 2003. 1–3.

Bly, Robert. "Leaping up into Political Poetry." *Poetry and Politics: An Anthology of Essays.* Ed. Richard Jones. New York: Morrow, 1985. 129–137.

Breslin, Paul. "Review Essay: The Cultural Address of Derek Walcott." *Modernism/modernity* 9.2 (2002): 319–325.

Brown, Joseph A. "Their Long Scars Touch Ours: A Reflection on the Poetry of Michael Harper." *Callaloo* 26 (1986): 209–220.

Bruce-Novoa, Juan. *Chicano Poetry: A Response to Chaos.* Austin: U of Texas P, 1982.

Brunner, Edward J. *Poetry as Labor and Privilege: The Writings of W.S. Merwin*. Urbana: U of Illinois P, 1991.

Burnett, Paula. *Derek Walcott: Poetics and Politics*. Gainesville: U of Florida P, 2000.

Burt, Stephen. "September 1, 1939 Revisited: Or, Poetry, Politics, and the Idea of the Public." *American Literary History* 15.3 (2003): 533–559.

Campo, Rafael. "Sturdy Boxcars and Exploding Pickle Jars: Review of *Small Congregations: New and Selected Poems* by Thylias Moss." *Parnassus: Poetry in Review* 21.1/2 (1996): 341–350.

Candelaria, Cordelia. *Chicano Poetry: A Critical Introduction*. Westport, CT: Greenwood P, 1986.

———. "Rethinking the "Eyes" of Chicano Poetry, or, Reading the Multiple Centers of Chicana Poetics." *Women Poets of the Americas: Toward a Pan-American Gathering*. Ed. Jacqueline Vaught Brogan and Candelaria. Notre Dame, IN: U of Notre Dame P, 1999.

Collins, Billy. "My Grandfather's Tackle Box: The Limits of Memory-Driven Poetry." *Poetry* 178.5 (2001): 278–287.

Cruz, Victor Hernández. "Mountains in the North: Hispanic Writing in the U.S.A." 1991. *Postmodern American Poetry: A Norton Anthology*. Ed. Paul Hoover. New York: Norton, 1994. 672–675.

———. *Panoramas*. Minneapolis, MN: Coffee House P, 1997.

Davis, William V. Introduction. *Critical Essays on Robert Bly*. Ed. Davis. Critical Essays on American Literature. New York: G.K. Hall & Co., 1992. 1–18.

DeShazer, Mary K. *A Poetics of Resistance: Women Writing in El Salvador, South Africa & the United States*. Ann Arbor: U of Michigan P, 1994.

Des Pres, Terrence. *Praises & Dispraises: Poetry and Politics, the 20th Century*. New York: Viking Penguin, 1988.

———. "Adrienne Rich, North America East." *Adrienne Rich's Poetry and Prose: Norton Critical Edition*. Ed. Barbara Charlesworth Gelpi and Albert Gelpi. New York: Norton, 1993. 357–369.

Dick, Bruce Allen. *A Poet's Truth: Conversations with Latino/Latina Poets*. Tucson: U of Arizona P, 2003.

Donzella, Niccolò N. "The Rage of Michael Harper." *Callaloo* 13 (1990): 805–806.

Doubiago, Sharon. "Towards an American Criticism : A Reading of Carolyn Forché's *The Country Between Us*." *American Poetry Review* 12.1 (1983): 35–39.

Elder, Arlene. "A MELUS Interview: Nikki Giovanni." *MELUS* 9.3 (1982): 61–75.

Engelmann, Diana. "'Speaking in Tongues': Exile and Internal Translation in the Poetry of Charles Simic." *The Antioch Review* 62.1 (2004): 44–49.

Evans, Stephen F. "'Open Containers': Sherman Alexie's Drunken Indians." *The American Indian Quarterly* 25.1 (2001): 46–72.

Folsom, Ed. "'What a Filthy Presidentiad!': Clinton's Whitman, Bush's Whitman, and Whitman's America." *The Virginia Quarterly Review* 81.2 (2005): 96–113.

Folsom, Ed and Cary Nelson. Introduction. *W.S. Merwin: Essays on the Poetry*. Ed. Folsom and Nelson. Urbana: U of Illinois P, 1987.

Forché, Carolyn. "El Salvador: An Aide Memoire." *Poetry and Politics: An Anthology of Essays*. Ed. Richard Jones. New York: Morrow, 1985. 243–257.

———. Introduction. *Against Forgetting: Twentieth-Century Poetry of Witness*. Ed. Forché. New York: Norton, 1993. 29–47.

Frazier, Jane. "Writing Outside the Self: The Disembodied Narrators of W.S. Merwin." *Style* 30.2 (1996): 341–350.

Gardinier, Suzanne. *A World that Will Hold All the People*. Poets on Poetry. Ed. David Lehman. Ann Arbor: U of Michigan P, 1996.

Gardner, Joann. "The Mirrored Self: Images of Kinship in Carolyn Forché's Poetry." *Women's Studies* 18 (1991): 405–419.

Gery, John. *Nuclear Annihilation and Contemporary American Poetry: Ways of Nothingness*. Gainesville: UP of Florida, 1996.

Gibbons, Reginald. "Political Poetry and the Example of Ernesto Cardenal." *Politics & Poetic Value*. Ed. Robert von Hallberg. Chicago: U of Chicago P, 1987. 277–300.

Gilbert, Roger. "Framing Water: Historical Knowledge in Elizabeth Bishop and Adrienne Rich." *Twentieth Century Literature* 43.2 (1997): 144–161.

Gillan, Jennifer. "Reservation Home Movies: Sherman Alexie's Poetry." *American Literature* 68.1 (1996): 91–110.

Gioia, Dana. *Can Poetry Matter?: Essays on Poetry and American Culture*. Saint Paul, MN: Graywolf P, 1992.

Good, Carl. "A Chronicle of Poetic Non-Encounter in the Americas." *The New Centennial Review* 3.1 (2003): 225–255.

Goodman, Jenny. "Politics and the Personal Lyric in the Poetry of Joy Harjo and C.D. Wright." *MELUS* 19.2 (1994): 35–56.

Greer, Michael. "Politicizing the Modern: Carolyn Forché in El Salvador and America." *The Centennial Review* 30.2 (1986): 160–180.

Halpern, Nick. *Everyday and Prophetic: The Poetry of Lowell, Ammons, Merrill, and Rich*. Madison: U of Wisconsin P, 2003.

Harper, Philip Brian. "Nationalism and Social Division in Black Arts Poetry of the 1960s." *Critical Inquiry* 19 (1993): 234–255.

Harrington, Joseph. *Poetry and the Public: The Social Form of Modern U.S. Poetics*. Middletown, CT: Wesleyan UP, 2002.

Harris, Victoria Frenkel. *The Incorporative Consciousness of Robert Bly*. Carbondale: Southern Illinois UP, 1992.

Hass, Robert. *Twentieth Century Pleasures: Prose on Poetry*. New York: The Ecco P, 1984.

———. "An Informal Occasion with Robert Hass." *The Iowa Review* 21.3 (1991): 126–145.

Hass, Robert, Yusef Komunyakaa, W.S. Merwin, and Joyce Carol Oates. "'How Poetry Helps People to Live their Lives': APR's 25th Anniversary Celebration." *The American Poetry Review* 28.5 (1999): 21–27.

Helms, Alan. "Over the Edge." Rev. of *They Feed They Lion*. *Partisan Review* 41 (1974): 151–153.

Henderson, Stephen E. *Understanding the New Black Poetry: Black Speech and Black Music as Poetic References.* New York: Morrow, 1973.

Herrnstein-Smith, Barbara. *Poetic Closure: A Study of How Poems End.* Chicago: U of Chicago P, 1968.

Herzog, Anne. "Adrienne Rich and the Discourse of Decolonization." *The Centennial Review* 33.3 (1989): 258–277.

Hirsch, Edward. "Naming the Lost: The Poetry of Philip Levine." *On the Poetry of Philip Levine: Stranger to Nothing.* Ann Arbor: U of Michigan P, 1991. 344–352.

———. *How to Read a Poem: And Fall in Love with Poetry.* New York: Harcourt, Brace, 1999.

Hussain, Azfar. "Joy Harjo and Her Poetics as Praxis: A 'Postcolonial' Political Economy of the Body, Land, Labor, and Language." *Wicazo Sa Review: A Journal of Native American Studies* 15.2 (2000): 27–61.

Islas, Arturo. "On the Bridge at the Border: Migrants and Immigrants." 5th Annual Ernesto Galarza Memorial Lecture. Stanford Center for Chicano Research. 1990.

Jaffe, Harold. "Picketing the Zeitgeist: The Writer in Wartime." *American Book Review* May–June 2005: 3 ff.

Kalaidjian, Walter. *Languages of Liberation: The Social Text in Contemporary American Poetry.* New York: Columbia UP, 1989.

———. "From Silence to Subversion: Robert Bly's Political Surrealism." *Critical Essays on Robert Bly.* Ed. William V. Davis. New York: G.K. Hall & Co., 1992. 194–211.

Kraver, Jeraldine R. "Revolution through Poetic Language: Bilingualism in Latina Poetry from *la Frontera.*" *LIT: Literature-Interpretation-Theory* 8.2 (1997): 193–206.

Levertov, Denise. "On the Edge of Darkness: What Is Political Poetry?" *Poetry and Politics: An Anthology of Essays.* Ed. Richard Jones. New York: Morrow, 1985. 162–174.

Levine, Philip. "Staying Power: A Lifetime in Poetry." Interview by Gary Pacernick. *The Kenyon Review* 21.2 (1999): 9–29.

Levis, Larry. "War as Parable and War as Fact: Herbert and Forché." *The American Poetry Review* 12.1 (1983): 6–12.

Limón, José E. *Mexican Ballads, Chicano Poems: History and Influence in Mexican-American Social Poetry.* The New Historicism: Studies in Cultural Poetics. Ed. Stephen Greenblatt. Berkeley: U of California P, 1992.

Lorca, Federico García. "The Irresistible Beauty of All Things." Trans. Christopher Maurer. *Harper's* September 2004. 26–28.

Marchant, Fred. "Cipriano Mera and the Lion: A Reading of Philip Levine." *On the Poetry of Philip Levine: Stranger to Nothing.* Ed. Christopher Buckley. Ann Arbor: U of Michigan P, 1991. 303–310.

McGrath, Thomas. "The Frontiers of Language." *North Dakota Quarterly* 50 (1982): 28–29.

McKenna, Teresa. *Migrant Song: Politics and Process in Contemporary Chicano Literature*. Austin: U of Texas P, 1997.

Mendieta-Lombardo, Eva and Zaida A. Cintron. "Marked and Unmarked Choices of Code Switching in Bilingual Poetry." *Hispania* 78.3 (1995): 565–572.

Mersmann, James F. *Out of the Vietnam Vortex: A Study of Poets and Poetry Against the War*. Lawrence: UP of Kansas, 1974.

Mills, Jr., Ralph J. *Contemporary American Poetry*. New York: Random House, 1965.

Milosz, Czeslaw. *The Witness of Poetry*. The Charles Eliot Norton Lectures 1981–1982. Cambridge, MA: Harvard UP, 1983.

Molesworth, Charles. "The Political and Poetic Vision of *Turtle Island*." *Critical Essays on Gary Snyder*. Ed. Patrick D. Murphy. Boston: G.K. Hall, 1991. 144–156.

Montenegro, David. "Carolyn Forché: An Interview by David Montenegro." *The American Poetry Review* 17.6 (1988): 35–40.

Mora, Pat. "Interview with Pat Mora." Interview with Elisabeth Mermann-Jozwiak and Nancy Sullivan. *MELUS* 28.2 (2003): 139–150.

Nelson, Cary. "The Resources of Failure: W.S. Merwin's Deconstructive Career." *W.S. Merwin: Essays on the Poetry*. Ed. Nelson and Folsom. Urbana: U of Illinois P, 1987. 78–121.

Newton, John. "Sherman Alexie's Autoethnography." *Contemporary Literature* 42.2 (2001): 413–428.

Ostriker, Alicia. "Dancing at the Devil's Party: Some Notes on Politics and Poetry." *Politics & Poetic Value*. Ed. Robert von Hallberg. Chicago: U of Chicago P, 1987. 207–224.

———. "Beyond Confession: The Poetics of Postmodern Witness." *The American Poetry Review* 30.2 (2001): 35–39.

Palmer, Michael. "'Dear Lexicon': An Interview by Benjamin Hollander and David Levi Strauss." *Acts* 5.2 (1986): 8–36.

———. "Conversation." Interview by Lee Bartlett. *Talking Poetry: Conversations in the Workshop with Contemporary Poets*. Ed. Bartlett. Albuquerque: U of New Mexico P, 1987: 126–43.

Pérez-Torres, Rafael. *Movements in Chicano Poetry: Against Myths, against Margins*. Cambridge Studies in American Literature and Culture 88. New York: U of Cambridge P, 1995.

———. "Chicano Ethnicity, Cultural Hybridity, and the Mestizo Voice." *American Literature* 70.1 (1998): 153–176.

Perloff, Marjorie. "Apocalypse Then: Merwin and the Sorrows of Literary History." *W.S. Merwin: Essays on the Poetry*. Ed. Folsom and Nelson. Urbana: U of Illinois P, 1987. 122–144.

———. "Poetry in Time of War: The Duncan–Levertov Controversy." *Poetry On and Off the Page: Essays for Emergent Occasions*. Evanston, IL: Northwestern UP, 1998.

Pinsky, Robert. *The Situation of Poetry*. Princeton, NJ: Princeton UP, 1976.

Pinsky, Robert. "Responsibilities of the Poet." *Politics & Poetic Value*. Ed. von Hallberg. Chicago: U of Chicago P, 1987. 7–20.

Ramazani, Jahan. *Poetry of Mourning: The Modern Elegy from Hardy to Heaney*. Chicago: U of Chicago P, 1994.

———. Author Head Notes: Thylias Moss. *The Norton Anthology of Modern and Contemporary Poetry*. 3rd ed. Ed. Ramazani, Richard Ellman, and Robert O'Clair. New York: Norton, 2003. 999–1000.

———. Author Head Notes: Ezra Pound. *The Norton Anthology of Modern and Contemporary Poetry*. 3rd ed. Ed. Ramazani, Richard Ellman, and Robert O'Clair. New York: Norton, 2003. 345–349.

Rasula, Jed. "The Politics of, the Politics in." *Politics & Poetic Value*. Ed. von Hallberg. Chicago: U of Chicago P, 1987. 315–322.

Rexroth, Kenneth. "The Function of Poetry and the Place of the Poet in Society." 1936. *World Outside the Window: The Selected Essays of Kenneth Rexroth*. New York: New Directions, 1987. 1–7.

Rich, Adrienne. *What Is Found There: Notebooks on Poetry and Politics*. New York: Norton, 1993.

Roberts, Andrew Michael and Jonathan Allison, eds. *Poetry and Contemporary Culture: The Question of Value*. Edinburgh: Edinburgh UP, 2002.

Rodriguez y Gibson, Eliza. "Love, Hunger, and Grace: Loss and Belonging in the Poetry of Lorna Dee Cervantes and Joy Harjo." *Legacy* 19.1 (2003): 106–114.

Rosman, Silvia N. "The Poetics of Politics and the Politics of the Poet: Experience and Testimony in Pablo Neruda." *Pablo Neruda and the U.S. Culture Industry*. Hispanic Issues, Vol. 25. Ed. Teresa Longo. New York: Routledge, 2002. 126–137.

Rueckert, William H. "Rereading *The Lice:* A Journal." *W.S. Merwin: Essays on the Poetry*. Ed. Folsom and Nelson. Urbana: U of Illinois P, 1987. 45–64.

Rukeyser, Muriel. *The Life of Poetry*. 1949. New York: Morrow, 1974.

Sack, Lisa. "Charles the Great: Charles Simic's *A Wedding in Hell*." *Charles Simic: Essays on the Poetry*. Ed. Bruce Weigl. Ann Arbor: U of Michigan P, 1996. 133–137.

Sáenz, Benjamin Alire. "I Want to Write an American Poem." *Currents from the Dancing River: Contemporary Latino Fiction, Nonfiction, and Poetry*. Ed. Ray González. New York: Harcourt Brace, 1994. 524.

Savin, Ada. "Bilingualism and Dialogism: Another Reading of Lorna Dee Cervantes's Poetry." *An Other Tongue: Nation and Ethnicity in the Linguistic Borderlands*. Ed. Alfred Arteaga. Durham, NC: Duke UP, 1994.

Scigaj, Leonard M. *Sustainable Poetry: Four American Ecopoets*. Lexington: UP of Kentucky, 1999.

Seator, Lynette. "Emplumada: Chicana Rites-of-Passage." *MELUS* 11.2 (1984): 23–38.

Selinger, Eric Murphy. "Important Pleasures and Others: Michael Palmer, Ronald Johnson." *Postmodern Culture* 4.3 (1994).

Shetley, Vernon. *After the Death of Poetry: Poet and Audience in Contemporary America.* Durham, NC: Duke UP, 1993.

Smethurst, James. "'Pat Your Foot and Turn the Corner': Amiri Baraka, the Black Arts Movement, and the Poetics of a Popular Avant-Garde." *African American Review* 37.2–3 (2003): 261–270.

Smith, David L. "Amiri Baraka and the Black Arts of Black Art." *Boundary 2* 15.1/2 (1986–1987): 235–254.

———. "The Black Arts Movement and Its Critics." *American Literary History* 3.1 (1991): 93–110.

Steele, Cassie Premo. *We Heal from Memory: Sexton, Lorde, Anzaldúa, and the Poetry of Witness.* New York: Palgrave, 2000.

Stein, Kevin. *Private Poets, Worldly Acts: Public and Private History in Contemporary American Poetry.* Athens: Ohio UP, 1996.

St. John, David. "Where the Angels Come toward Us: The Poetry of Philip Levine." *On the Poetry of Philip Levine: Stranger to Nothing.* Ed. Christopher Buckley. Ann Arbor: U of Michigan P, 1991. 277–295.

Tapscott, Stephen. Introduction. *Twentieth-Century Latin American Poetry: A Bilingual Edition.* Ed. Tapscott. Austin: U of Texas P, 1996. 1–20.

Thompson, Denys. *The Uses of Poetry.* New York: Cambridge UP, 1978.

Thompson, Jon. "A Turn toward the Past." Rev. of Forché's *The Angel of History. Postmodern Culture* 5.2 (1995).

Vendler, Helen. "Totemic Sifting: Charles Simic's *The Book of Gods and Devils, Hotel Insomnia, and Dime-Store Alchemy.*" *Charles Simic: Essays on the Poetry.* Ed. Weigl. Ann Arbor: U of Michigan P, 1996. 119–132.

———. "Poet of Two Worlds." *Bloom's Modern Critical Views: Derek Walcott.* Ed. Bloom. Broomall, PA: Chelsea House Publishers, 2003. 25–33.

Villatoro, Marcos McPeek. "In Search of Literary *Cojones:* Pablo Neruda, U.S. Latino Poetry, and the U.S. Literary Canon: A *Testimonio.*" *Pablo Neruda and the U.S. Culture Industry.* Hispanic Issues, Vol. 25. Ed. Longo. New York: Routledge, 2002. 163–178.

von Hallberg, Robert. *American Poetry and Culture 1945–1980.* Cambridge, MA: Harvard UP, 1985.

———. Introduction. *Politics & Poetic Value.* Ed. von Hallberg. Chicago: U of Chicago P, 1987. 1–6.

Walters, Jennifer. "Nikki Giovanni and Rita Dove: Poets Redefining." *The Journal of Negro History* 85.3 (2000): 210–217.

Weigl, Bruce. Introduction. *Charles Simic: Essays on the Poetry.* Ed. Weigl. Ann Arbor: U of Michigan P, 1996. 1–5.

Welty, Eudora, "Must the Novelist Crusade?" 1965. *Eudora Welty: Stories, Essays, & Memoir.* Ed. Richard Ford and Michael Kreyling. New York: Library of America, 1998. 803–814.

Yamazato, Katsunori. "How to Be in This Crisis: Gary Snyder's Cross-Cultural Vision in *Turtle Island.*" *Critical Essays on Gary Snyder.* Ed. Murphy. Boston: G.K. Hall, 1991. 230–247.

Zimmerman, Lee. "Against Vanishing: Winnicott and the Modern Poetry of Nothing." *American Imago* 54.1 (1997): 81–102.

Primary Sources:
Hip-Hop Recordings

Atmosphere. *Lucy Ford*. Minneapolis: Rhymesayers Entertainment, 1998.

Coup, The. *Party Music*. San Francisco: 75 Ark, 2001.

dead prez. *let's get free*. New York: Loud Records, 2000.

Edan. *Beauty and the Beat*. London: Lewis Recordings, 2005.

Grae, Jean. *Attack of the Attacking Things*. New York: Third World Music, 2003.

J-Live. *All of the Above*. New York: Coup d'État Entertainment, 2002.

KRS-One. *KRS-One: A Retrospective*. New York: Zomba Recording Corp., 2000.

Little Brother. *The Listening*. Oakland: ABB Records, 2002.

Mobb Deep. *The Infamous*. New York: Loud Records, 1995.

Mos Def. *The New Danger*. New York: Geffen Records, 2004.

Mr. Lif. *Emergency Rations*. New York: Definitive Jux, 2002.

Nas. *Illmatic*. New York: Sony, 1994.

Notorious B.I.G., The. *Ready to Die*. New York: Bay Boy Entertainment, 1994.

Perceptionists, The. *Black Dialogue*. New York: Definitive Jux, 2005.

Roots, The. *Things Fall Apart*. New York: MCA Music, 1999.

Williams, Saul. *Not in My Name*. New York: Synchronic Records, 2003.

Primary Sources:
Live Hip-Hop Shows

Atmosphere. Concert. Cat's Cradle, Carrboro, NC. November 17, 2003.

Best Damn Rap Tour, The. Concert. Cat's Cradle. Carrboro, NC. June 27, 2005.

Coup, The. Concert. Cat's Cradle, Carrboro, NC. April 12, 2002.

Cunninlynguists. Concert. Cat's Cradle. Carrboro, NC. September 30, 2004.

Living Legends. Concert. Cat's Cradle, Carrboro, NC. February 15, 2003.

Mos Def and Talib Kweli Are Black Star. "What's Beef." Live Performance. *Chappelle's Show*, Comedy Central, 2003. April 9, 2003.

Prince Paul. Concert. Cat's Cradle, Carrboro, NC. June 13, 2003.

Secondary Sources:
Hip-Hop

Ards, Angela. "Rhyme and Resist: Organizing the Hip-Hop Generation." *The Nation* 269.4 (07/26/1999–08/04/1999): 11–20.

Baker, Jr., Houston A. *Black Studies, Rap, and the Academy*. Chicago: U of Chicago P, 1993.

Costello, Mark and David Foster Wallace. *Signifying Rappers: Rap and Race in the Urban Present*. Hopewell, NJ: The Ecco Press, 1990.

Damon, Maria. "Was that 'Different,' 'Dissident,' or 'Dissonant'?: Poetry (n) the Public Spear: Slams, Open Readings, and Dissident Traditions." *Close*

Listening: Poetry and the Performed Word. Ed. Charles Bernstein. New York: Oxford UP, 1998.

Dimitriadis, Greg. "Hip Hop: From Live Performance to Mediated Narrative." *Popular Music* 15.2 (1996): 179–194.

Dyson, Michael Eric. *Reflecting Black: African-American Cultural Criticism.* Minneapolis: U of Minnesota P, 1993.

George, Nelson. *Hip Hop America.* New York: Viking Penguin, 1998.

Hillburn, Robert. "Checking in with Chuck D. *Los Angeles Times* November 8, 1992. Calendar section 65.

Keyes, Cheryl L. *Rap Music and Street Consciousness.* Music in American Life. Urbana: U of Illinois P, 2002.

Kitwana, Bakari. "The Cotton Club: Black-Conscious Hip-Hop Deals with an Overwhelmingly White Live Audience." *The Village Voice* June 24, 2005. Available at <http://www.villagevoice.com/music/0526,-kitwana,65332,22.html>.

Neate, Patrick. *Where You're at: Notes from the Frontlines of a Hip-Hop Planet.* New York: Riverhead Books, 2003.

Perkins, William Eric. "The Rap Attack: Introduction." *Droppin' Science: Critical Essays on Rap Music and Hip Hop Culture.* Ed. Perkins. Philadelphia, PA: Temple UP, 1996. 1–48.

Potter, Russell A. *Spectacular Vernaculars: Hip-Hop and the Politics of Postmodernism.* SUNY Series, Postmodern Culture. Albany, New York: SUNY P Albany, 1995.

Rose, Tricia. *Black Noise: Rap Music and Black Culture in Contemporary America.* Hanover, NH: Wesleyan UP, 1994.

Saddik, Annette J. "Rap's Unruly Body: The Postmodern Performance of Black Male Identity on the American Stage." *The Drama Review* 47.4 (2003): 110–127.

Shusterman, Richard. "The Fine Art of Rap." *New Literary History* 22.3 (1991): 613–632.

Smith, Christopher Holmes. "'I Don't Like to Dream about Getting Paid': Representations of Social Mobility and the Emergence of the Hip-Hop Mogul." *Social Text* 21.4 (2003): 69–97.

Secondary Sources: Theory and Various

Agamben, Giorgio. *Infancy and History: The Destruction of Experience.* Trans. Liz Heron. New York: Verso, 1993.

Arendt, Hannah. *Between Past and Future: Eight Exercises in Political Thought.* New York: Penguin, 1954.

———. *The Human Condition.* Chicago: U of Chicago P, 1958.

———. *On Revolution.* New York: Penguin, 1977.

Barthes, Roland. "The Discourse of History." Trans. Stephen Bann. *Comparative Criticism* 3 (1981): 7–20.

Basso, Keith H. *Portraits of "The Whiteman": Linguistic Play and Cultural Symbols among the Western Apache.* Cambridge: Cambridge UP, 1979.

Beckett, Samuel. *Molloy.* New York: Grove P, 1955.

Bell, Jr. Bernard W. *The Afro-American Novel and Its Tradition.* Amherst: U of Massachusetts P, 1987.

Benjamin, Walter. *Illuminations: Essays and Reflections.* Trans. Harry Zohn. Ed. Arendt. New York: Shocken Books, 1969.

Bérubé, Michael. *Public Access: Literary Theory and American Cultural Politics.* London: Verso, 1994.

Beverley, John. "The Margin at the Center: On Testimonio (Testimonial Narrative)." *The Real Thing: Testimonial Discourse and Latin America.* Ed Georg M. Gugelberger. Durham, NC: Duke UP, 1996: 23–41.

Blanchot, Maurice. *The Writing of the Disaster.* Trans. Ann Smock. Lincoln: U of Nebraska P, :1995. Trans. of *L'Ecriture du désastre.* 1980.

Bourdieu, Pierre. *The Logic of Practice.* Trans. of *Le sens pratique.* 1980. Trans. Richard Nice. Stanford, CA: Stanford UP, 1990.

Burke, Kenneth. *A Rhetoric of Motives.* 1950. Berkeley: U of California P, 1969.

Caruth, Cathy. *Unclaimed Experience: Trauma, Narrative, and History.* Baltimore, MD: The Johns Hopkins UP, 1996.

Castillo, Debra A. *Redreaming America: Toward a Bilingual American Culture.* SUNY Series in Latin American and Iberian Thought and Culture. Albany: SUNY P, 2005.

Cixous, Hélène. "Conversations." *Twentieth-Century Literary Theory: A Reader.* Ed. K.M. Newton. New York: St. Martin's P, 1997. 225–233.

Colás, Santiago. "What's Wrong with Representation: Testimonio and Democratic Culture." *The Real Thing: Testimonial Discourse and Latin America.* Ed. Gugelberger. Durham, NC: Duke UP, 1996. 161–171.

Crews, Frederick. "The Trauma Trap." *The New York Review of Books.* March 11, 2004.

Davis, Mike. "Planet of Slums." *Harper's* June 2004. 17–22.

de Soto, Hernando. *The Mystery of Capital: Why Capitalism Triumphs in the West and Fails Everywhere Else.* New York: Basic Books, 2000.

Ellison, Ralph. *Invisible Man.* 1952. 2nd ed. New York: Vintage, 1995.

Fanon, Frantz. *The Wretched of the Earth.* New York: Grove P, 1963.

Gates, Jr., Henry Louis. *The Signifying Monkey: A Theory of African-American Literary Criticism.* New York: Oxford UP, 1988.

Geyh, Paula, Fred G. Leebron, and Andrew Levy, eds. Introduction. *Postmodern American Fiction: A Norton Anthology.* New York: Norton, 1998. IX–XXX.

Giddens, Anthony. *Central Problems in Social Theory: Action, Structure, and Contradiction in Social Analysis.* Berkeley: U of California P, 1979.

Gugelberger, Georg M. "Introduction: Institutionalization of Transgression: Testimonial Discourse and Beyond." *The Real Thing: Testimonial Discourse and Latin America.* Ed. Gugelberger. Durham, NC: Duke UP, 1996. 1–19.

Hall, Stuart. *Stuart Hall: Critical Dialogues in Cultural Studies.* Ed. David Morley and Kuan-Hsing Chen. New York: Routledge, 1996.

Hansen, Miriam. Foreword. *Public Sphere and Experience: Toward an Analysis of the Bourgeois and Proletarian Public Sphere.* By Oskar Negt and Alexander Kluge. Trans. Peter Labanyi et al. Minneapolis: U of Minnesota P, 1993. ix–xli.

James, William. *Pragmatism and Other Writings.* 1907. Ed. Giles Gunn. New York: Penguin, 2000.

King, Martin Luther, Jr. "Beyond Vietnam." April 4, 1967. Available at: <http://www.stanford.edu/group/King/publications/speeches/contents. htm>.

Massumi, Brian. *Parables for the Virtual: Movement, Affect, Sensation.* Durham, NC: Duke UP, 2002.

McGowan, John. *Hannah Arendt: An Introduction.* Minneapolis: U of Minnesota P, 1998.

O'Brien, Tim. *The Things They Carried.* New York: Penguin, 1990.

Parenti, Michael. *Democracy for the Few.* 7th ed. Boston: Bedford/St. Martin's, 2002.

Sanders, Leslie Catherine. *The Development of Black Theater in America: From Shadows to Selves.* Baton Rouge: Louisiana State UP, 1988.

Sennett, Richard. *The Fall of Public Man.* New York: Knopf, 1977.

Stiglitz, Joseph E. *Globalization and Its Discontents.* New York: Norton, 2003.

Yúdice, George. "Testimonio and Postmodernism." *The Real Thing: Testimonial Discourse and Latin America.* Ed. Gugelberger. Durham, NC: Duke UP, 1996. 42–57.

West, Cornel. *The American Evasion of Philosophy: A Genealogy of Pragmatism.* Madison: U of Wisconsin P, 1989.

Wright, Richard. *Black Boy: A Record of Childhood and Youth.* 1945. New York: Harper Collins, 2005.

Zinn, Howard. *A People's History of the United States: 1492–Present.* New York: Harper Collins, 1999.

INDEX

abstraction, 78–80, 87, 92–3,
    101–2, 105–6, 129, 189, 191
    see also indirection
accessibility
    of hip-hop, 156, 182–4
    of political poetry, x, 94–7, 103
    of scholarship, xi–xii
action
    call to, 59–63, 157, 172–5
    determining constraints on, x, 21,
        31, 155–6, 162–6
    social, 23
    symbolic, 21–2, 39–40, 55–6,
        130, 198–9
African American culture
    and AAVE, 63–7, 104–5
    and call-and-response, 171–2
    and signifying, 7, 21, 55, 190,
        202 n. 15
Agamben, Giorgio, 36
agency, x, 2, 4, 11
    authoritative, 9–10, 26–7, 52–3,
        191–2
    collective, x, 21, 29, 31, 59–60,
        89–91, 106–7, 141–4
    contestatory urban, 9–10, 29–31,
        153–6, 166
    embodied, 9–10, 21–5, 35–40,
        67, 190–1
    equivocal, 9–10, 27–8,
        77–84
    experiential, 9–10, 21–6, 40–1
    as framework for reading poetry,
        9–10, 21–3, 32
    and imagination, 89–91
    individual, 21, 31

individual *v.* collective, 56–7,
    166–7
and live hip-hop, 166–84
migratory, 9–10, 28–9, 117–26,
    191
types of equivocal, 79–80, 97–8
types of in poetry, 9–10, 21–4,
    189–94
Alegría, Claribel, 28–9
Alexie, Sherman, 84, 206 n. 7
    "Evolution," 107–10, 134
Altieri, Charles, 41, 51, 72, 190
American literature
    poetic tradition in, 123–4
    terminology for, 13–14, 120–1
    v. U.S. literature, 13, 28–9
Ammons, A.R., 114
anthologies, 19
Anzaldúa, Gloria, 81
Ards, Angela, 164, 180
Arendt, Hannah
    on "acting in concert," 31, 167–84
    on action, 23
    on imagination, 91
    on performance, 180
Arias, Santa, 146
Aristotle, 9
Ashbery, John, 73, 150
Atmosphere, 16, 173–4, 179–80
Auden, W.H.
    "In Memory o W.B. Yeats," 1–3
    "September 1, 1939," 7
audience
    and action, 55–7, 60–3
    for hip-hop *v.* printed poetry, x,
        15–16